# WILLIAM JENNINGS BRYAN

## Champion of Democracy

TWAYNE'S TWENTIETH-CENTURY AMERICAN BIOGRAPHY SERIES

John Milton Cooper, Jr., General Editor

# WILLIAM JENNINGS BRYAN

## Champion of Democracy

## LeRoy Ashby

TWAYNE PUBLISHERS • BOSTON
*A Division of G. K. Hall & Co.*

Copyright 1987 by LeRoy Ashby
All rights reserved
Published by Twayne Publishers
A Division of G. K. Hall & Co.
70 Lincoln Street, Boston, Massachusetts 02111

Twayne's Twentieth-Century
American Biography Series No. 4

Photographs courtesy of the Nebraska State
Historical Society unless otherwise noted

Designed by Marne B. Sultz
Produced by Janet Zietowski
Copyediting supervised by Lewis DeSimone
Typeset in 11/13 Goudy by Compset, Inc.

Printed on permanent/durable acid-free paper
and bound in the United States of America

First Printing

Library of Congress Cataloging in Publication Data

Ashby, LeRoy.
William Jennings Bryan : champion of democracy

(Twayne's twentieth-century American biography series ; no. 4)
Bibliography: p.
Includes index.
1. Bryan, William Jennings, 1860–1925.
2. Statesmen—United States—Biography.   3. Presidential candidates—United States—
Biography.   4. United States—Politics and government—1865–1933.   T. Title.
II. Series.
E664.B87A85   1987   973.91'092'4   [B]      87–8407
ISBN 0-8057-7760-1 (alk. paper)
ISBN 0-8057-7776-8 (pbk. : alk. paper)

To Sam and Marion Merrill

# CONTENTS

# FOREWORD

From the time William Jennings Bryan was 30 years old, in 1890, until his death in 1925, he seldom strayed from the center of public attention and controversy. Except for Presidents Theodore Roosevelt and Woodrow Wilson, Bryan shaped American politics more than anyone else during those years. No one was a more familiar sight. Photographs and political cartoons made him recognized everywhere, both as a handsome young candidate and later as a balding, middle-aged crusader. Tireless speaking on campaign trails, at religious revivals, and on lecture tours made his powerful, mellifluous voice better known than anyone else's in the era before radio. His string of nicknames— "the Great Commoner," "the Peerless Leader," "the Prince of Peace," "the Boy Orator of the Platte," "the Fundamentalist Pope"—attested the contrasts of adulation and derision, faith and ridicule, devotion and contempt that he aroused over three decades. Champion of many causes—including silver money, world peace, regulation of big business, woman suffrage, prohibition of alcoholic beverages, and banning the teaching of evolution—Bryan indisputably helped to change the course of American history.

Yet his influence always seemed mysterious. The three times he ran for President, in 1896, 1900, and 1908, Bryan lost. The only elections he won were twice to the House of Representatives from a Nebraska district in the early 1890s. He dominated the Democratic Party from 1896 to 1912 and permanently reoriented their approach to the major issues of the industrial revolution, but he repeatedly flopped as a political organizer. Social and religious causes often suffered as much as they profited from his championship. By the time of his death, Bryan had become a pathetic, bypassed figure. His last two major public appearances, at the fractious 1924 Democratic convention at Madison Square Garden and at the Scopes trial in Dayton, Tennessee, in 1925, featured him in postures of apparently defending prejudice and ignorance. Yet no one ever questioned Bryan's sympathy toward poor, ordinary, struggling people or his vigilance against privilege, exclusiveness, and plutocracy. In all, he embodied the best and worst aspects of the nation's white Protestant heartland.

The great contribution of LeRoy Ashby's engaging biography is to view Bryan completely and consistently. Unlike all but a few previous interpreters, Ashby does not try to separate the sweet from the sour or to distinguish between a "good" and a "bad" Bryan or an "early" and a "late" one. As Ashby shows so clearly, the man displayed the same traits and held the same views throughout most of his life. Likewise, Ashby demonstrates that Bryan always remained an exponent of the political, economic, social, and religious values that he drew from his family and his region. Bryan was, genuinely, a great commoner, essentially simple in his outlook, but not foolish or simplistic. Bryan's thorough identification with his people gave him equally his strengths and his weaknesses as a leader, together with the adoration and repulsion that he inspired. Ashby views Bryan with sympathy and criticism, with understanding but without excuses. This book presents the most balanced and insightful portrait that has ever been done of Bryan. It illuminates the figure who personified, better than anyone else, the mixed success and failure of democracy in America.

John Milton Cooper, Jr.

# ACKNOWLEDGMENTS

I am deeply grateful to John Milton Cooper, Jr., for inviting me to contribute to Twayne's American Biography Series. His shrewd editorial insights and impressive knowledge of the field have helped the manuscript immensely. From beginning to end, he has been an ideal editor—encouraging, prompt, and insightful.

Robert H. Zieger of the University of Florida, whose critical talents and friendship I have drawn on many times, and my fine colleague Gene Clanton, whose knowledge of populism and progressivism is formidable, read the entire manuscript and offered valuable suggestions. So, too, did Horace Samuel Merrill and Marion Galbraith Merrill, generous friends and discerning critics. This book is far better because of the advice and comments of all these individuals, to whom I owe much.

I appreciate as well the support of two departmental heads at Washington State University, David Stratton and Richard Hume. Both not only encouraged me in this project but did everything they could to provide the time and resources to complete it. Thanks, also, to John Rindell, my teaching assistant, who helped me gather sources. And, as always, I wish to thank my wife, Mary. One could ask for no better partner, and I am delighted to share this book and my love with her.

# INTRODUCTION:

## THE GHOST AT THE CONCERT

"And you shall not crucify mankind upon a cross of gold." The words rang out with suggestions of their original power, but the time and setting had changed dramatically. It was no longer 1896 in Chicago but 22 October 1985, in the University of Illinois football stadium. Moreover, the speaker's voice carried not simply to the back of a packed auditorium but coast to coast over national television.

Almost ninety years after William Jennings Bryan had electrified twenty thousand people with his Cross of Gold speech at the 1896 national Democratic convention, an actor from a popular television series read Bryan's concluding sentences in a quite different setting. It was the Farm Aid concert, an entertainment extravaganza that country-and-western singer Willie Nelson and others had put together to help raise funds for America's beleaguered farmers, thousands of whom were facing foreclosures because of mounting debts. In the midst of electric guitars, microphones, and television cameras, Bryan's stirring words were poignant reminders of a rapidly fading past. In 1985, the peroration to his famous Cross of Gold address still seemed appropriate enough to include on a program that featured movie stars and well-known singers. At the same time, those haunting words from the previous century seemed anachronistic. Probably when the actor identified Bryan as the source of his quotation, most people barely recognized the name, if they did so at all.

Yet from the mid-1890s until his death in 1925, few Americans were better known than William Jennings Bryan. Three times—in 1896, 1900, and 1908—he ran for president on the Democratic ticket. He lost each time, but in his first unsuccessful effort he received more votes than had the winners of any previous election. Between 1896 and 1912 no Democrat was more influential. Even after Woodrow Wilson claimed leadership of the party in 1912, Bryan continued to be enormously influential. He served for over two years as Wilson's secretary of state, before resigning office to challenge the administration's foreign policy on World War I. His ability to stir grass-roots excitement and galvanize public emotions ended only with his death, a few days after his appearance in the celebrated Scopes "monkey trial" in Tennessee. The "Great Commoner," as his followers called him, was for his era what later generations would call a "celebrity candidate" or political "superstar." Even though he built his career in the sparsely settled state of Nebraska at a time when no serious presidential candidate lived west of the Mississippi River, he rose to the heights of leadership. And he did so without benefit of personal wealth or a highly organized political machine, and against opposition that was often fierce. A brilliant speaker, he dominated for years not only the nation's political stump but also the centerpiece of American mass culture from the 1890s into the 1920s, the Chautauqua. "The newspapers ought to put up the money to build a memorial for William Jennings Bryan," wrote one individual several days after the Commoner's death, "because he was to the world of news what Babe Ruth is to baseball—the real drawing card."[1]

As much as anyone from the end of the nineteenth century through the first quarter of the twentieth, he helped to define the great issues and policy questions that the nation faced. These included the relevance of the nation's democratic traditions in an industrialized, corporate society, the role of common citizens in an age of specialized knowledge and expertise, the place of morality and individual conscience in defining foreign policy, and the goals of the United States in a world of empires and revolution.

He also demonstrated an ideological ambivalence so common in American history, especially that of grass-roots movements. Much as the movements with which Bryan was most sympathetic—populism and progressivism—he moved along divergent ideological paths, economic and cultural. On political and economic issues, his inclinations were leftward in terms of his suspicion of concentrated wealth, as well as his commitment to the democratic principles of majority rule and the rights of ordinary people to participate in their government. On cultural matters, his course was nostalgic and defensive.

Politically and economically, he was concerned with protecting the power and status of common citizens against organized privilege, especially that of big business. The question that he posed in his 1908 presidential campaign summed up the issue: "Shall the people rule?" He championed direct primary laws, woman suffrage, the direct election of United States senators, and campaign regulations that would help curb the power of wealthy groups over the economy and government. Convinced that government existed to defend and aid the common folk, he tried to curtail the influence of big business, to establish a graduated income tax and guaranteed bank deposits, and to improve the economic conditions of what he called "the producing classes"— farmers, laborers, and small businesspeople.

Although such causes opened him to charges of radicalism, his ardent defense of traditional values was strikingly old-fashioned. A firm believer in "the old time religion" as well as the time-honored values of family, hard work and self-discipline, he resisted many of the trends that characterized the emerging twentieth-century culture of consumerism and social permissiveness. Intellectually, he stood on moral bedrock, certain of unchanging absolutes and the eventual triumph of truth and justice. Confident that he was on the side of righteousness, he spent little time examining either himself or the values that he had inherited from his family and the mid-nineteenth-century small-town culture of his youth.

Few things have been more volatile in America's past than this combination of cultural traditionalism and the democratic desire to protect the little folk. The main battleground of American democracy has time and again rested on the emotional soil of fear and hope—fear that conspiracies are underway to destroy old values, and hope that the common people will prevail. Social and political movements have typically erupted out of suspicions that "fat cats" or other privileged groups are enjoying unfair advantages or special favors, thereby threatening the nation's most cherished beliefs in economic mobility and the inherent worth of the individual citizen.

This was political ground that Bryan occupied as forcefully as any American. Not surprisingly, his reputation varied from that of an arch disturber of the peace to that of an outdated and quaint throwback. On the one hand, he recognized a central challenge: the need to find ways of salvaging democratic traditions in a nation moving toward larger, more distant, and more powerful economic units. Convinced that government is the logical and most accessible means by which a majority of citizens in a democracy can exert its influence, he helped to sketch out the protective and welfare responsibilities of the modern state. On the other hand, he was increasingly uncomfortable with the emerging mass culture of consumerism and leisure, which he warned was eroding the moral base of American life.

If Bryan could have attended the 1985 Farm Aid concert, he would probably have had mixed feelings. He would certainly have been pleased that later generations were still quoting him. Moreover, a number of cultural and social signposts would have been gratifyingly familiar. In the 1980s the word *populism* was again much in fashion. Direct democracy was manifesting itself with remarkable energy as citizens used initiatives to get proposals immediately before the people and not await sluggish legislative action. In mid-1984 alone, at least three hundred initiative movements were under way across the nation. There was also considerable discussion of the place of morality in politics, especially among numerous preachers, some of whom classified themselves as representatives of the "moral majority." And a resurgent religious fundamentalism had once again, as in the 1920s, turned the teaching of Darwinism in public school classrooms into a turbulent political issue.

For all the familiarity of such developments in the 1980s, Bryan would nevertheless have had difficulty understanding some of the new manifestations of causes with which he had identified. Among a new generation of people who described themselves as "populist," he would have discerned echoes of his own earlier speeches advocating economic fairness for plain people; but he would have been at a loss trying to comprehend something called "conservative populism" that portrayed the federal government as the people's foe, that opposed taxes, and, even more horrifying to Bryan, that advocated the reinstatement of gold as the nation's money standard. Similarly, the use of political initiatives by well-funded private groups to overturn such reforms as inheritance taxes might have bothered him as examples of organized wealth's capacity to pervert participatory democracy. Equally troubling to him might have been the suavely dressed television ministers who, while preaching morality, seemed to have little sympathy for what Bryan had deemed essential: a Social Gospel religion that aligned itself not with the economically comfortable but with the downtrodden and disadvantaged.

Although Bryan had been dead for sixty years by the time of the 1985 Farm Aid concert, the decision to quote from him was both timely and incongruous. The glitter, the fashion, the television advertising, and much of the technology assuredly represented aspects of the very commercialism that had appalled him. Yet from the concert stage came numerous appeals for Americans to help those within the nation, specifically small family farmers who were struggling to survive economically. There were also numerous references to government's responsibility to aid and protect the little people. And there were occasional suggestions of populist distaste for wealthy business and financial managers who were destroying in the name of profit what had been a proud feature of American life for generations—the family farm. These angry messages and desperate appeals at the concert were sandwiched between selections of country-and-western music—music that since its origins had focused on the lives of common folk, their miseries, hopes, failures, strengths, and their homely virtues of hard work, honesty, family, and piety.

In notable ways, William Jennings Bryan was a ghost at the concert. It was fitting that one of the performers invoked his memory. Years earlier, in 1924, journalist William Allen White claimed that Bryan had "influenced the thinking of the American people more profoundly than any other man of his generation."[2] As America neared the end of the twentieth century, the world of Bryan receded ever more into the past. But that past was not without meaning—a fact that was touchingly clear on that cloudy and rain-threatened day in central Illinois in October 1985. Even ghosts have their purposes, and it was fitting that Bryan's was summoned forth in that part of the country. For it was in that very region, 125 years earlier, that the story of William Jennings Bryan had begun.

# I

# FORMATIVE YEARS
## (1860–1887)

In the prairie country of south-central Illinois in 1860, the promise of spring heralded new beginnings and fresh starts. Silas and Mariah Bryan were still trying to escape from the physical bleakness that annually settled over the region in winter, but also from the emotional pall of an even longer season of grief. The nineteenth of March provided them with special evidence of renewed possibilities and awakened hope. On that date, two years after the deaths of their first two children, there was again new life in the household. His name was William Jennings, and he joined the Bryans' other surviving child, Frances.

William's childhood was stable, secure, and full of assurance. Growing up in a locally distinguished and respectable family in small-town, Middle America, he accepted without question the traditional values of the mid-nineteenth century. The certainties of progress, the rewards of religious faith, the fruits of hard work, close social bonds, and a need for an orderly, self-disciplined life formed his moral landscape as decisively as the rich farmland shaped Marion county, where his father owned five hundred acres. To a remarkable extent William would never leave the world of his childhood, despite the fact that he traveled widely, lived through sixty-five years of profoundly turbulent change in American history, and became one of the best-known political figures of his era. Novelist Thomas Wolfe's famous statement "You can't go home again" never applied to Bryan because spiritually and emotionally he never ventured from his place of origin.

The rural, village Illinois settings where Bryan spent his first twenty-one years left an indelible influence on him. His world seemed permanent and secure. In the little town of Salem where he initially resided, there were notable reminders of the pioneer spirit, with its celebration of social mobility and its confidence that success comes through diligent effort and pursuit of the main chance. It was that very spirit that had sent Silas as a young man scurrying out of the rugged mountain country of western Virginia and eventually to Illinois, and that had persuaded Israel Jennings, Mariah's grandfather, to move from Kentucky to Marion county, where he purchased cheap government land. Salem's three small mills, producing flour and lumber, and the surrounding miles of farmland likewise testified to a vision of business achievement that went beyond potential profits to include nothing less than a philosophy of life. Economic independence seemed the natural order of things. In the township of Salem, where the population in 1870 was barely two thousand, only a few people worked for wages in the several local shops and businesses. Eighty percent of the adults were self-employed. For most of the area's residents, farming was the source of income and the way of life. In his autobiography, Bryan described his origins as indeed fortunate. He believed that he had been "born in the greatest of all ages" in "the greatest of all lands."[1]

One of the most important staples in young Bryan's cultural diet was a rich and profoundly complex tradition of evangelical Protestantism. For huge numbers of nineteenth-century Americans, it provided a whole cosmology, as ubiquitous as the air they breathed. Bryan absorbed this religion easily and, except for a brief moment in college, held to it fiercely. "The spread of Christian religion" was among his early resolves. "In his zeal for souls," according to his spouse, "he was like an evangelist." Theodore Roosevelt, who described the White House as a "bully pulpit," once declared of him, "By George, he would make the greatest Baptist preacher on earth." And Bryan himself viewed his decision at age fourteen to join a church as more influential "for good" than anything else he had done.[2]

Certainly his devout and upstanding parents helped to chart his course. His father, a Baptist farmer-politician-judge who set aside time for prayers and Scripture reading at least three times a day, provided firm direction. When William, not yet six, contemplated becoming a Baptist minister it was because, as he recalled years later, his father belonged to that church. It was, however, his mother who dominated his first years. While he was young, she struggled with grief. The deaths of her first two children from whooping cough unquestionably continued to haunt her. And when William was still small, she suffered the death of her new baby, Harry. Such tragedy no doubt reinforced her search for spiritual answers and strengthened the protective embrace that she threw around her surviving children—Frances, William, and two younger brothers and sisters. She was a constant presence in William's life, caring for him day to day, serving as his schoolteacher until he was ten, and singing her favorite gospel songs to him.

It was probably more from his mother than from anyone else that William obtained his preference for the emerging sentimental side of American Protestantism. During the pre–Civil War era famed revivalists such as Charles Grandison Finney had jolted established churches by appealing directly to the passions of their listeners. The gospel according to Finney and his counterparts stressed individual emotional commitments to salvation, an avenue reportedly available to anyone who sought it. Divine mercy and Christian martyrdom received prominent attention. Such preaching was part of an ongoing shift within evangelical Christianity away from the angry God of Jonathan Edwards's prerevolutionary, Calvinist preaching that emphasized sin and damnation. The popular hymn "What a Friend We Have in Jesus"— undoubtedly part of Mariah Bryan's repertoire for William—exemplified this religious transformation. By the mid-nineteenth century, more and more hymns celebrated a "gentle," "tender," "sweet" Savior, who affectionately welcomed sinners to his loving arms. This was the variety of Christian faith that Bryan always favored. Throughout his life, he drew upon this religion of feeling, as opposed to one of abstract doctrines.

While evangelical Protestantism molded Bryan's view of a loving community infused with intense feelings, so too it pushed him strongly toward an active, public-spirited life. Throughout the nineteenth century, ringing appeals that converts must recognize the social responsibilities of their faith shook the nation's churches and generated powerful reform currents. Granted, the pulpit messages in behalf of self-discipline and temperance squared neatly with the emerging ethos of commercial or industrial capitalism. New entrepreneurs could find in the revivalist doctrines a rationale for being less sensitive to the needs of others (employees, for example) on grounds that, after all, each person was responsible for his or her own fate. But this was not the legacy of religion to the family of Silas and Mariah Bryan. In their home, public service and the model of the Good Samaritan always held a special place.

William Jennings Bryan grew up believing in a moral universe that was as fixed as Sir Isaac Newton's physical universe: harmonious and without friction, constituting proof that God was a reasonable and benevolent creator. From this perspective, such precepts as the general welfare and individual morality were as natural as gravity. Unselfish benevolence was not only a means of salvation; it also conformed to God's larger purpose. The long-range prognosis for humans was thus optimistic: it was possible to bring their activities and institutions in line with God's desired ends. This meant that politics was loaded with moral meaning, a point that Judge Silas Bryan could not make often enough and that William echoed again and again as he grew older. In this respect the Bryans were in large company. Such concern with morality fed a rich reform tradition in American religion, pushing many believers from spiritual retreat to worldly activism. Indeed, the historical links between Christian moralism and politics were so strong in the United States that, years later, a political scientist half-seriously suggested there was a "need to study theology in order to follow American politics." Bryan, as much as anyone of his generation, represented this "seminarian strain," as another cultural commentator has described it.[3]

While the daily devotions, hymns, and example of his parents were the main agencies through which Bryan encountered evangelical Protestantism, the outside world initially provided no shocking disparities. He much enjoyed Sunday school. For a while he attended the Baptist school in the morning and the Methodist in the afternoon. Eventually he settled on the Presbyterian group because it included many of his school chums and a popular superintendent.

His academic education was in many respects an extension of his Sunday school lessons. _The McGuffey Reader_ was a centerpiece of his early instruction, whether at home with Mariah or later in public school. It was as good a guide as any to nineteenth-century evangelical Protestantism and village maxims. Designed in 1836 by a Presbyterian minister from Pennsylvania, the books were enormously popular for decades in rural and small-town America. Their purpose was not simply to provide instruction in the mechanics of reading, but also to teach morals and to reaffirm agrarian, rural life-styles. Heavily religious, the brief stories and poems indicated that a divine plan guides events, that virtue triumphs, that evil must fail, that God-given truths are easily discernible, that responsibilities are clear, and that, short of dying, one can get no closer to heaven than America's villages and farms. To succeed and be happy, children must master the ideals of self-help, hard work, frugality, loyalty to family, honesty, and courage. They must avoid unclean thoughts, tobacco, gambling, and liquor— "the Worm of the Still."

None of this surprised or offended young William Jennings Bryan, of course. It simply gave him, as it did so many of his contemporaries, a neat summary of well-known, eternal truths that were simple and uncomplicated. A schoolboy speech of his, loaded with sentimentality and optimism, could have come directly from _McGuffey_. William stated confidently that the unvirtuous were destined for "defeat, misery, and shame" in an unequal contest with diligent, committed individuals. "No class of men can cease from labor," he argued. "There is a place for all, there is a work for all. No drones are needed in the human hive. The idle are not only unnecessary, but dangerous to society." Throughout his life Bryan would continue to make such statements with complete conviction and utterly without embarrassment.[4]

If evangelical Christianity constituted the bedrock of received wisdom for Bryan and his generation, so did the Enlightenment legacy of the American Revolution. From one angle, this combination of influences may have seemed unlikely. Enlightenment theory was rooted in the emerging perspectives of modern science; evangelical Protestantism rested on religious faith and the Bible. Indeed, Bryan's career often suggested the collision of these worlds, rather than their mutuality. Yet in important ways the two apparently competing world-views shared significant premises. Both envisioned a natural order of human affairs; both stressed individual responsibility; and both were heavily moral. The theory of republicanism, unquestionably one of the Enlightenment's most vital bequests to the era of revolution and constitution making, not only focused on the proper structure of government, with divided powers and delicately balanced parts, but also trumpeted the role of virtuous citizens who enjoyed personal liberties while committing themselves to the larger public good. "Virtue" signified the necessary willingness of patriotic people to subsume personal interests to the needs of the "commonwealth"; it was the cultural cement of a harmonious society. Selfishness, vice, unchecked ambition, and the pursuit of "luxury" abetted either tyranny or anarchy. None other than the famous patriot Thomas Paine had written that "the word *republic* means the *public good*, or the good of the whole."

William Jennings Bryan, several generations removed from the revolutionary era, placed among his good fortunes the fact that he was a citizen of "the greatest of the republics of history." Again and again, he praised America's republican foundations and appealed to virtuous citizens to defend the public welfare. As ardently as a Paine or a Samuel Adams, he believed that true patriots must place their duty to their government above any pleasure or convenience. And as much as his revolutionary heroes, he always worried about the enervating influences of great wealth. It was an axiom to him, as it was to the generation of 1776, that "all nations which have grown strong, powerful and influential . . . through hardship and sacrifice . . . have gone to decay through the enjoyment of luxury."[5]

By Bryan's time, however, it was evident that the ideology of republicanism, like that of evangelical Protestantism, had several uses. Just as the emerging industrial capitalism of the pre–Civil War era had begun to fragment the traditional craft relationships of the workshop, so too it had infused republicanism with a growing class consciousness. Both opponents and advocates of economic change claimed the mantle of republicanism. With equal fervor in the years after the Civil War, multimillionaire industrialist Andrew Carnegie and union leader and budding socialist Eugene Debs invoked the revolutionary heritage. New corporate leaders, such as Carnegie, championed individualist self-discipline and independence as the means by which to enlarge personal profits, and thereby to elevate the economic base of all citizens and aid the commonwealth. But journeyman workers and members of the nascent union movement worried that the emerging corporate forms were susceptible to luxury, privilege, and tyranny. Labor leaders such as Debs thus used republican ideals to counter industrial capitalism by elevating honorable work above the accumulation of property and privilege.

During Bryan's youth the ideological arena for this debate was still very much under construction, and his immediate experiences helped to determine which side he eventually joined. By the 1870s, his father was no longer enthusiastic about the railroads, preeminent symbols of the new corporate, industrial era. Like most of his neighbors, Silas came to see the railways as steel bands that were squeezing midwestern farmers into debt. Silas's suspicions of railroads and eastern financial interests mirrored those of his disgruntled Marion county neighbors, equally restive over discriminatory shipping rates and the privileges that large industrial and financial corporations enjoyed. When William was twelve, Abraham Lincoln's former law partner William Herndon summed up the anger of many midwestern farmers: "They are down on railroads and rings, and conspiracies, and monopolies, and *treason* against the general welfare."[6] William Jennings Bryan's political education thus started when he was young, and his school extended to the dusty streets of downtown Salem, where local agrarians commiserated with each other about growing debts and powerful outside business interests. He came naturally to the view that an apocalyptic struggle was under way with a corporate, industrial order that struck at the very roots of republicanism.

The culture out of which Bryan came, and which he defended to his death in 1925, thus rested on what historian John Thomas has described as "the twin truths of natural law and Christian faith"— embodied in those pillars of "political rights and Christian duties," the Declaration of Independence and the New Testament. The compatibility between republicanism and Protestant evangelical influences had been evident as far back as the revolutionary era, when numerous nonclerical republicans had allied with the clergy. The result was nothing less than a form of "political religion" that blended the civic duties of republicanism with evangelical piety. Political religion was ingrained in William Jennings Bryan. His father, a devout Baptist as well as a judge and legislator who admired republican institutions, had once said, for example, that "politicians and divines" had first claim on the family's guestroom.[7]

When Bryan was a youth, the "twin truths" of republicanism and evangelical Christianity were important aspects of a culture that seemed intact and inviolate. All around him were reassuring signposts. Life was congenial and well-ordered—at home, where each Sunday the "Bryan choir" gathered in the parlor around the piano to sing hymns, at Sunday school, and in the village settings of rural Illinois.

This did not mean, however, that growing up was always easy or without disappointment. Although Bryan later claimed that no one could have asked for a happier childhood, he sometimes hinted at another aspect of his youth, physically harsh and emotionally anxious. Curiously, Bryan's incredible ability on the political stump to remember names and faces faltered badly when he tried to recall details from his youth.

Looking back, he waxed eloquent about the virtues of agrarian living, but in fact as a boy he had looked forward to escaping "the hardships of work" by hunting rabbits with his dogs. The county fair had been fun; trying to keep his white pig clean had not. Only in retrospect had his farm chores offered valuable instruction in the work ethic; at the time, they had been "drudgery," characterized in the winter months by numb fingers, a runny nose, and even softly uttered oaths lamenting his plight. In some respects his life on the farm one mile outside Salem had actually been rather special. The family had not moved there from town until he was six; the house was new and large; most of the five hundred acres were rented out; and Silas, no farmer at heart, was a college graduate with an M.A. degree, who had taught school, become a locally prominent attorney, served in the state legislature, and (during William's first twelve years) been a circuit judge. Although William's experience with the soil had thus been limited, it had nevertheless been sufficiently hard to provide the days that he "least enjoyed." Nor was there much about his public school years that he believed "worth recording" other than the "strict disciplinarian" teacher, Mary Lemon (whose name Bryan somehow transposed into "Mrs. Lamb"), a huge woman whose ready use of a willow switch attested to her belief that sparing the rod only spoiled the child.[8]

He conceded that his parents, loving and responsible, had also been "quite strict." He admitted that as a child he had sometimes envied friends "who were given more liberty." Indeed, he had sometimes felt so restless during prelunch discussions of Bible chapters with his father that even work in the fields looked attractive. His playmates observed that Silas, tall and lean, kept especially rigid rules and handed out catechisms to memorize, rather than candy or toys. And William himself remembered "more than once" being "chastised and tied to the bed-post as a punishment." He responded by being a model child. A Salem woman who had helped to care for him and his siblings said that "he never argued or refused to do what was required of him." The closest he got to trouble may have been when he used his jackknife to carve his initials on a school desk, for which he received a switching. Otherwise, neither fighting nor swearing marked his conduct.[9]

Perhaps the most coercive aspect of Silas and Mariah's upbringing, however, was not the threat of punishment, or the firm rules, but the force of their own example and personalities. William's admitted fascination for "the lure of prizes" may have reflected his desire to please his parents as well as his need to prove himself worthy of their respect. If so, it was a difficult assignment. Indeed, when William at the age of thirty read one of his father's speeches about "honor, truth, sincerity, justice, and Christianity," he was moved to tears. "I felt so unworthy to take my father's place," he wrote.[10] Such feelings of inferiority were not unique to him. Many of his contemporaries, also of pioneer stock but one or two steps removed from the cutting edge of settlement, worried as well that they were made of less substantial stuff than their parents. They felt more privileged, less useful. Hence Theodore Roosevelt judged himself weak as compared with his recently deceased father. So did others such as Jane Addams, born the same year as Bryan and in the same state, and destined to be a famous reformer in her own right, and Lincoln Steffens, who became one of the nation's most famous journalists.

Given the sway of Silas and Mariah Bryan over their son, William's move at age fifteen from his parents' home to Jacksonville, Illinois, to finish high school and attend college, must not have been easy. Silas had originally hoped to send him to a prestigious eastern school, or at least to a Baptist college in Missouri; but depleted family funds owing to the depression of 1873 narrowed the alternatives. Jacksonville, less than one hundred miles away, was a satisfactory option for several reasons: Whipple Academy and Illinois College had fine reputations; and Silas's cousin, Hiram Jones, a medical doctor and college trustee, offered William a place to stay in return for odd jobs and chores. However acceptable this was to William, the choice had not been his to make. He could not recall choosing to attend college. "It was decided for me by my parents and when I was too young to fix the day." Silas's occasional insensitivity to his son's needs could hardly have helped. Once William wrote home requesting a new pair of pants because he had outgrown his others and was ashamed to wear them. Silas urged him to be patient and added, "You might as well learn now that people will measure you by the length of your head and not by the length of your breeches." The advice was sound; the timing was not.[11]

However difficult the fifteen-year-old's move was to Jacksonville, he quickly discovered a cultural environment that differed little from what he had known. The religious commitments of Whipple Academy and Illinois College were clear. "Jesus the Christ Himself" was the institution's "chief cornerstone," according to the president. The setting was small and friendly. Seventy-eight students attended the academy; sixty more were enrolled in the college. The college faculty numbered eight, several of whom were noted classicists. Indeed, Bryan's education was oriented heavily toward the classics, including three years of Latin and four of Greek. Like most schools of the time, the academy and college refrained from encouraging independent or critical thinking; instead, the academic regimen consisted of reading and memorizing textbooks. As a student, Bryan was industrious enough, although he hardly compiled an outstanding record. He did very well in American government and moral philosophy, but sparkled far less in his other studies, especially science and geology. Insofar as he encountered the world of books, it was not in the college library, which mainly featured rare volumes and reference works and was open only one hour daily. His contact with books and intellectual exchange came mostly in the home of his relative Hiram Jones, who had a large personal library and hosted a local literary group. At school Bryan was popular enough, but preferred being with the quieter, more disciplined students. He was more interested in performing well on the debate team than on the athletic field and, although his debating record was far from distinguished, when he graduated in 1881 he delivered the valedictory address as well as the class oration.

In many respects, Jacksonville turned out to be a larger edition of Salem. Located in the rich farmland country of central Illinois, near the shallow, muddy Mauvaise Terre river, the town of ten thousand very much reflected the history and values of Middle America. By living there for six years of schooling and, after a brief hiatus, for four more to practice law, Bryan continued to imbibe deeply from the cultural waters of nineteenth-century village society. Just as the world of his parents had shaped his early childhood, so too did the decade in Jacksonville reinforce firmly held impressions of American life and values. Throughout his career, he bore the stamp of Jacksonville and thousands of communities like it.

Jacksonville, as well as Salem, mirrored vividly the social processes and ideals that gave birth to numerous midwestern frontier towns in the 1800s. Myths eventually obscured the histories of such places, leaving fond memories of "the good old days" when people were reportedly bound tightly together, caring for each other, helping each other, and enjoying an existence that seemed quieter, friendlier, and more united than what followed. Bryan subscribed to such sentimentalized village mythology as tenaciously as anyone, and he later filled his speeches with celebrations of gentle folk, shaded streets, and simple, shared life-styles.

The contradictions and social strains that in fact often lay beneath the mythology were just as essential to Bryan's character as to the histories of Jacksonville, Salem, and their many counterparts. He, like other citizens of such towns, felt profoundly the competing currents of nineteenth-century village life: individualism versus community, voluntarism versus coercion, rootedness versus geographical mobility, localism versus nationalism, and optimistic boosterism versus often grim realities.

His inveterate optimism, which again and again buoyed his spirits through setbacks and failures, surely reflected the positive spirit so central to the community-building process of towns where he lived, whether in Illinois or, subsequently, in Nebraska. Boosterism represented more than backslapping salutes to success and progress, although certainly it had plenty of those. While it tended to play down misery and overlook misfortune and trouble, it also served as a kind of buffer against the kind of unbridled individualism that could produce adversity and suffering. By trumpeting the ideal of a united, happy, prospering community, the booster ethos made much of collective goals, self-sacrificing citizens, and a strong public spirit. And while it invariably had its shallow, hypocritical and self-serving aspects, it also contained remnants of the revolutionary era's celebration of classical republicanism in which virtuous citizens were to subsume purely personal gain to community needs. Within the booster mentality, selfish ambition did not go uncontested; the community exerted claims of its own.

Throughout his life, William Jennings Bryan would exhibit the booster spirit. Sometimes it verged toward a shallow hucksterism. Invariably, however, a strong sense of public responsibility and duty overshadowed his pocketbook concerns.

His enthusiastic temperament may have helped him, as surely as it did many other Americans, to cope with a world in which realities often fell short of ideals. Jacksonville's residents for over half a century had adjusted to growing divisions and fragmentation, along with the unpredictable nature of external developments. The town's growth from a few families in the 1820s to around ten thousand by the 1870s—development to warm any booster's heart—brought problems of its own. By the 1850s the cheap shacks and apartments that constituted "the Patch" near the railroad depot were already becoming alien territory. As the historian of Jacksonville, Don Doyle, notes, "from high on College Hill," where Bryan subsequently lived, "the Protestant elite could look down upon the Patch and witness the Catholic menace intruding, not as a stealthy conspiracy of the priesthood, but as a rowdy band of Irish railroad workers—rough young men who drank too much, and who gambled and wenched." Portuguese and German immigrants, along with a small black population of almost five hundred, who came from the South mainly after the Civil War, superficially attested to the community's open door. Uneasiness about the newcomers nevertheless revealed significant social fault lines that belied the image of a contented and united population. Added to this demographic fact were the thwarted dreams of Jacksonville's leaders, who time and again lost out to rival communities such as nearby Springfield, Peoria, or Champaign in the race for economic and social status.[12]

Bryan presumably could have sympathized as much as anyone with the setbacks of the town that for ten years was his home. His own life would be in many ways a study in thwarted aspirations and lost causes. But he, like his cultural mentors in Jacksonville, was typically able to paper over such disappointments with imagined history. "Inverted boosterism" characterized Jacksonville's rendering of its past, as community leaders, in retrospect, interpreted failures as desired results. The town, left behind by the successes of Springfield and other neighboring places, supposedly was what its residents had always intended—relatively small, without the problems of industry and a large ethnic work force, and in no hurry to rush into the frantic future. That Bryan learned well the lessons of such "inverted boosterism" may have sustained him through major disappointments. He was able to look back with equanimity, sentimentally viewing his life as proof of what anyone, with comparable luck, diligence, and opportunity, "can accomplish in this favored land of ours."[13]

While this ability to reorder and view events in a favorable way was a product of his Jacksonville culture, so too was his capacity to square such contradictory ideals as geographical mobility and social rootedness. The fact that the population of Jacksonville, like most nineteenth-century communities, had a rapid turnover was due, in part, to people like Bryan. In the two decades before he first moved there, less than half the population had stayed for as long as ten years, a turnover rate roughly comparable to the national figure. Bryan twice left the town, once to attend law school in Chicago, and then permanently because he found the career and political pickings more attractive in Nebraska. Years later, owing partly to his wife's health, he switched his residence to Florida. Even while he resided in Nebraska, however, he spent much of his time on the road, traveling, lecturing, and campaigning. His roots ran deep, but less geographically than culturally.

For this reason the period from roughly 1880 to 1884 was especially important in his life. These were wrenching, bittersweet years. A brief crisis of identity in college threatened to sunder the cultural assumptions of his youth. Then came shocking news of the unexpected deaths of his father and younger brother. He next encountered urban America firsthand for an extended time, while he attended law school in Chicago, before returning to Jacksonville to enter law, marry, and gain his first child.

His identity crisis was perhaps not surprising, given the coercive power of his parents. Nor was the crisis unique. A striking number of Bryan's contemporaries plunged into harrowing emotional times as they reached maturity. These included some of the most celebrated reformers of his generation—Jane Addams, one of the pioneers of the settlement house movement; Ben Lindsey, Denver's famed "kid's judge"; Richard T. Ely, the noted economist; Tom Johnson, who served as mayor of Cleveland; and defense attorney Clarence Darrow.

Bryan's personal crisis had several dimensions. One involved a collision between his religious beliefs and what he was learning in his college science courses. In his first encounter with the evolutionary ideas of Charles Darwin, the scientist scored heavily. For a short while, Bryan wrestled with serious doubts as he tried to reconcile his childhood views of God and the universe with Darwin's theories. For a moment, he wavered. He even toyed with thoughts that he would not join a church in Jacksonville. In his search for answers about God and immortality, he turned to an unexpected source, the famed agnostic Robert Ingersoll, a man whose freethinking was so controversial that he had been pelted with fruit and vegetables in some towns. But Ingersoll's response to Bryan's letter proved disappointing, probably because Ingersoll was temperamentally indisposed to offer clear-cut answers to the young student's questions.

Something less theological than familial added to Bryan's anxiety. For the first time in his life, he had pushed away from his parents, flirting with nothing less than a rejection of their most basic beliefs. Although he later shrugged off these brief challenges to accepted family authority as merely silly examples of youthful exuberance, at the time his doubts and assertions of independence must have seemed considerably more significant.

Only in retrospect could he have dismissed as brash and fatuous his strong sense as a student of possessing new personal powers and encountering new intellectual possibilities. For a person whose childhood contained no documented examples of youthful misconduct, his abbreviated courtship with the world outside of church and home had been an uncharacteristic example of risk taking. His experiment in skepticism lasted only briefly. He joined Jacksonville's Presbyterian church and never again let his religious compass waver. Still, the momentary loss of his theological bearings had been searing enough that, decades later, when he publicly staged his last famous battle with Darwinian theories and modernist thought, he worried about the vulnerability of college students to unorthodox ideas. In his own case he had survived the challenge. He held firmly to the certainties that were rooted in his childhood, in the cultural and social settings of Salem and Jacksonville, and in the intellectual universes of republicanism and evangelical Protestantism.

His college encounter with Darwinian thought ultimately demonstrated that he was no cultural rebel. His steadfast resistance subsequently to many of the changes that marked the modern intellectual world ultimately took a considerable toll, opening him to criticism as inflexible, ignorant, simpleminded, and undistinguished in ability. For Bryan, however, his fixed intellectual reference points were continuing sources of comfort and security. They sustained his confidence through numerous setbacks and allowed him to keep up the good fight. They also unquestionably accounted for much of his appeal to hundreds of thousands of Americans who believed deeply in him, who trusted him, and who gave him genuine affection as well as votes.

While he was in college, his only other recorded departure from accepted rules and beliefs involved his future wife, Mary Baird. The daughter of a retired country storekeeper in a tiny community some thirty miles away, she was a student at nearby Jacksonville Female Academy, or the "Jail for Angels," as young men in the area labeled it. Attractive and charming, she quite simply dazzled the nineteen-year-old Bryan. In turn, she found him very attractive, with his strapping physique, finely textured black hair, dark eyes, firm chin, and confident, dignified manner. Although she described his nose as "prominent—too large to look well"—she found captivating his "expansive and expressive" smile.[14]

Soon, romance pushed them into a conspiracy against proper etiquette and, indeed, against academy rules concerning chaperoned dating. Their secret meetings, when discovered by the school authorities, led to Mary's temporary suspension. Even then, Bryan hid in a baggage car as the principal escorted Mary to the train to send her home. Once the train pulled away from the principal's watchful eyes, Bryan emerged from the baggage car and sat with her. It was a memorable trip. Not far out of Jacksonville, on that late spring day in 1880, they agreed to marry. Few decisions could have worked out so well. Mary Baird was a remarkable person, bright, talented, resourceful, and energetic. A year younger than her husband, she quickly became the central figure in his life. Regrettably, his father never had a chance to meet her. Silas died the very day that William had planned to introduce them.

15

Silas Bryan's sudden death after a stroke at age fifty-eight stunned William, who was halfway through his junior year in college. Difficult months followed. Added to William's grief was a deep concern that he might not be able to finish college because of Silas's debt-ridden estate. Eventually the problem was resolved, but in a way that brought additional pain, when William's brother Russell also died suddenly. The tragedy liberated money that Russell planned to use for college, thereby sparing William from a forced return to the farm. In 1881, William was even able to scratch out enough money to go on to law school.

Operating on the leanest of budgets, Bryan spent two years at the Union College of Law in Chicago, which he had selected upon the recommendation of his father's law partner, who had gone there. Not only was he separated from Mary, his fiancée, but for the first time he had to deal on a day-to-day basis with a tumultuous urban setting. In sharp contrast to the relative tranquility of Salem and Jacksonville, Chicago was for him a very unsettling place. He lived in a windowless, battered room. To save money, he walked the four miles to and from school. The bitterly cold winds that blew off Lake Michigan in the winter only added to the emotionally chilly surroundings of a city on the make, halfway in time between the Great Fire of 1871 (which had wiped out four square miles of densely populated area) and the famed Columbian Exposition of 1893. To many people, Chicago symbolized America's can-do spirit. When Bryan arrived, its population already exceeded half a million, 40 percent of whom were either foreign-born immigrants or their children. Over the next ten years, it would more than double in size, thereby becoming the second largest city in the Western Hemisphere.

The whirl of change was so great that, according to Mark Twain, it was "hopeless for the occasional visitor to try to keep up with Chicago."[15] As the great crossroads and trading center of Middle America, building especially upon the meat-packing industry, it had quickly become a place of startling contrasts, with conspicuous wealth and huge commercial buildings on one hand, and, on the other, the ugly, stinking sprawl of the stockyards and endless stretches of filthy and dilapidated shanties.

Bryan may have found the sheer energy of Chicago somewhat exhilarating, but his reaction was apparently more like that of Rudyard Kipling, the well-known English writer who in India and elsewhere had already witnessed urban poverty. "I urgently desire never to see it again," Kipling wrote of Chicago in 1889. "And I went away to get peace and rest." To Bryan's impressionable eyes, Chicago's notoriously corrupt machine politics was especially unnerving. "I am wrought up to such a pitch that I cannot hold in," he wrote Mary. "There are reports of recent jury packing in this city and they only indicate how criminally negligent and selfish we as a people are becoming."[16]

Equally repugnant to him were the squalor and suffering of the poor in contrast with the staggering wealth of the new corporate millionaires. On one icy day near the city courthouse he observed a number of shabbily clad youngsters—newsboys and "street arabs"—desperately trying to keep warm. The pathetic scene, so common in Chicago and other cities, shocked him and made him wonder what was happening to the American dream of opportunity. His visit to the industrial shops of George Pullman, the railroad car magnate, also agitated him greatly. The workers there were unlike those he had observed in Salem and Jacksonville, and he worried that their anger and frustration might soon erupt into violence. His fears were not unjustified. Within three years after he left Chicago, the bloody strike at the McCormick Harvester plant and the subsequent horror of the Haymarket Square riot provided the chilling spectacle of class warfare. Similarly violent labor confrontations in nearby Pullman, Illinois, and during the tumultuous 1894 railroad strike made the Windy City and its environs shattering symbols of urban, industrial conflict.

Little wonder, then, that Bryan's letters to Mary in the early 1880s painted a bleak picture of Chicago. And little wonder that Bryan, whose points of reference were Salem and Jacksonville, felt out of place in a sprawling urban center. Even later, after he moved to Lincoln, Nebraska—in many respects simply a larger Jacksonville—he never shrugged off his basic discomfort with big-city America.

Bryan was unquestionably delighted in 1883 to finish his law training and escape Chicago. Probably the most valuable lessons that he brought away with him were those he had learned while working part-time in the law office of Lyman Trumbull, who had known his father and was one of Illinois's political giants. Trumbull, who as a senator had cast a long shadow, especially during Reconstruction, was an aging but outspoken critic of economic monopoly and concentrated wealth. His opinions confirmed what Bryan had already heard in downstate Illinois from the rumblings of unhappy and financially troubled farmers who complained about the power of railroads, manufacturers, and bankers. Although Bryan's academic record at Union College of Law was respectable, his presence was most conspicuous as a budding orator with a keen interest in political questions. "Will was eagerly impressed with the idea that the people are being unjustly burdened by monopolies," observed one of his classmates. "He maintained even then that the menace of the country was the encroachment of wealth on the rights of the commonwealth, and he thought there was serious trouble ahead for the country."[17]

In 1883, back in the friendly, familiar confines of Jacksonville, and sporting for a short while a long beard that he had grown in law school, he joined one of the town's prominent law firms. The next year, in October, more confident that he could now support a family, he married Mary Baird. Their first child, Ruth, was born on 30 September 1885.

Two years later, in 1887, Bryan made a momentous decision. He abandoned the state of his birth and moved to Nebraska. Over the previous few months he had become increasingly discouraged with his still-struggling law practice, even though he submitted stories to the local newspapers describing himself as "a promising young lawyer." He recalled weary days in which the chair at his desk, as he put it, "stared at me vacantly." His earnings one month were a paltry $2.50. Similarly, even though in some news stories he indicated that he was "one likely to go far in the political world," he now recognized how limited his political prospects were in Jacksonville. For an aspiring young Democrat, remaining loyal to the party of his father, Jacksonville's strongly Republican constituency offered little hope. He thus took advantage of an offer to join the law practice of a former college classmate in the capital city of Lincoln. After twenty-seven years of living in Illinois, he was off to Nebraska, a sprawling prairie state, sparsely settled, largely dependent on agriculture, and a place whose politics were becoming as volatile as its weather patterns.[18]

# 2

# POLITICAL
# BEGINNINGS
## (1887–1892)

When Bryan moved to Nebraska in October 1887, the state and much of the nation were on the edge of a major political transformation. Within the next few dramatically turbulent years, profound economic developments shattered the traditional political bargaining system. That system, despite religious and ethnic tensions, had rested upon a large consensus that government's main purpose was to promote growth and productivity. Democrats and Republicans alike were agreed on the goals of economic expansion and development. During the 1890s, however, as it became terrifyingly clear to a number of groups that they were too often victims of such expansion and development, the nation experienced a massive political upheaval. Small farmers and laborers in particular concluded that the emerging corporate, industrial society threatened to render them powerless and push them ever closer to the margins of national life. At issue were not simply economic trends but, also, matters of culture that affected nothing less than the American way of life.

In this greatly agitated setting, Bryan emerged as a conspicuous figure. Although he often followed paths that voters had already charted, he pressed himself to the forefront of American political history. His genius was in his ability to articulate the economic anger of the era, as well as the growing fears of social and cultural vulnerability.

In the fall of 1887, none of the residents of Lincoln, Nebraska, of course had any reason to suspect that the twenty-seven-year-old attorney from Illinois would be at the center of the political convulsions soon to shake the country and, within less than a decade, would be one of the best-known people in the United States. When he first arrived in Nebraska, he seemed little more than an extremely personable, civic-minded young man who was bursting with energy. Although he was not distractingly handsome, he had pleasant features— a firmly set mouth, a solid chin not yet starting to sag, a slightly hooked nose, and luminous, dark eyes. The beard that he had worn for a while in Illinois was now gone, and his cleanly shaven face had a boyish quality. His black hair was starting to thin, but there were only suggestions of his future baldness. His six-foot, muscular frame was moving toward bulkiness but still free of the ample girth that subsequently characterized him. He, the effervescent Mary, and their small daughter constituted an attractive family. And the law firm with which he was associated put him in contact with some of the community's social and political leaders. In sum, he was a promising—but hardly outstanding—figure.

Politically, the Nebraska situation offered Bryan more challenge than hope. He was a strongly committed Democrat in solidly Republican country. Since the state's territorial days, the GOP had controlled public offices at every level and, in 1880, claimed two voters for every Democrat.

There was much about Bryan's background, ironically, that seemed to mark him as ideal Republican material. In the Midwest and Great Plains areas, certainly in Illinois and Nebraska, the GOP had relied historically upon old-stock evangelical Protestant groups. Among the so-called "pietistic" denominations friendly to the Republican party were Methodists and Baptists—sects that had directly influenced Bryan's childhood. Such religious groups were much concerned with the conversion experience and looked to government to root out sin. They tended to see the Democratic party as the province of various immigrant groups, especially Irish Catholics, who appeared far too lackadaisical on moral issues. Many Democrats, for their part, took religion seriously; but, because they were often relative newcomers to the United States and belonged to minority religious denominations, they resented the intrusive character of the Republicans. The GOP seemed too willing to dictate personal behavior in public schools, on Sunday, and especially in drinking liquor. For people outside the nation's mainstream Protestant culture, the Democratic reputation as "the party of personal liberty" was appealing; to their Republican opponents, such emphasis on personal liberty was downright dangerous, threatening to replace public morality with individual passion. But even some Republicans fretted, as did one in Iowa, about the dangers of turning the GOP into "a police sergeant."[1]

Given the tone of evangelical Protestantism in Bryan's family—his parents' firm opposition to gambling, tobacco, and alcohol, and their willingness to use government as a moral agency—William on paper was a prime candidate for the GOP. Before he left Jacksonville, he had stumped throughout the county in behalf of clean living and prohibition. Moreover, few historical figures impressed him as much as Abraham Lincoln, whom he lauded as "a perfect model."[2]

Nebraska's political setting should also have nudged Bryan toward the GOP. Republicans in the state were more likely than Democrats to be old-stock, evangelical Christians who supported moral reforms, especially Prohibition. Democrats controlled the few counties that opposed liquor laws. In 1882, one of the state's leading Democrats, and, for a while, a man with whom Bryan worked closely, claimed that "not a single Prohibitionist in the state of Nebraska" was in the Democratic party. "Show me," he said, "a radical pulpit-hanger of any denomination or sect—one who preaches politics every Sunday mixed with the Puritan Doctrine of prohibition and I will show you always, without exception an individual who is voting for . . . the Republican ticket throughout."[3] As a group, Nebraska's Republican leaders had more education than the Democrats, were more closely tied to finance or the law, and were less liable to be directly involved in agriculture. Bryan easily fitted this profile. Also, his booster optimism squared nicely with the Nebraska GOP, which, as the majority party, claimed credit for the state's growth and pointed to the Democrats as dissatisfied nay-sayers.

Bryan, however, was not a Republican; nor did he ever consider joining the party of Lincoln. An ethno-religious line divided voters' affiliations in perhaps a majority of cases, but at least some families, Bryan's included, seemed oblivious to it. Undoubtedly, William's loyalty to the Democratic party started with his father. Silas, a devout Baptist who believed in public prayer and enforced morals, was nevertheless a lifelong Democrat. The Irish and, subsequently, Virginia roots of Silas's ancestors may have predisposed him somewhat toward the Democratic party, but the most important factor was the appeal of Andrew Jackson. In Silas's estimation, Old Hickory's 1828 election symbolized a victory of small farmers over the corrupt monied interests of the East. Silas had, moreover, served eight years as a Democrat in the state senate before the Civil War and had clearly felt the influence of Illinois's Little Giant, Stephen Douglas. Illinois was Abraham Lincoln country, but it also belonged to Douglas, who had bested Lincoln in the famous senate contest of 1858. Although Douglas lost the presidential race two years later to his rival, he ran strongly in their home state; and in Marion county, home of the Bryan family, he beat Lincoln by a margin of two to one.

William Jennings Bryan came happily and early into the Democratic fold, and stayed in it. As a twelve-year-old, he had accompanied his father during Silas's unsuccessful campaign for Congress. At age sixteen, he had sold enough corn to pay for a trip to St. Louis to observe the 1876 party convention. Although he had not been able to gain formal admission, he had breathlessly looked down upon the proceedings from a window. Shortly thereafter he had become an active volunteer in local Democratic activities. His reading in college of George Bancroft's *History of the United States* surely helped to confirm his political allegiances. Bancroft glorified Andrew Jackson by pitting him as the voice of the people against un-American forces of special privilege. No political image would ever be more appealing to Bryan than that of a champion of the little folk battling wealthy elites and unfair advantages. For him the party of memory was thus Democratic, and his emotional ties to it were strong. The sorry state of the Democratic party in Nebraska did not much discourage him. Struggling against Republican currents, it desperately needed young, vigorous political activists—men like the increasingly ambitious young Bryan.

The timing of Bryan's arrival in Nebraska was also fortuitous. A surging population and booming land values made the state in the 1880s a place of exhilarating opportunities—a booster's dream come true. Between 1880 and 1890 the overall population more than doubled, to over one million. The southeastern area, where Bryan settled, shared substantially in this increase. During the two years before his arrival, Lincoln had doubled in size, reaching forty thousand and encouraging enthusiastic predictions that by the decade's end it would be one hundred thousand. All around was striking evidence of boom times. The city established an electric light plant, began to pave its streets, and put in a sewer system. Every day forty-six passenger trains stopped there. The state capital and university made Lincoln the political and educational center of the state, but even in that bustling community the strongly rural nature of the state was apparent. Some citizens, for example, still grazed their livestock on the university campus, and, invariably, the number of farmers who visited the city provided reminders of agriculture's central place in a state that by 1889 produced a whopping 10 percent of America's corn.

Although Nebraska's political scene, like that of the United States generally, was soon to experience a wrenching reorientation, in the 1880s it was characterized by pronounced features. For one thing, local interests still prevailed over those of the larger national society. For another, the major political parties agreed that government's primary role, especially at the federal level, was to promote growth and economic productivity. Voters, interest groups, and elected officials united around the agenda of progress and prosperity. Towns, counties, states, and regions competed for various kinds of largesse, from railroad lines to other forms of business. At issue within states, for example, were such questions as the location of colleges, prisons, state hospitals, and other institutions, all of which promised local jobs and other forms of income. At the more distant federal level, tariff protection and land grants constituted important kinds of economic aid. Debates swirled around the distribution of resources, raising questions about who was to get what—not whether there was anything to get.

This political landscape was beginning to experience tremors at the very time that Bryan settled in Nebraska. Indeed, during the late 1880s and most of the 1890s the Great Plains felt with particular force a political earthquake that staggered the nation. For a young man with elective ambitions of his own, the upheavals provided welcome opportunities as well as severe tests.

Balanced against Nebraska's relative isolation and scattered population was the fact that its politics was more fluid than that of older states. Unlike the northeastern section of the nation, Nebraska was relatively free of strong political party networks and well-established groups. The patronage system, for example, so important for controlling political loyalties, was still quite shaky. And certainly Bryan's chances of attracting attention were better than those of, say, a young immigrant living in New York City's Mulberry Bend tenement district, where by 1890 some 290,000 people (almost one-third of Nebraska's total population) were packed into one square mile of territory. In this sense, it was relatively easy for Bryan, a young attorney in a comparatively small capital city, to strike up acquaintances with key power brokers in the state. This he promptly set out to do, launching his own political talents in what proved to be the right place at the right time.

The law practice that he shared with his partner and former classmate, Adolphus Talbott, provided a convenient base of operations. Bryan never made much money as an attorney, but his profession for a while facilitated contacts with colleagues around the state and even allowed him the opportunity to argue several cases before the Nebraska Supreme Court. He also joined virtually every service organization or club in the area—from the Chamber of Commerce to the Knights of Pythias. As if these were not enough, he and Mary organized other groups, usually informal gatherings to discuss books and issues. He was very active in the local Presbyterian church, worked actively with the Young Men's Christian Association, and delivered sermons to other Protestant denominations.

In early 1888, shortly after arriving in Nebraska, Bryan was on the move politically. He quickly cultivated contacts with one of the state's leading Democrats, J. Sterling Morton, already a three-time gubernatorial candidate. This relationship was not destined to last, given Morton's political conservatism and his role as a lobbyist for the railroad interests. Bryan, in contrast, disliked the railroads so much that he refused to do legal work for them. Despite the differences between the two men, they struck up a political alliance for several years that served each well, but was particularly useful to Bryan, who was trying to establish himself in Nebraska's Democratic party.

As a participant at the state Democratic convention in May 1888, Bryan chose not to be a mere observer. Even though at age twenty-eight he was the youngest delegate present, he scrambled from his chair to deliver a rousing speech on tariff reform. The delegates were so fired up when he finished that the party's central committee invited him to stump Nebraska that year on behalf of the reelection of President Grover Cleveland. More incredibly, he impressed the convention leaders so much that they offered to nominate him for either lieutenant governor or attorney general, but even at that giddy moment, he was shrewd enough not to lose his perspective. He declined both nominations. He knew that it was one thing to dazzle Nebraska's Democrats; it was another to put his young political head on the state chopping block for the Republican majority to lop off.

Within several months in 1888 Bryan established himself with stunning speed as the rising political star in Nebraska. His speeches for Cleveland in twenty-four counties did far more for his future than for the incumbent president (who lost the election to Benjamin Harrison). Again and again, with impassioned addresses sometimes lasting for two hours, he stoked his audiences' emotions. Besides endorsing Democrats, he attacked high protective tariffs as exemplifying Republican favoritism for manufacturers and insensitivity to the needs of farmers. His ringing eloquence, his uncanny ability to paint understandable and strikingly vivid word pictures, and his superbly resonant voice invariably brought his listeners to their feet. He spoke clearly and forcefully, with a fine feel for the dramatic. His marvelously expressive face and easy smile were captivating. Above all, there was the force of his sincerity—of deeply held beliefs. The press labeled him "Bryan the Invincible."

Bryan's rise over the next eight years was meteoric. Within less than a decade, he would move from complete obscurity to national prominence. He did so without great wealth, without wartime achievements to capture the public's attention, and initially without the kinds of status and connections so often necessary to budding politicians. No wonder that he was always willing to work within the established political structure; his own success seemed to offer abundant proof that the system worked. It was to his credit, however, that he did not allow his career to settle into smug self-satisfaction. He never drew the moral from his own life story that his political fortunes hinged simply on his own talents, dedication, morals, and hard work—although certainly he celebrated such virtues and took pride in his own manifestations of them. Instead, again and again, he was alert to the role that sheer luck had played. One of his most admirable traits was his sensitivity to the difficulties that plague most people, and to the ways in which circumstances dictate behavior, success, and failure.

It was during the 1888 campaign that the excited response of a noisy small-town crowd made Bryan himself pause. As he looked out over the completely captivated audience, he felt an exhilarating sense of power, of being able to control the moment, to set the mood, to persuade, to ignite emotions, to command the scene. One observer recalled that the crowd wanted Bryan to continue his speech into a third hour: "I believe they would have listened all night." Bryan came away exalted, but also a little nervous at the prospects. "I could move them as I chose," he told Mary, awakening her early in the morning after his return from the speech. He then reportedly prayed never to misuse what was indeed a very special talent.

Two years later, in 1890, his oratorical abilities were unquestionably instrumental in an election victory that made him only the second Democrat in Nebraska's history to win a seat in the United States Congress. Barely thirty, he was known as the "boy congressman." After less than four years in Nebraska, the Bryan family, which now included two more children (William Jennings, Jr., born in mid-1889, and Grace, born in early 1891), moved again—this time to an apartment on Washington, D.C.'s Capitol Hill.

More than Bryan's speaking ability and his sensitivity to the problems of individuals propelled him from Nebraska newcomer to member of Congress. In his successful first bid for the House of Representatives, he astutely turned rapidly changing state politics to his advantage. He shrewdly shaped alliances with volatile factions to emerge as a skillful power broker and campaigner. And he did so while portraying himself as a modern David taking on Goliath—or as he put it, by "trusting to the righteousness of my cause." It was a considerable achievement, especially given Nebraska's stormy political environment in 1890.

The agrarian protests that shook not only Bryan's Nebraska, but other western and southern states as well, grew out of a severe economic crisis and profound social and cultural stress. The most immediately visible sources of farm discontent sprang from a horrendous drop in agricultural prices in the late 1880s. In the Great Plains states, a series of droughts, fierce winters, and mortgage problems battered already struggling farmers. Creditors in Kansas alone from 1889 to 1893 foreclosed on more than eleven thousand mortgages, moving one person to write sadly, "We worked through spring and winter, through summer and through fall / But the mortgage worked the hardest and steadiest of them all." In the South, where the Civil War had shattered the economy, small farmers plunged deeper into debt, falling more and more under the control of merchants and bankers, until many previously independent agrarians became impoverished sharecroppers. In the Ozark country of Arkansas, the economy was in such bad shape that, in the words of one journalist, "a dollar looked at least as big as the moon and was only slightly easier to lay hands on."[4]

For many farmers far more was at stake than just their pocketbooks. In jeopardy was nothing less than a way of life. The America of small, independent producers—an America that lay at the very core of the nation's history and imagination—was looking into its own grave. The series of economic depressions that culminated in the devastating years of the middle 1880s made this all too clear. Nervous farmers, as early as the 1870s through organizations such as the Grange, and subsequently through the Farmers' Alliances, had already tried to establish more control over their destinies.

In 1890 their various movements fused into populism, a major development that was political, economic, and cultural. As a political phenomenon, populism encompassed third-party tickets in many states and, starting in 1892, in national elections. Its strongest centers were in the South, the Great Plains, and the West. Dedicated to keeping political power in the hands of the rank-and-file, Populists advocated such political reforms as the initiative and referendum (by which the people could bypass unresponsive legislatures and pass or repeal laws), the secret ballot (which many states did not yet have), and direct election of senators. Economically, they favored a cooperative commonwealth that would move control of the major transportation, banking, and communication networks to the public sector. Culturally, they championed a traditional value system in which producers, or the actual makers of goods, enjoyed dignity and respect, as well as the fruits of their labors. One angry Georgia Populist articulated the central concern of his embittered and frightened counterparts when he charged that "an idle, do-nothing class of people" was gaining inordinate and undeserved wealth, power, and influence.[5]

Nowhere did the Populists describe more forcefully the magnitude of the nation's problems than in the preamble to the 1892 Omaha platform of their new political party: "We meet in the midst of a nation brought to the verge of moral, political, and material ruin." Evidence of this was both overpowering and frightening. "The fruits of toil of millions are boldly stolen to build up colossal fortunes for a few," the Populists warned, "and the possessors of these, in turn, despise the republic and endanger liberty." The Omaha platform described a nation of demoralized and exploited citizens, victims of unprecedented corruption and "governmental injustice."

Such a critique grew not from abstract theory but from the personal experience and observations of troubled agrarians. People like themselves who labored directly with the soil—people with sweat on their brows who brought forth tangible goods such as food and clothing—were staggering under growing burdens of debt. In contrast, huge wealth flowed into the hands of railroad officials, industrialists, mine owners, lawyers, bankers, and merchants—those without calloused hands, those who simply moved paper around on desks and scratched numbers in ink. "Sharp, unprincipled men," as an angry Kansas farmer characterized them. How was it possible, for example, that railroad corporations thrived while the workers plunged into hardship? "Did the stockholders throw up the embankments?" asked a North Carolina Populist rhetorically. "Did they make the ties, lay the rails, or string the wires? Do they run the trains, keep up repairs, collect receipts, or run the engines?" Or why was it, wondered a Georgia Populist, that local farmers, "intelligent, economical and industrious," slid further into debt despite bountiful harvests of cotton?[6]

On a sweltering Fourth of July in 1890, a long parade of farm wagons down one of Lincoln's streets served notice that populism had arrived in Nebraska, and that the state's political ground was shifting dramatically. Actually, the farmers' protest on that sun-baked day should have come as no surprise to those familiar with Nebraska's recent past. For eight years, the state's Alliance party had angrily objected to the growing control of a few people over land, transportation, and finances. It had, among other things, objected to unfair railroad rates and land monopolization, had advocated public ownership of the telegraph and telephone system, had urged the expansion of the money supply through government-issued fiat money, had endorsed woman suffrage and secret ballots, and had opposed convict leasing and "political organizations based on religious prejudices." The agrarian protests in Nebraska grew directly from encounters with politically powerful groups that lent money, bought grain, and set insurance and shipping rates.

Despite at least eight years of growing Alliance activity, the various factions within Nebraska's Democratic and Republican parties continued to view politics in the promotional terms so familiar elsewhere across the nation. The goal was to insure economic growth, whether through trade, investments, or technological advance. While farmers were as supportive as anyone of economic expansion, they were more and more convinced that the benefits accrued only to nonagrarian groups.

It was along an axis of villages and countryside that Nebraska populism swung into prominence. Certainly, the rage that fueled Nebraska's agrarian upheaval was a product of harsh economic times, as beleaguered farmers battled undercapitalization, rising debts, summer droughts and frigid winters, unpredictable markets, and rampantly vacillating commodity prices. But also important was the farmers' sense that town and city courthouse cliques—whether Republican or Democratic—were not only unresponsive to the rural plight, but guilty of making a bad situation worse.

The farmers had a point. Political leadership at both the local and state levels, regardless of political affiliation, came overwhelmingly from professional and nonagricultural groups. Rural residents had acquiesced to this during Nebraska's boom years through most of the 1880s; but as hard times pressed down on the state late in the decade, they were increasingly resentful of village and urban dominance. Typically suspicious of nonagrarians anyhow, farmers grew more and more distrustful of merchandisers and bankers—local elites who resided in comfortable Victorian houses along restful, tree-lined streets. One Populist farmer, writing a letter to the local editor, sounded a warning: "You just wait till we control things and we'll make you town fellows hump yourselves."[7] To nervous town residents, such outbursts were disconcerting. Village leaders often shared farmers' concerns about railroad rates or the eastern money powers; but they worried that agrarian radicalism would only be counterproductive, scaring away investors and future settlers, relegating Nebraska to an economically stagnant backwater, and sacrificing town needs for narrow country interests. And in 1890 villagers suddenly had plenty to worry about, when an electoral "revolution" rattled the state with such force that, incredibly, the new Populist party (although it would not carry that title for several more years) grabbed control of the state legislature and various local offices.

Against this backdrop in 1890, William Jennings Bryan won election to Congress. That he did so attested to his political skills within the state's Democratic party, as well as his ability to gain support in his district from the surging farmers' Alliance party. At first glance, Bryan's success with the new, independent party seemed unlikely. He was a newcomer to the state, a town dweller in the state's capital, and an attorney in a firm that worked on retainer for the Missouri Pacific Railroad (although, as noted, he himself refused to take cases from any railroad).

From another perspective, however, Bryan's emotional kinship with Nebraska's populist movement was hardly astonishing. Although his contact with farm life had been rather fleeting and special, he nevertheless had some understanding of the travails of agricultural existence. Perhaps more important were the values that he and many Populists held in common.

Populists, like Bryan, were very much products of a deeply rooted culture that expounded the virtues of private property, of profits, of individual self-interest, of competition among small, independent producers, and of an orderly society resting on honest labor, individual character, middle-class respectability, and material progress. Socialism held little more attraction for many Populists than it did for Bryan. They prided themselves as landowners or aspiring landowners, and they fretted that society would falter without the incentives of profits and private property. According to one leader of the third-party movement, Tom Watson of Georgia, Populists rejected "Socialism, with all its collective ownership of land, homes, and pocketbooks." They were most assuredly not "destroyers of private property," emphasized a Virginian. Nor did they have a basic quarrel with the advantages of manufacturing and industrial growth, which could boost the local economy and benefit everyone. Thus, for example, Populists in one Alabama town pushed for the establishment of a local cotton factory, and farmers generally had little difficulty appreciating the benefits of new machinery for plowing and harvesting, or of railroad lines that expanded markets. "It is not the railroads of which the people complain," asserted a Texan, "but the abuses of their power."[8]

The populist vision, then, was one in which small, independent producers advanced themselves while supplying the larger community with needed goods and overall prosperity. This was a vision that William Jennings Bryan shared. And he, as well as discontented agrarians, was aware by the 1890s of jarringly disturbing developments: harsh economic times for masses of people, striking disparities in wealth, and a growing concentration of power in the hands of a few. Moreover, especially in southern and western states, new (and often absentee) landowners were intensifying their efforts to shift the traditional agrarian concepts of property rights, such as customary usage laws (common rights to unenclosed lands, for example), to sharply restrictive fencing regulations that squeezed out small farmers and herdsmen. Few ideals were dearer to Bryan than one that typically appeared in fights against these new fencing laws: "Equal rights to all and special privileges to none."

There were, of course, undeniable differences between Bryan and many Populists. For one thing, although like them he called for expanded governmental powers to protect common citizens, he did not advocate the kinds of radical structural changes that they sketched out in their 1892 Omaha platform—a public banking system, for example. More important, his own life reflected less the world of struggling farmers than that of College Hill in Jacksonville, Illinois, or neat, respectable middle-class neighborhoods in Lincoln, Nebraska. Unlike some residents in such neighborhoods, however, he never felt uncomfortable with the poor farmers and laborers with whom he might rub shoulders in town squares. In terms of background and social status he undoubtedly had much in common with the College Hill resident who unexpectedly stumbled into a large, raucous Fourth of July celebration; but he did not share her feelings of fright during such encounters with "the other half." In this respect, contrary to the views of many local elites, he had absolutely no quarrel with the Omaha platform's demand that government must rest in "the hands of 'the plain people.'"

Granted, there were limits to the social leaps he could make. Later in his life, he was visibly shaken after speaking to a forlorn group in one of New York City's waterfront missions. "It takes a man who has been saved from the depths to reach men like these," he told his wife. "I cannot do it. I lack the necessary past." He had no trouble, on the other hand, identifying with even the most deprived residents of village and rural America. "Mingle with them," he said with absolute sincerity; "know them and you will trust them and they will trust you."[9]

More than most Americans of his class and background, he was able to move from the social and cultural orbits of neighborhoods like College Hill, or his pleasant country home outside Lincoln, to the world of those who lived at the forks of the creeks, or in the isolated sod houses on the Great Plains. And that partially explained why he did not, as did so many of his contemporaries, shudder at the specter of populism. Temperamentally, he was predisposed to sympathize with small farmers who shouted, "Down with monopolies!" or who pleaded, as did those opposing barbed-wire fences that would deny them access to water and roads, "Give us homes as God intended and not gates to churches and towns and schools."[10]

Opponents of special privileges and of the growing influence of industrial and financial interests thus found an ally in Bryan. He shared their dislike for "money kings," "speculative parasites," and corporate capitalists who fattened themselves at the expense of farmers and laborers. And he joined them on common ground when he stated his conviction that the individual entrepreneur must "not stand always in the fear that some great trust will run him out of business." In this respect, like the Populists, he placed himself squarely at odds with trends that were shaping industrial America. That was why small farmers in distant states such as North Carolina eventually classified themselves as "Bryan Populists," and why, in 1890, he appealed to many members of the Alliance party in Nebraska's First Congressional District.[11]

Following his election, as he awaited the seating of the new Congress, he read widely to enhance his understanding of a subject that was rapidly gaining public attention—the money question. At issue was the quantity and the basis of the nation's money supply. The United States could, for example, base its monetary system upon gold, or a bimetallic combination of gold and silver, or something else such as paper dollars backed by the credit of the government. For more than eighty years, from 1792 to 1873, the nation had recognized both gold and silver as legal tender in the payment of debts. By law since at least 1832, the Mint had used sixteen times as many grains of silver to make a silver dollar as it did grains of gold for a gold dollar—hence the terminology "sixteen-to-one." During the Jackson era, however, silver dollars had virtually disappeared. Many Americans, with little thought or concern, simply assumed that gold alone was the monetary standard.

After the Civil War, discoveries of huge silver deposits in the West had made the white metal more conspicuous than before. The timing was significant. At the very time silver became more abundant, debates flared up with greater frequency over matters of credit, prices, wages, interest rates, industrial growth, and agricultural production. To debt-ridden farmers, as opposed to industrial groups and creditors, the enlarged money base was a godsend, facilitating loans and pushing interest rates down. Lenders and creditors, in contrast, understandably preferred money that was less accessible and thus more valuable. When they lent one hundred dollars at interest for a farmer to buy a plow, they wanted to make sure that when the money got back to them it could still pay for a plow, as well as something else. The profit on the loan, after all, was what made lending a satisfying investment. A dramatic increase in the amount of available money could jeopardize such an investment by pushing prices up. This would mean that the farmer would have to sell fewer bushels of wheat than previously in order to pay off the loan—a boon to the farmer surely, but hardly good news for the creditors, who would get their hundred dollars back with interest, but would be unable to buy as much with it as before. The creditors would in effect have lost money. A shrunken supply of money, on the other hand, would work to their advantage and to the despair of borrowers.

Policymakers who hoped to balance the competing needs of people who needed money with those who provided it faced formidable challenges under the best of circumstances, and the troubled decades after the Civil War further complicated the situation. While the population of the United States doubled between 1865 and 1895, the money supply actually contracted, tripling the value of a dollar and skewing the economy decidedly against borrowers. Hence the anguished cry of many farmers and other financially strapped groups, "Let us pay back the kind of dollars we borrowed."

In 1873, during a brief hiatus in the growing public concern over the money issue, Congress passed the Coinage Act, demonetizing silver, and placing the nation on a single standard of money—gold. The bill's supporters were convinced that they were insuring economic stability and progress, but groups especially vulnerable to the sickening economic slumps of the late nineteenth century were outraged. To

33

them the "crime of '73," as these critics called it, assumed conspiratorial proportions, symbolic of the insidious control of "bloated bondholders" over the producing classes.

During the last decades of the nineteenth century, the United States clearly faced a dilemma. In a nation with a rapidly growing population, a monetary standard tied to a limited gold supply hardly made sense. The problem was in coming up with a solution that did not make things worse. Defenders of the gold standard worried that shifting away from it was bad, because such a policy could produce runaway inflation, rendering money virtually worthless, bringing on economic collapse and financial chaos, and jeopardizing American currency in the international markets. From this perspective, "sound" money was essential, however much discomfort it might bring at particular times to unfortunate groups. Gold's advocates thus feared the long-range economic consequences that might flow from a short-term remedy. The coinage of silver, they contended, would produce panic, not a panacea.

The money question had many "experts." It was a subject about which emotions were intense, even though comprehension was often limited. People on opposing sides of the issue reacted passionately with arguments that often resembled articles of faith. Journalist Harold Ickes, for example, recalled that he was "unquestionably a gold man," a true believer in "the gold cause," although he did not know why and understood little about the money issue.[12]

When William Jennings Bryan in the early 1890s immersed himself in the literature of the money question, it was not as a neutral observer simply seeking information. His early education had predisposed him to dislike the gold standard. His father had been an ardent "greenbacker" who favored paper money that the government guaranteed. At Illinois College, William believed that he had learned about the virtues of bimetallism from his economics teacher, Julian M. Sturtevant, even though Sturtevant was no great advocate of silver and would have been surprised at such a misunderstanding of his course. Certainly the anger of midwestern farmers over the "Crime of '73" had also influenced Bryan. As a student he had expressed concern over ways in which the "money power" endangered republican institutions—a prominent theme in the writings of Wendell Phillips, the great abolitionist whose words he had sometimes copied in notebooks.

Bryan was thus being disingenuous when, as a young congressman in the early 1890s, he claimed that he favored free silver because the people of Nebraska preferred it and he would look up the reasons later. Some Nebraskans, including his political ally and Democratic wheelhorse J. Sterling Morton, wanted to stay with the gold standard. In order to agree with Morton, Bryan needed to reject what he had learned about money in his first several decades. He was not inclined to do so. The political possibilities with which Nebraska's agrarian uprising loaded the silver cause simply reassured him that he was on the right side.

Certainly as a congressman he was extremely attentive to the needs of his constituents. In Washington, D.C., he quickly demonstrated his political talents and sympathies. Rather than waiting for pressure from back home to push him toward particular causes, he conscientiously anticipated special needs of local residents. Just as important, the power of his oratory thrust him into the national spotlight. His initial major speech in Congress not only delighted most Nebraskans but filled the galleries and gained widespread attention.

As he rose to his feet on 16 March 1892, to make his first extensive comments in the House of Representatives, he was initially quite nervous, although perhaps only Mary Bryan, sitting in the galleries, knew the extent of his uneasiness. He stood for a few moments, a handsome figure with striped pants, a string tie, western boots, and hair that was relatively long and curly along the back of his head. As the richness and cadence of his voice cast its spell over the growing audience, few would have guessed how long and hard he had worked to become an effective public speaker.

Years earlier, in his first declamation contest at Whipple Academy, he had not impressed the judges. Indeed, they had ranked him near the bottom of the competition. Insecure and bashful as a youth, and well aware of his father's reputation as an excellent lecturer, he had worked hard to develop his forensic abilities. Increasingly competitive in outlook, he had been an ambitious college debater bent on winning prizes. He had sought out private instruction, practiced speaking with pebbles in his mouth, and rehearsed endlessly, sometimes in the woods with trees as his audience. On one occasion, his ringing voice in the woods had frightened away some picnickers, who had mistaken him for an escapee from a nearby insane asylum. His labors had paid off.

By the time he addressed Congress on 16 March 1892, he had honed a magnificent voice into a marvelously controlled instrument. And on that spring day in the nation's capital, he electrified spectators and colleagues alike.

His topic at first glance seemed hardly the stuff out of which to ring the rafters. It concerned the protective tariff, and specifically the duty on binding twine. In fact, however, he could not have picked a better subject for his first congressional speech. The Omaha *World-Herald* had already dubbed him "the young tariff orator of Lincoln," because of his speeches on the topic.

At the time, moreover, the protective tariff was an emotionally charged issue, loaded with partisan and regional interest. From one angle it seemed indispensable and promised something for all Americans. It was a source of domestic revenue, and it struck patriotic chords by sheltering the American economy from foreign competition. Yet few subjects were more controversial or engendered fiercer debates.

Republicans had long prided themselves as the party of protection, actively using government to shield infant industries from outside competitors. Farmers ostensibly benefited as much as anyone. The tariff was supposed to keep foreign produce from flooding the American market and pushing agricultural prices down. Actually, farm imports from abroad were minimal, and falling prices were largely the results of domestic overproduction; but farmers often had difficulty understanding this, especially when Republican politicians warned of ships steaming toward America with foreign grain or vegetables. Even tariffs that primarily protected industries reportedly had a spillover effect that aided the entire nation; the rising profits of America's industry would buoy up other sectors of the economy. According to the Republican scenario, protection was a key to prosperity for all citizens.

Democrats rejected this rosy interpretation. Most of them had little quarrel with a tariff for revenue purposes only, but they balked at high protective duties as surcharges that consumers ended up paying in order to bolster the profits of a few. Indeed, Democrats seized the opportunity to elaborate on their traditional defense of limited government. The government that imposed these surcharges on consumers, they argued, was the same one that endangered "personal liberty" and convictions. The slogan of Iowa Republicans in the 1880s, "A school house on every hill, and no saloon in the valley," was to

Democrats a clear reminder of the intrusive nature of the GOP. Republicans had another reading of events. In the words of Thomas B. Reed of Maine, "Progress is the essence of Republicanism. . . . The Republican party does things, the Democratic party criticizes; the Republican party achieves, the Democratic party finds fault." And few things better signified the GOP's commitment to progress than the protective tariff.[13]

Underlying such partisan differences were intensely felt economic concerns. Tariffs that helped one group could in fact easily hurt another. Producers who were dependent on foreign markets or materials typically favored free trade, or at least low tariffs. From their perspective, tariffs too often inspired other countries to impose protective barriers of their own. On this level, battle lines over the tariff reflected regional as well as party disposition.

By the 1890s events had superimposed upon the United States an invisible set of boundaries, distinctly sectional and suffused with economic, political, and cultural meaning. One of the best illustrations of this was a cartoon that showed a cow astride much of the United States. While farmers fed the cow in the West, bankers and manufacturers milked it in the East. William Jennings Bryan liked this image so much that he used it in his first political address in Lincoln. It was an effective way to illustrate a situation that to many Americans was all too real. The Northeast was the center of the nation's industry, finance, and education; in contrast, other parts of the country seemed to have little more than a colonial status. As Mary Elizabeth Lease, the noted Kansas Populist, said in 1890, "The West and the South are bound and prostrate before the manufacturing East." By 1896, even an anti-Populist Republican editor complained, "The West has lots of labor; the East has lots of capital. . . . Heretofore the capital end of the bargain has been given the best of it. . . . The farmer and his friend have paid the fiddler long enough to have a right to dance some."[14]

In virtually every way, the undercapitalized western and southern "colonies" depended heavily upon the marketing and financial resources of the northeastern industrial region. This relationship by its very nature encouraged suspicions in outlying areas about "the interests." Such suspicions, moreover, were not misplaced. Railroad shipping rates in border areas, for example, were sometimes double those paid within the northeastern area. Colorado's mining industry was so dependent on absentee bankers and entrepreneurs that it resembled, in the words of one historian, "little more than a pocket borough of the corporate oligarchy."[15] The agricultural South, struggling to recover from the Civil War and starved for funds, increasingly fell under the control of northern capital so vital to economic revitalization. And in William Jennings Bryan's Nebraska, the sad joke by the 1890s was that the state produced two crops: corn and mortgages. Tariff schedules in this context assumed particular importance. Increasingly, they fed "colonial" grievances against eastern industries, which seemed to enjoy economic advantages and special protection.

In his 16 March 1892 foray into the dense thicket of the tariff issue, Bryan forcefully presented the case for Americans who were convinced that they needed protection from "protective" tariffs. "Out in Nebraska we are so far away from the beneficiaries of a tariff," he laughingly noted, "that the arguments in justification of protection in traveling that long distance become somewhat diluted." Turning deadly serious by the end of his three-hour speech, he described the sorry status of regions outside the Northeast. In Kansas, 65 percent of the farms were mortgaged, and in ten years the number of renters there had increased from 13 to over 35 percent. Charging that "these mortgages are held in the East," Bryan asked: "If these manufacturing States, when their industries are 'infants,' own themselves and have a mortgage on us, what is going to be the result when they get full grown?" Protection was part of an egregious system that was turning America into "a land of landlords and tenants"—a beleaguered place in which "the great majority of its citizens are tenants of a small minority."[16]

Carefully and relentlessly, Bryan portrayed protective tariffs as weapons of greedy manufacturers anxious to skewer other Americans, especially farmers and consumers, in order to gain unfair economic advantages and enlarged profits. He warmed to his subject as a growing audience filled the galleries and as more and more of his colleagues stopped to listen. His denunciations of high tariffs as "vicious" examples of "favoritism" echoed throughout the chamber. He argued that the additional costs of binding-twine, due to taxes that made foreign twine more expensive in order to protect some thirty-five factories in the United States (most owned by one corporation), were trivial in comparison with the larger issue involved. Because some twenty-five hundred other articles were on the tariff list, the duty on binding-twine served primarily as an outrageous symbol to oppressed farmers, "who have been made to bleed at every pore by your infamous system." Unlike a highway robber, who at least confronted his victim face to face, a high protective tariff was more like a burglar who "steals into your house in the night while you are asleep and robs you of your treasures." It lifted "money from one man's pocket to another man's pocket." It violated the rights of "forgotten men" so that a few might prosper. In Bryan's view, the protectionist response to the depressed farmer was a mean-spirited "Bleed him again."[17]

During a long series of questions, Bryan handled himself with poise and authority. His quick ripostes, humorous jabs, and clever asides evoked laughter. When an Iowa Republican taunted him with the alleged misdeeds of a Democratic city council in Sioux City, Bryan slipped around the barb by giving credit to the town for choosing a Democratic majority. When the Republican countered that the Democrats had lost control of the council in the last election, Bryan expressed regret "that the news must go out over this great country that Sioux City is on the decline." Occasionally, amid cries that he continue, he paused for effect, sometimes by peering at the clock.

Bryan's main argument was against "special legislation" that aided "the strong and the powerful" at the expense of common citizens. He rebuked wealthy defenders of "home industries" who enjoyed $10-per-plate dinners while other Americans lacked the money for a ten-cent meal. The real American home industry—the one rich industrialists actually harmed—was "the home of the citizen." In this sense, Bryan claimed that the Democrats constituted the party of legitimate protection because they said, "'Hands off, and let that home industry live.'" He concluded on a stridently partisan note, asserting that in 1890 angry citizens had struck back at the Republicans: "You rioted in power, you denied their petitions, and now you have felt their wrath. At last justice has overtaken you." In Bryan's estimation, it was folly to destroy "the peasantry of this country. We cannot afford to degrade the common people of this land."[18]

Seldom had any speech on the floor of Congress struck with such force. In a few dramatic hours Bryan had established himself as one of the premier orators on the national scene. Even one leading Republican admitted "that Bryan made the best tariff reform speech I have ever heard." Predictably, the Democrats cheered loudest.[19]

Ironically, Bryan's rise to prominence was placing him on a collision course with his own party's leadership. Over the next few years he would increasingly challenge the old guard Democratic leadership, nationally as well as in Nebraska. And in doing so, he would place himself more and more in the camp of the nation's discontented—especially its unhappy and struggling farmers.

# 3

## "FIRST BATTLE"
### (1893–1896)

As the train approached Chicago in the early summer of 1896, William Jennings Bryan, like other visitors to that city, may have noticed the long stretches of depressingly drab shanties, the massive and dirty gray smoke cloud on the horizon, and the "sudden smudge" of factory life intruding on the "great green plains."[1] Chicago had assuredly never been his favorite place. His memories of law school there, far removed from Mary and the village setting that he preferred, were perhaps almost painful. He had no way of knowing for sure that in a few more days he would, at age thirty-six, receive the presidential nomination of the Democratic party. Indeed, the year 1896 would prove to be pivotal not only for Bryan but for American politics, encompassing changing leadership within the Democratic party, a shifting balance of power between the major parties, and the fate of populism.

Peering out the train window as he neared the Windy City, Bryan was certainly not without hopes for his own ascendancy within the

nation's convulsive political universe. Indeed, he was probably thinking primarily about the exciting opportunities that perhaps awaited
him over the next few days at the Democratic convention. But he
may have reflected somewhat upon the frantic pace of personal and
national events that had marked the past few years, including his
growing identification with free silver, the economic crisis that had
deepened rapidly, and the shattering turmoil that continued to disrupt
the Democratic party.

Three years earlier, in 1893, the party had seemed in splendid
shape. Grover Cleveland had just recaptured the presidency, which
he had held for one term before relinquishing it to the Republicans in
the 1888 election. A huge man with a walruslike shape and countenance, he impressed his admirers as a man of "weight, power, greatness."[2] And in 1893 he enjoyed an advantage that had escaped him
in his earlier term: the Democrats controlled both houses of Congress.
With the resurgent Democrats in command of the executive and legislative branches of government for the first time since before the Civil War, there was even speculation that the Republican party might
be headed for extinction.

But the new administration had hardly taken office before economic
disaster struck. Following a financial panic in late 1893, the nation
plunged into its worst depression to that date. The next year was terrifyingly grim. Bankruptcy staggered some of the largest industries,
including fifty-six railroads that controlled some thirty thousand miles
of track. Even such prestigious lines as the Union Pacific went into
receivership. Thousands of industries closed down. Unemployment
soared to around 20 percent. Hordes of "tramps" roamed the countryside seeking work. Violence shook countless locations, from Boston,
where the police repulsed some six hundred jobless and desperate men
demanding relief, to the western states where angry citizens battled
local authorities and even commandeered trains in futile efforts to take
their appeals directly to Congress. As the body in power, the Democratic party suddenly fell victim to public wrath. Grover Cleveland
became a political pariah to many Americans who saw him as directly
responsible for their misery. In homes such as that of the young Walter
Lippmann, later a famous journalist, Cleveland's name "was uttered
with monstrous dread" and the president loomed as "a sinister figure."
For the Democratic party, such impressions were to take a terrible and

lasting toll. Years later, Lippmann still held "a subtle prejudice against Democrats that goes deeper than what we call political conviction."[3] He spoke not just for himself but for many citizens whose memories of the awful nineties inextricably linked Democrats and hard times.

Although Bryan had not anticipated the panic of 1893 and the severity of the national depression, he was more prepared for what happened than Cleveland. For one thing, Nebraska and other farm states had been experiencing serious economic woes for several years, and with especial severity since 1887. For another, although the 1892 elections had indeed been good to Democrats as a group, in Nebraska the party was in trouble. Bryan had barely hung on to his congressional seat, narrowly surviving by a mere 140 votes a reapportionment plan that had recast his old district. As before, he could not have won without populist support; indeed, James B. Weaver, the Populist presidential candidate, and Mary Elizabeth Lease, the third party's firebrand from Kansas, had campaigned in his behalf. After the election, Bryan resembled a political Lazarus in Nebraska's Democratic graveyard.

Given the tenuous position of the Democratic party in his home state, he cringed when Cleveland appointed Nebraska's J. Sterling Morton as secretary of agriculture. The political ties that had earlier pulled Bryan and Morton together had long since frazzled. Their alliance, once so important to Bryan's career in Nebraska, had fallen victim to personal rivalries and disagreements over issues such as fusion with the Populists and the coinage of silver money. Moreover, the 1892 election had confirmed Bryan's suspicions: Morton, finishing a distant third in the gubernatorial race, spoke for a wing of the Democratic party that had obviously fallen out of favor in Nebraska. Cleveland, apparently unmindful of Morton's declining home base, or—even worse from Bryan's point of view—deliberately turning his back on party reformers, named Morton to his cabinet. The new secretary promptly astounded Bryan and millions of farmers by suggesting that agriculture's problems flowed primarily from organizations such as the National Grange, whose leaders "farmed the farmers." Already well known for his staunch defense of the railroad corporations, Morton now pointed up the administration's insensitivity to agrarian America.

It was, however, Cleveland's decision to limit the nation's money standard to gold that produced the largest political explosion. As the nation's economy collapsed in the rubble of the mid-nineties depression, the already smoldering money issue burst into a political firestorm. For a while, the fury of that inferno seared American politics as few issues had done.

Ultimately, the money question struck at deeply held values concerning work, opportunity, obligations, and morality. At stake in the 1890s seemed to be nothing less than the very future of the nation: Whose country was it, anyhow? As the nation polarized along class and sectional lines, each of the competing groups believed that it stood on the side of truth and light; the opposition, either ignorant or malicious, represented the forces of darkness.

Following the "crime of '73," when Congress had placed the nation on the gold standard, the restoration of a bimetallic money system became for many Americans a cause that transcended politics. Indeed, throughout the 1880s and into the 1890s few issues packed the emotional clout as that concerning the free and unlimited coinage of silver. Congress had on several occasions allowed for the coinage of limited amounts of silver, but Grover Cleveland in late 1893 halted this. Cleveland, to whom a monometalist gold standard was an Eleventh Commandment, persuaded Congress to stop the mints from purchasing any silver at all. In the fierce battle to reach his goal, however, the president turned substantial numbers of his own party into adversaries. "I hate the ground the man walks on," said Alabama's senator John T. Morgan.[4] The politics of the silver issue increasingly resembled a war.

Bryan had by then already thrown down his own gauntlet against Grover Cleveland. He staunchly opposed Cleveland's nomination in 1892, largely because of the former president's vociferous and uncompromising commitment to the gold standard. During the campaign itself, he not only refused to stump for Cleveland, but even went so far as to deliver speeches for the Populist candidate, James B. Weaver. Under pressure from the Democratic hierarchy in Nebraska, whose support he could not ignore in terms of his own reelection hopes, he finally stated that he would vote for Cleveland, even though he preferred Weaver. Subsequently, when conceding that Cleveland "might be honest," he added the chilling remark that "so too were the mothers who threw their children in the Ganges."[5]

Twice in 1892 at state conventions he openly challenged J. Sterling Morton and other party regulars. Striking a pose that reminded one observer of the famous actor Edwin Booth, Bryan at one point evoked a thunderous response from his audience by arguing that the battle was on between silver—the choice of the people—and gold, the favorite of "the money power." In his own successful bid for reelection to Congress he campaigned on a personal platform calling for silver coinage. The differences between him and the gold wing of Nebraska's Democratic party were substantial enough to produce "some very cross-eyed Democrats," according to an Omaha editor. Morton privately lamented that Bryan was worse "than any pinfeathered economist" but realized that to many voters he was "Bryan the Great." There was no doubt about it: within Nebraska Bryan was a growing political power. Eventually, in fact, Morton swallowed his pride and urged the First District to reelect Bryan despite the young congressman's refusal to endorse Cleveland and gold.[6]

In Congress Bryan quickly established himself as one of the most articulate and informed silverites. Before packed galleries on 16 August 1893, for example, he spent several hours discussing the money question. In a speech loaded with statistics, quotations, historical and biblical allusions, colorful analogies, and passionate emotional appeals, he denounced the gold dollar "as the most dishonest dollar we could employ." Bimetallism was no panacea, he emphasized, but it would be more equitable and stable because it would keep the money supply more in line with the demands of an expanding population. "If we are given a choice between a change which will aid the debtor by reducing the size of his debt and a change which will aid the creditor," Bryan believed firmly that "the advantage must go to the debtor." As long as the advocates of gold demanded "unconditional surrender," there could be no peace in the nation, only "war—eternal war." The army of the "work-worn and dust-begrimed" was locked in a desperate but unequal struggle against the staggering wealth of the corporate interests, "imperious, arrogant, compassionless," and ever in search of special favors and privileges. On which side, he wondered, would the Democrats take their stand? With President Cleveland, who in Bryan's opinion had backed down in the face of "the money power"? Or, in the grand tradition of Jefferson and Jackson, on the side of the common people? Two weeks later, when it was clear that Bryan's argument had persuaded neither Congress nor the administration, he solemnly promised, "There will be a day of reckoning."[7]

In just two congressional terms Bryan had clearly emerged as one of the most promising newcomers in national politics. He had captured the attention and respect of bimetallists across the nation. As an outspoken critic of the Cleveland administration, he had won praise from Democrats, primarily from the West and South, who were furious at the president's apparent indifference to economic turmoil and suffering. His success in capturing Populist votes had distinguished him as Nebraska's only successful Democrat of note.

But in 1894 the steep and rapid trajectory of Bryan's political career suddenly hurtled downward. He chose not to seek reelection to Congress, possibly because he suspected that it would be foolish to do so. The deepening depression certainly jeopardized his chances of victory, especially in light of the unnervingly close contest two years earlier. As events turned out, the alternative to seeking a third term in the House worked out no better. His bid for a senate seat crashed in the Republican-dominated legislature.

However audacious his race for the Senate appeared, it was far from crazy. By capturing the Democratic nomination in a hard-fought battle at the state convention, he scored heavily against the Cleveland-Morton faction and virtually made the Democratic party in Nebraska his own. The Populists' decision not to run their own candidate for the Senate kept open the possibility of fusion, so crucial to Bryan. He entered the race knowing what had happened two years earlier. At that time, he had convinced enough Democrats in the legislature to align with third-party members and thus to elect a Populist, William V. Allen, to the Senate. In 1894–95, however, Bryan fared less well. The fusion strategy, which he carried out with remarkable acuity, failed to overcome the three-to-one Republican control of the legislature. By 4 March 1895, despite his accomplishments within the state's Democratic and Populist parties, he no longer held political office. One delighted Cleveland supporter, in a letter to J. Sterling Morton, referred to "the shattered prayer wheel which looms on the prairie of Nebraska that was the pious Bryan."[8]

Incredibly, sixteen months later Bryan not only led the charge when his party savagely repudiated the incumbent president, but he himself captured the Democratic nomination. As he was quick to point out, events had helped his cause. But equally important was his own political cunning. Through a series of well-calculated steps he pushed his way to the forefront of the free silver movement, ending up at the 1896 Democratic convention in the right place at the right time.

It was not accidental that at a crucial point in the tumultuous Chicago gathering the silver enthusiasts looked to him for leadership of their party. In Congress, he had become one of their heroes. After leaving office, he had traveled around the nation, attending various silver conferences and eloquently championing the cause of bimetallism. He succeeded in connecting the cause of silver and the name of Bryan in many people's minds.

More than silver was on the Nebraskan's mind, however. Otherwise he might have been less inclined to ignore Mary's request that he settle into private life in Lincoln, practicing law and writing. "It will be more pleasant for you, me, and the whole family," she told him. But Bryan, burning with political fever, chose as he rarely did to reject her appeal. "It would seem to me as if I were born for this life," he explained candidly as he ventured back onto the political stump. He was perhaps being less than honest with her or himself when he added that it made no difference if he personally ever actually held office again. Similarly, his decision to leave law practice for journalism (becoming political editor of the weekly edition of the Omaha *World-Herald* in the mid-nineties) was misleading insofar as it suggested the role of political observer rather than office-seeker. By turning to journalism, Bryan, who had never found a great deal of satisfaction practicing law anyhow, was able to free himself for more travel and speaking engagements. He could also use the newspaper as another forum for his opinions on a range of issues, increasingly that of free silver. In sum, despite his departure from elective office, he had not left, nor did he intend to leave, politics. He was on the road so much that his actual contribution to the *World-Herald* was minimal. Typically, he sent notes for his assistant to put in editorial form—evidence that he had no real commitment to journalism as a career. Politics was still his main concern. The letter that he received in late 1894 from his good friend and devoted silverite James Dahlman probably fertilized rather than planted an idea. The rangy ex-cowboy who had actively campaigned for Bryan in Nebraska reported, "I have begun to talk you for President,—and I mean it. . . . No gift in the hands of the people is too high for you."[9]

One of the most important factors behind Bryan's political ascendancy by the summer of 1896 was the disastrous record of Grover Cleveland's administration, which in turn dramatized ways in which the national political system was sagging under the weight of new developments. From the era of Andrew Jackson to the post–Civil War era, political parties had been lively centers of activity, engaged in brokering power but also providing sources of information and even entertainment. As early as the 1870s, however, public dissatisfaction with parties and politicians was apparent. The struggle over the distribution of resources and privileges—the driving engine of mid-nineteenth-century political life—produced losers as well as winners. Many observers, especially among the losers, pointed angrily to corrupt deals, bribes, and payoffs. Political parties fell under a growing wave of criticism for being unrepresentative, too narrowly partisan, and too much the captives of courthouse cliques, urban bosses, and monied interests. Governing bodies seemed either uninterested in people's problems, or answerable only to a powerful few. Mark Twain's jest underlined serious concerns: "Suppose you were an idiot. And suppose you were a member of Congress. But I repeat myself."[10]

Grover Cleveland, elected in 1884 and again in 1892, shared the expanding public distrust of legislatures. Always in executive roles (whether as sheriff, mayor of Buffalo, governor of New York, or president), he viewed with disdain the warring factions that dominated state houses and Congress. By battling corruption and inefficiency, he became a model of integrity. From his perspective, he was the needed wedge that would bring the wheel of "distributive politics" to a halt. In place of the politics of graft and grab, he intended to substitute a principled government that spoke in the public interest.

However laudable his goals and vision, Cleveland proved painfully unsuited to the task. For one thing, his self-righteousness made him stubborn and unyielding, lacking in flexibility and political savvy. For another, his assumption that business interests and the public interest were one and the same generated its own winners and losers. He was oblivious to the complaints of suffering farmers and wage earners, as well as to the need for any kind of social legislation. In better times, such personal and political liabilities might not have mattered as much. But the mid-1890s were not good years for the United States. Cleveland's administration collapsed in the ruins of the depression while a wave of criticism swept over the befuddled president. "He is not a Democrat, he's a stomach," stated one angry opponent. "He is an old bag of beef," declared South Carolina senator Ben Tillman, who intended to go "to Washington with a pitchfork and prod him in his fat ribs."[11] Cleveland, lamenting that there was not one member of the Senate upon whom he could count, stayed in character. With firm resolve, he stuck with his convictions, including his reverence for a monometallic gold standard. This political captain would remain at the wheel, no matter how severe the storm. Unfortunately for Cleveland, his ship of state was no match for the tidal wave of economic crisis, free silver, populism, and William Jennings Bryan.

By the time the Democrats gathered in Chicago in July 1896, the money issue was so pervasive that no political party could escape it. "The battle of the standards"—gold against silver—engaged Republicans, Democrats, and Populists alike. The GOP tried in its platform to placate various factions by endorsing gold, as well as promising to pursue an international agreement to place the United States and other leading nations on a bimetallic money system. A small group of noisy westerners, suspecting that the commitment to silver was more pose than promise (a plausible assumption, given the strength of the "sound money" advocates), angrily bolted the Republican party. The Populists, on the other hand, assumed that the Cleveland faction would commit the Democrats to the gold standard, thereby allowing the People's party to win over silverites from around the nation. When this did not happen, the ensuing debate over the importance of silver in the Populist movement left the party so wounded that it never recovered. And the Democrats, by endorsing bimetallism, repudiated their incumbent president, forced a fatal dilemma upon the Populists, and emerged as the party of Bryan.

When Bryan arrived in Chicago for the Democratic convention in early July, he carried only one hundred dollars—hardly the bankroll of a serious candidate intending to wine and dine delegates in order to win the party's nomination. He nevertheless very much saw himself as a genuine Democratic contender. As he later admitted, he invited Mary so that she could be on hand in case he was the nominee. And he brought with him a weapon worth far more than any large entertainment fund for uncommitted delegates: he came armed with a speech that he had been honing on the stump and in numerous silver conventions for months. This, combined with his recent efforts to draw attention to himself, just might be sufficient to capture the nomination—assuming that what he described as "the logic of the situation" developed in his favor.[12]

He could not have written a better convention script for himself. For one thing, the silver forces as well as representatives from many other reform organizations turned out in huge and thunderous numbers. Even before the convention, a Cleveland backer, West Virginia congressman William L. Wilson, confided to his diary that "we find perverts where we least expected them, and a madness that cannot be dealt with." The president himself privately conceded that he had "never before been so depressed" regarding his party and the nation. A conservative Chicago minister told his congregation that "unfortunately, the Populist and anarchist have come with this great Democratic gathering." And millionaire William C. Whitney, one of Cleveland's advisers, after mingling with the convention delegates, was genuinely alarmed: "For the first time I understand the scenes of the French Revolution." In sum, backers of the Cleveland administration and the gold standard were overwhelmingly on the defensive; expectations for a revamped Democratic party were high; and the convention setting was fluid, with substantial numbers of uncommitted delegates.[13]

Also working to Bryan's advantage was a schedule of events that allowed him to deliver the last of the convention's addresses on the money issue. The delegates were primed to hear him long before he took the floor. His reputation as an orator was already legion, and people knew him by such nicknames as the "Nebraska Cyclone," "Knight of the West," the "Boy Orator of the Platte," and the "Silver-tongued Orator." On the morning of 9 July, the day of the platform debates on the money question, the Chicago *Tribune* focused the spotlight even more on the Nebraskan by carrying a front page headline: "Bryan, Boy Orator of the Platte in the Presidential Race." The newspaper's story argued that Bryan was "more than a dark horse candidate for the Presidency."

Before the debates started, Bryan felt faint and his stomach was churning—physical signs that he usually experienced before delivering an address. Without any opportunity to lie down, he had to settle for coffee and a sandwich to ease his nervousness. But as he listened to the speakers who preceded him, his confidence grew. The more than twenty thousand people jammed into the sweltering hall were increasingly restless and disappointed. In the far reaches of the massive Chicago Coliseum, the largest permanent exhibition building in the world, it was impossible even to hear some of the speeches. Speakers who peered toward the distant galleries saw not faces but row upon row of newspapers rolled up into trumpets or cones that people were holding to their ears. For Bryan the situation was perfect. During an era that preceded the public address system, his superbly modulated voice could reach the incredibly large number of thirty thousand people outdoors, and his perfect enunciation made him understandable. Now, in the densely packed and highly charged convention setting, the inadequacies of the speakers who preceded him helped to turn into prophecy his confidential remarks to Mary and a friend the evening before. He had optimistically told them that they could sleep comfortably in the knowledge that the nomination would be his: "I am what they call 'the logic of the situation.'" He promised to make "the greatest speech of my life tomorrow. . . . I will be at my best."[14]

Even before Bryan bounded two steps at a time to the coliseum's platform, the silver delegates were leaning forward in anticipation. Frustrated because the first speakers had not done justice to the bimetallist cause, they kept reassuring each other, "Wait until you hear Bryan." Now as he finally appeared on the stage, thousands in the gallery and on the floor surged to their feet with deafening applause, cheers, and foot pounding. For several minutes he stood proudly, his head slightly uplifted, a trace of a smile on his thin lips, while the wildly enthusiastic crowd chanted his name.

In retrospect, Bryan wrote that there had probably never been "such a setting for any other political speech ever made in this country, and it must be remembered that the setting has a great deal to do with a speech." What he later described as "a revolt" was shaking the Democratic party. The silverites, whose cause had become a crusade, eagerly awaited the opportunity to claim a definitive leader. Bryan rose magnificently to the occasion, drawing upon words, phrases, and arguments that he had tried out in Congress and in front of audiences for several years. He paced himself brilliantly, played carefully upon the emotions of his listeners, and disarmed his critics with sweet reasonableness. "The audience acted like a trained choir," he recalled. "In fact, I thought of a choir as I noted how instantaneously and in unison they responded to each point made." Even one spectator who huffed that he did not intend "to stay to hear that crazy Populist, Bill Bryan of Nebrasky," ended up throwing his hat in the air, pounding his chair with his coat, and shouting his support.[15]

For forty minutes Bryan mesmerized his listeners. As he spoke, people in the galleries put away their paper ear trumpets. "His wonderful voice filled the auditorium," recalled Harold Ickes, who at age twenty-two sat "spellbound" in a far corner and who, despite his political allegiance to gold Republicans, was positively "thrilled" by Bryan's words.[16]

Bryan opened with a modest, if somewhat disingenuous, claim that he could not hope to match in ability "the distinguished gentlemen" who had just spoken. But this was "not a contest between persons." Indeed not. It was "a question of principle." In this case the principle was "a cause as holy as the cause of liberty—the cause of humanity." Bryan identified himself and the free silver movement with "the plain people of this country," "the common people," "the humbler members of society," and against "the encroachments of organized wealth." His listeners should make no mistake: "The humblest citizen in all the land, when clad in the armor of a righteous cause, is stronger than all the hosts of error."

In response to those who argued that gold was essential for business, he argued that their definition of business was too narrow. "The broader class of business men" for whom he spoke included wage earners, small-town attorneys, village merchants, farmers toiling in their fields, and numerous other producers. Miners who labored underground "and bring forth from their hiding places the precious metals to be poured into the channels of trade are as much business men as the few financial magnates who, in a back room, corner the money of the world."

Against the Republicans, who in their 1896 party platform pledged to seek an international bimetallist agreement (a position with which some gold Democrats agreed), Bryan struck a patriotic note. "The avenging wrath of an indignant people" simply would not abandon "the right of self-government and place the legislative control of our affairs in the hands of foreign potentates and powers." Why, he wondered, should desperate American citizens have to await the decision of other nations? Why not "let England have bimetallism because the United States has it?" To believe otherwise would be to betray the ideals of 1776 and to "declare that we are less independent than our forefathers."

For residents of the Northeast who might fail to recognize the importance of the other geographical regions of the nation, he issued a reminder. Raising his arm and pointing westward, he spoke of "the pioneers away out there"—hardy types who raised their children close to nature and constructed schools, churches, and houses. "It is for these that we speak. . . . We are fighting in the defense of our homes, our families, and posterity." But ultimately, he emphasized, more was at stake than the interests and fate of one group. The future of the entire United States depended upon the survival of the great expanse of agricultural America. "Burn down your cities and leave our farms, and your cities will spring up again as if by magic; but destroy our farms and the grass will grow in the streets of every city in the country."

To the delegates in the sweltering Chicago Coliseum, on hand to select a platform and a presidential candidate, Bryan posed what in his view was the fundamental question: "Upon which side will the Democratic party fight; upon the side of 'the idle holders of capital' or upon the side of 'the struggling masses'?" Several minutes later, as the audience sat in stunned silence, he concluded with a ringing challenge to opponents of bimetallism. "Having behind us the producing masses of this nation and the world, supported by the commercial interests, the laboring interests, and the toilers everywhere," he roared, his marvelously resonant voice bouncing off the furthest walls of the auditorium, "we will answer their demand for a gold standard by saying to them: You shall not press down upon the brow of labor this crown of thorns, you shall not crucify mankind upon a cross of gold."

With his arms stretched out parallel with the ground, and his head tilted slightly as if he were hanging from a cross, Bryan stood motionless for several seconds while the audience sat in awed silence. Initially, he feared that something had gone wrong. Finding the hush "really painful," he started toward his seat. At that point the convention broke into a deafening roar and a wild demonstration of approval. One young reporter, swept up in the contagion of the moment, believed that Bryan was nothing less than "a young David with his sling, who had come to slay the giants that oppressed the people. . . . Clean of limb, clean of heart, and clean of mind, he was a vital figure."[17]

53

That evening, in a different setting, Bryan inspired another aspiring journalist, Ray Stannard Baker, who was already convinced that he had never heard a better orator. Baker had gone to the Palmer House, Chicago's famous hotel, where throngs of people awaited Bryan's appearance. The room was so crowded that individuals stood on chairs and desks. An outpouring of cheers from the corridor signaled that Bryan had arrived. When he got to the room, he ended up addressing the crowd from the huge bridal bed, the only place left for him to stand. As Bryan spoke, seemingly oblivious to his unsteady footing, Baker believed that he "had never seen a handsomer man: young, tall, powerfully built, clear-eyed, with a mane of black hair which he occasionally thrust back with his hand." His delivery in this more intimate setting was markedly different from what it had been earlier in the massive coliseum. Here, Baker wrote, the Nebraskan was "among old friends," and his "beautiful, deeply modulated voice" expressed profound feeling and sincerity. Baker, much impressed, had no trouble accepting Bryan as "the representative of the underprivileged."[18]

It was, however, that very image of Bryan that shocked and frightened other individuals such as budding Kansas reporter William Allen White. "Here," recalled White, "was a new figure" who spoke for "the downtrodden. It was the first time in my life and in the life of a generation in which any man large enough to lead a national party had boldly and unashamedly made his cause that of the poor and oppressed." But White found no comfort in this. "I was moved by fear and rage. . . . To me he was an incarnation of demagogy, the apotheosis of riot, destruction, and carnage."[19]

The day after his Cross of Gold speech—and after the Democrats had overwhelmingly endorsed the free and unlimited coinage of silver—Bryan, in his hotel room, received the good news. On the fifth ballot, he had won his party's presidential nomination. In a sense it was incredible. Earlier, Colorado's senator C.S. Thomas had shrugged off as absurd any chance that this "young man barely thirty-six, living in a comparatively unimportant Republican state west of the Mississippi River," might lead the Democratic ticket. And when the disbelieving Republican candidate, Ohio's William McKinley, learned that Bryan was about to receive the Democratic nomination, he snapped, "That is rot."[20] Certainly Bryan's rousing speech to the convention had played an important role in accomplishing what a Thomas or a

McKinley believed was impossible. Without it the delegates might not have chosen him. But the speech alone hardly told the entire story. Bryan had for months worked to make himself an available and attractive candidate. Days on the stump had built essential grass-roots support. It was certainly not by accident that he had been one of the featured speakers during the platform debate, or that so many delegates had awaited his appearance with such expectancy. But if Bryan's nomination was far from a miracle, it would nevertheless take something of that magnitude for him to win the election.

For the Populists, Bryan's nomination presented more immediate problems. After the Democratic convention, their major challenge was how to handle the money issue. They favored silver coinage, but much more as well. Indeed, their famed Omaha platform of 1892 was genuinely radical in its call for such things as government ownership of the railroads, telephone, and telegraph; its opposition to monopolizing natural resources for speculative purposes; and its labor theory of value—namely that "wealth belongs to him who creates it, and every dollar taken from industry without an equivalent is robbery." The movement toward farmer-owned cooperatives, especially in a state such as Texas, had also offered significant alternatives to corporate capitalism. Although Populists specifically demanded the free and unlimited coinage of silver at the ratio of sixteen to one, and in 1896 hoped to lead the bimetallist forces, some of them were alert to the dangers that a preoccupation with silver could pose. A shift from the broad Omaha platform to a narrower reform agenda could force the Populists off their own turf and onto the ideological ground of corporate America. Silver coinage, after all, would hardly lead to enlarged popular control of the financial and banking structure of the country. As a Kansas editor asked, "Are we ready to sacrifice all the demands of the Omaha platform on the cross of silver?"[21]

This was precisely the dilemma that some leading Populists believed the Democrats had presented them. The alternatives seemed stark. Fusion with the Democrats might aid the silver cause while keeping the allegiance of pro-Bryan western Populists; but it could also render the People's party irrelevant. As Tom Watson of Georgia put it, merging with the Democrats would mean "we play minnow while they play trout; we play June bug while they play duck; we play Jonah while they play the whale."[22] The option was to maintain an independent, or middle-of-the-road, anti-fusionist position, thus ensuring the integrity of the third party. But this would mean almost certain victory in November for the Republicans and gold, and by then the Populists might have lost substantial numbers from their ranks to the Democrats. The challenge, in sum, was how to preserve the People's party while keeping the silver forces united.

Some Populists shuddered at the very prospect of joining the Democrats. In much of the South they had defined themselves against the hated Democratic party, which had sometimes literally gunned down third-party members. To rejoin the Democrats at this point would be, as Tom Watson saw it, to "return as the hog did to its wallow." In the North, on the other hand, were people such as Kansas's Mary Elizabeth Lease, who detested the Democrats for reasons going back to the Civil War. "My father and brothers died," she wrote, "on the field of battle defending the flag and the Union that the Democratic party, represented by Bryan . . . sought to destroy."[23]

But if such memories exerted enormous pressures upon political allegiances, so did the emotional impact of the rapidly escalating silver issue. This was immediately clear in late July at the Populist convention in St. Louis when the prairie and western states took the lead in pressing for Bryan's nomination—in other words, for fusion. "Sockless" Jerry Simpson, the flamboyant congressman from Kansas, believed that if the Populist party failed to endorse Bryan it "would not contain a corporal's guard in November." Even in the South there was some early enthusiasm for the Nebraskan. The leader of the Alabama delegation saw no choice but to back him: "I'm a middle-of-the-road Populist, but I've got sense enough to walk around a mud hole." Marion Butler, the Populist senator from North Carolina and eventually the party's national chairman, was inclined to agree with William M. Stewart, Nevada's silver Republican. The Nevada senator, after attending the Democratic convention in Chicago, wrote Butler that Bryan was "more of a Populist than a Democrat," and that "there was nothing left of the Democratic party at Chicago but the name."[24]

In the stifling midsummer heat of St. Louis, some fourteen hundred Populist delegates finally struggled to a compromise position: they nominated Bryan but rejected the Democrat's vice-presidential choice, Arthur Sewall, in favor of Tom Watson, one of the giants within the People's party. The compromise did not come easily. Emotions ran high and tempers occasionally flared into fistfights. Hostile reporters, looking for evidence of woolly-headed radicalism, joked about the proceedings. "There is a dangerous glitter in most of the eyes," wrote a Boston journalist, "and nearly every face has some normal feature lacking. Queer chins, queer noses, uneven temples—something out of the common is conspicuous on every hand."[25]

Then, and later, some people believed that Bryan's nomination was the product of deception, betrayal, and the manipulations of pseudo-Populists—of individuals more committed to their own political fortunes or to silver than to the heart and soul of the People's movement. Ignatius Donnelly, the embittered Minnesota Populist, charged that "the Democracy raped our convention while our own leaders held the struggling victim."[26]

Middle-of-the-roaders who suspected fusionist treachery pointed, for example, to the vice-presidential issue. The Democrats, with Bryan's approval, had picked Sewall of Maine because he might be able to attract votes from the Northeast (the section where the Nebraskan was weakest); because he favored silver; and because as a wealthy financier and industrialist he might reassure moderate voters that the Democrats had not fallen victim to the great unwashed. Populists could only wince at the selection of Sewall, a multimillionaire eastern banker, shipbuilder, and director of the Maine Central Railroad. He was "a warty excrescence on the body politic," according to a third-party publication. One could hardly find a better example of ways in which silver offered the illusion, rather than the substance, of reform. The fact that Bryan had accepted Sewall on the ticket in itself raised questions about the Nebraskan's willingness to trade principles for political expediency. Bryan's subsequent message to the St. Louis convention made his priorities clear. "If Sewall is not nominated," he said, "have my name withdrawn." The recipients of his telegram—Senator James K. Jones of Arkansas, who chaired the Democratic party's national committee and who was in St. Louis working for fusion, and Nebraska's Populist senator William Allen, who presided over the third-party convention—chose not to inform the delegates of Bryan's instructions. When the Populists went on to select Watson for vice-president they thus ended up with a compromise to which Bryan had not agreed. No wonder, then, that Henry Demarest Lloyd angrily described the convention as "gagged, clique-ridden, and machine ruled."[27]

It was, however, easy to exaggerate the extent to which duplicity shaped the Populists' decisions. Although Bryan did not attend the convention, he was overwhelmingly the dominant force. Even the most dedicated antifusionists challenged his candidacy only indirectly; by focusing on Sewall or on platform issues, they assumed that Bryan would remove himself from contention. And when Bryan did precisely that by asking the Populists not to nominate him without Sewall, a vast majority of delegates remained in his camp. In only four state delegations, most conspicuously Texas, which gave all of its 103 ballots to S. F. Norton of Illinois, did he fail to carry a majority of votes. Secrecy had nothing to do with this result. Newspapers had already made available the telegram that Allen refused to read to the convention. On the floor there was much discussion of it. When James B. Weaver, the party's candidate four years earlier, nominated Bryan, he referred specifically to the message: "You have all read the papers this morning; you have all read the manly dispatch from . . . Bryan. No man could have done less and be a man." According to Weaver, the convention would have to speak its own mind and name him anyhow. "Let us signal to him to hold the fort—that we are coming." Among those seconding the nomination were such Populist heavyweights as Jerry Simpson, Mary Elizabeth Lease—and Ignatius Donnelly.[28]

In a sense, of course, antifusionists had good reason to question Bryan's Populist credentials. He never joined those among them who actively championed a cooperative commonwealth. By ignoring the Omaha platform's most fundamental tenets, he raised suspicions among some Populists, as well as historians, that he was essentially a sham reformer who in his own way thwarted the Populist cause as effectively as any advocate of the gold standard.

Defenders of Bryan could nevertheless marshal persuasive arguments of their own. The Omaha platform, unquestionably a major political document, was in some respects a problematic litmus test of populism. Whatever the People's party had been in 1892, by 1896 it was different, and for reasons that had little to do with William Jennings Bryan.

As the agrarian protest of the 1880s and 1890s grew in size, it became less cohesive and more complex and contradictory. Local events and attitudes also took a toll. In Kansas, for example, the Populists suffered a terrible beating in the 1894 elections; the worsening depression was a political boon for the resurgent Republicans, not the agrarians. Populists lost their hold of the governor's mansion, the house side of the legislature, and four seats in Congress. Jubilant Republicans commemorated the supposed death of the third party with a public funeral in the state capital, and journalist William Allen White crowed that populism was "a fizzle—and not even a glorious fizzle, just a dreary[,] soggy, fagged-out, limber-kneed, red-eyed fizzle," leaving behind "a roomful of sad visages, seedy citizens and a terrible past." To some Kansas Populists the lesson was clear enough. Fusion and a narrower reform agenda were essential in order to capture a larger constituency. After 1894 Kansas populism thus changed considerably.[29]

To some observers populism had fallen victim to "the subversive tendencies of politics." "Practical politicians," like Bryan, had blunted its radical edge. The closer the movement had been to its grass-roots base, and the wider the distance between it and the established political system, the more genuinely responsive it had been to social problems and local needs. From this perspective, Ignatius Donnelly correctly perceived the dangers of placing votes ahead of principles. "Do not," he warned, "let us subordinate the cause to success."[30]

Without a larger political influence, however, populism could never have offered more than a critique of the massive changes affecting American life. To be a force, populism had to be political, with all the dangers to first principles that such a "practical" course suggested. And, in this sense, it could have met a far worse fate than its eventual alliance with William Jennings Bryan. Indeed, he may have injected new hope and energy into a political movement that by 1895 was fighting for its life at the polls in a number of states, including North Carolina, Kansas, and Colorado.

Some of the best-known Populists and opponents of corporate power in the United States found Bryan genuinely appealing. Whatever their reservations about silver as a major issue or fusion as a strategy, they saw him as an ally. James Weaver lauded him as "a gallant knight," and a "matchless champion of the people." Davis "Bloody Bridles" Waite, who had fought to make sure that Colorado populism was never limited to silver alone ("I can never agree to the Omaha platform being whittled down to that single issue"), said that Bryan was "the only man outside of the Populist party I could heartily endorse." The noted defense attorney Clarence Darrow—convinced that "the greatest battle of modern times" was under way "between the plutocrats and the producers"—endorsed the Nebraskan. Labor leader Eugene Debs, already on his way to becoming one of the nation's foremost socialists and the person whom some middle-of-the-road Populists favored for the nomination in 1896, wasted no time in rallying to Bryan. Shortly after the Democratic convention, Debs heaped praise upon him. "In the great uprising of the masses against the classes," Debs told him in a letter, "you are at this hour the hope of the Republic—the central figure of the civilized world. . . . The people love and trust you . . . and under your administration the rule of the money power will be broken."[31]

Even Ignatius Donnelly, furious at the Democratic "rape" of the third party in July, decided that Bryan was "a very able, shrewd, wise man." During a conversation between the two in October, the Nebraskan quite simply overwhelmed him. "His purposes are pure and noble," an ebullient Donnelly wrote in his diary. "He is a great man; and if he is the choice of the people he will give the country an administration the greatest and best it has ever enjoyed." In Donnelly's revised opinion, nothing less than Providence accounted for Bryan's candidacy.[32]

Equally suggestive of Bryan's reputation was the reaction of people who set themselves apart from reformers and radicals. In Emporia, Kansas, the young journalist William Allen White was not alone in viewing the Nebraskan's nomination with considerable trepidation. When word of Bryan's Democratic candidacy first arrived at the Emporia newspaper office, someone shouted, "Marat, Marat, Marat has won!" White himself feared that the analogy to the French Revolution might be correct. "Rude hands" appeared to be ripping at "the tabernacle of our national life."[33]

Such reactions assuredly told as much about the observers as about Bryan. The Nebraskan was no "agrarian revolutionist," despite that description of him in the *Atlantic Monthly*. Yet readers of that journal who worried in 1896 about "The Political Menace of the Discontented" had reasons to be uneasy about him.[34]

Although Bryan never came close to the heart of the populist movement—the self-help, cooperative alternatives to corporate capitalism, or the Omaha Platform that sought to democratize the nation's monetary, transportation, and communications systems—he was in touch with its soul. The ecstatic, and sometimes almost worshipful, response to him at the grass-roots level, especially in rural America, attested to this. After his nomination a flood of letters from humble folk, some barely literate, poured into his office. "You are the first big man that i [sic] ever wrote to," said an Iowa farmer. From Indiana came a message addressing him as "Dear father of our Country . . . God has sent you amongst our people to save the poor from starvation and we no [sic] you will save us." In Arkansas Bryan stirred more excitement among more people than had any previous politician in the history of the state. And in Kansas, the frenzy for Bryan among the "hayseeds" struck William Allen White as "a fanaticism like the Crusades."[35]

In a very real sense, entrenched, traditional power groups had reason for concern about this rising political star who was already building a legendary reputation as "the Great Commoner." His candidacy galvanized huge numbers of common citizens with a new sense of power and possibility. A middle-of-the-road Populist like Henry Demarest Lloyd could only have snickered at William Allen White's view of Bryan's candidacy as so radical that it resembled "the swinging of a firebrand in a powder mill." There was nevertheless genuine social dynamite in letters describing Bryan as "the new Christ of Humanity," who had come "to loose the chains of plutocracy from the people."[36]

Here was the populist soul with which Bryan identified. It drew upon some of the deepest wellsprings in American culture, including evangelical Protestantism and a fear of outside corruption and power. Members of the Farmers' Alliances, and later of the Populist movement, were typically "Bible people" to whom religion was both a source of comfort and a call to action. Strongly moralistic, often supporters of Prohibition, they staged political rallies that resembled religious camp meetings. They warmed to scriptural allusions and rhetoric. One Methodist minister who became an Alliance organizer claimed that if he was "a calamity howler," he stood in good company: "So was Jesus." A North Carolinian asserted that the Farmers' Alliance was "next to a religion with us." For impoverished, rural people who encountered condescension and social disapproval within town-based Protestant denominations, populism became a substitute church.[37]

Populists and Bryan often saw themselves as "missionaries" who needed to restore the true message of Christianity to American life. "The battle is between God's people and the worshippers of the golden calf," proclaimed Kansas's Populist congressman John Davis. Here was a gospel for the producer class. One member of the People's party argued that "in the economy of God there is no room for a *usurer or a landlord.*" Someone else guessed that "surely Heaven without lawyers or bankers is not a violent conception." Such words made clear that the old-time religion contained both a radical critique of the emerging industrial society and a rationale for political opposition. Bryan's ringing peroration at the Chicago convention—"you shall not crucify mankind upon a cross of gold"—thus fell upon ears that for some time had listened approvingly to what the Kansas Populist William Peffer labeled "the new gospel." Orthodox ministers were aghast at the use of such imagery, but to Bryan it came as naturally as it did to millions of Americans who, like one Kansas Alliance leader, took their words from the Scriptures: "'We were hungry, and ye took our bread.'"[38]

While the populist sensibility owed a great deal to the radical legacy of a strong Protestant tradition, it was also the product and expression of another enduring national theme—the fear of concentrated wealth and power. One of the most compelling scenarios in American culture has involved the struggle of "the little guys" against "the big guys." Images of embattled colonists standing up to the martial pomp of John Bull during the American Revolution, or (especially significant to a Silas Bryan) of Andy Jackson's battle against entrenched financial interests, assumed favored places in the nation's political memory. In the late 1800s no threat to the common folk seemed more dangerous than that of expanding business corporations, especially industrial and financial monopolies. "Wall Street owns the country," insisted Mary Elizabeth Lease. "It is no longer a government of the people, for the people, by the people, but a government of Wall Street, for Wall Street, and by Wall Street. . . . Monopoly is the master." A Nebraska Populist was far from alone when he cheered for "the farmers, laborers, and legitimate businessmen of the country, as opposed to the giant corporations and monopolists."[39]

No theme was more important to Bryan's 1896 campaign than that of fighting back against "the heads of these great trusts." Although he emphasized that the money question was paramount, in some respects he used it as a stalking horse for the larger topic of corporate greed and irresponsibility. "I have found it difficult to express, in language entirely parliamentary, my indignation when I consider our financial system." Again and again, he criticized "the bondholding classes," "the money changers and the attorneys of the great trusts and corporations," the "great combinations of money grabbers," the "'idle holders of idle capital,'" "the Wall Street syndicates which have been bleeding this country," and "the class which owns money, and trades in money, and grows rich as the people grow poor." The money question pitted "the capitalistic classes" against "the struggling masses"; the election was "between Plutocracy and Democracy." Bryan left no doubt about which side he was on. "If I am elected," he candidly told a gathering of Chicago businessmen, "the trusts will not select the Attorney General." On another occasion, he admitted that there was good reason to suspect that his "election would be a menace to those who have been living on what other people have earned."[40]

When Bryan described the struggle between the producing class and those of idle wealth as a moral issue, he not only sounded like a middle-of-the-road Populist; he also presented himself as a righteous defender of common people who "are despised and spit upon." Here again he evoked some of the richest political images in American culture, and ones to which Populists especially related. In important respects, as historian James Turner notes, "Populism became the refuge of the shutout." Its support came mainly from farmers who were generally isolated from towns, villages, established churches, and existing courthouse factions. However appealing they might have found aspects of the expanding, metropolitan, industrial society, the sad fact was that such changes came at their expense, separating them further from power and respectability, leaving them increasingly removed from the political and cultural mainstream. They felt, in Turner's words, "at sea in the society in which they lived."[41]

Their anger could only grow when hostile reporters described them as "anarchists, howlers, tramps, highwaymen, burglars, crazy men, wild-eyed men, men with unkempt and matted hair, men with long beards matted together with filth from their noses . . . men whose feet stank" and whose smelly armpits "would have knocked down a brazen bull." In contrast, Bryan vigorously defended the economic and cultural importance of plain people. As he told a small-town audience during the campaign, "Abraham Lincoln said that the Lord must have loved the common people, because He made so many of them. He was right about it." On another occasion, he predicted that if an average farmer and an average banker tried to discuss money and finances, "the banker could not hold his own with the farmer."[42]

Moreover, Bryan himself—like the Populists—faced continuing ridicule from large newspapers, prominent members of the clergy, and corporate groups. One conservative Republican dubbed him "the blatant wild ass of the prairie," and a "half-baked, glib . . . jack-leg lawyer"; and a New York City minister described him as "a mouthing, slobbering demagogue." The *Nation* magazine dismissed his supporters as "Populist and Anarchist groups." Such criticism in itself, according to some members of the People's party, had earned the Nebraskan wholehearted Populist support. S. F. Norton, the solidly middle-of-the-road Populist editor from Illinois, indicated his sympathy for the candidate on grounds that "Mr. Bryan's bitterest and most relentless opponents" had long been enemies of reform. The Nebraskan drew the same inference: "You can know a cause, as you know an individual, by the company it keeps."[43]

By continually demonstrating his affection for the common people, Bryan worked a special kind of political magic at the grass-roots level. Novelist Willa Cather had recently watched "rugged, ragged men of the soil weep like children" when Bryan addressed them in Red Cloud, Nebraska. Now, as the candidate logged an incredible eighteen thousand miles between August and November, sometimes delivering up to thirty speeches per day, he transformed American politics. According to one description, after his speeches hundreds of "the poor, the weak, the humble, the aged, the infirm" pressed toward him, reaching out "hard and wrinkled hands with crooked fingers and cracked knuckles to the young great orator, as if he were in very truth their promised redeemer from bondage." Illinois governor John Peter Altgeld, one of the best-known reformers of the era, marveled at "the effect on humble citizens of seeing and hearing the man they were asked to vote for," or "of knowing that he was doing his utmost to get among them, and talk to them face to face." Moreover, the candidate's audiences grew larger and more exuberant as the campaign continued. Some farm families traveled a hundred miles to hear him. A carnival atmosphere of fun and expectation swirled around his train stops. When he toured through North Carolina, jubilant partisans lit tar barrels along the tracks from Asheville to Raleigh to light his way.[44]

In many respects, then, Bryan was far from a disastrous Populist candidate for president. Indeed, insofar as populism was a "movement culture" that opened up social possibilities and altered the political imagination, he served the third party with distinction—perhaps as well as anyone in 1896 could have. "Our appeal," he happily told one rural Iowa audience, "has been to the great producing masses and to those who believe that the prosperity of the nation must begin with those who toil." That was sound Populist doctrine. None other than Ignatius Donnelly, one of the most committed of the middle-of-the-road Populists, thus wrote in his diary after the election, "We had a splendid candidate and he . . . made a gigantic campaign."[45]

Bryan's impact on the Democratic party was even more striking. In 1896, he may have saved it from the fate of the Whigs, the major party that disappeared just before the Civil War. More than anyone, the Nebraskan infused it with strong doses of Populist thought, particularly regarding the role of an active government. "The government which does not restrain the strongest citizen from injuring the weakest citizen fails to do its duty," he argued. When he called for government to curb the power of the corporations, he drew the analogy of farmers who put rings in the noses of hogs—not to prevent the hogs from getting fat, but to keep them from destroying more property than they were worth. "One of the duties of government is to put rings in the noses of hogs." He specifically rejected the theory that wealth trickled down to the lower classes. Instead, he subscribed to the view that "if you legislate to make the masses prosperous, their prosperity will find its way up through every class which rests upon them."[46]

Bryan also led the charge that displaced the old guard Democratic leadership. President Cleveland, as Bryan proudly told an Illinois audience, had "been thrown overboard by his own party." In North Carolina the new presidential candidate announced that the Democratic party would never be the same. Individuals "in the employ of trusts and syndicates and combinations" were no longer welcome in the party. If people from the large corporations wanted back in, now that it was in the control of common citizens, they needed to put on "sack cloth and ashes." Part of this was pure rhetoric, of course, but Bryan unquestionably moved his party to the left. By offering the example of himself—young, dynamic, eloquent, and principled—he energized the party and attracted rising new stars to it. In Arkansas, for example, where excitement over Bryan's campaign continued for several years, a wave of antimonopolist sentiment swept over the Democrats; although some of the moderate Bryanites were admittedly only lukewarm reformers, there were more radical disciples as well.[47]

Such grass-roots excitement for Bryan caught the Republicans by surprise. Initially, the GOP leadership had confidently dismissed him as only a minor threat. He seemed too young for one thing; and his bases of support were far removed from traditional power centers. Also, the stigma of Grover Cleveland seemed too much for any Democrat to overcome. But the popular frenzy that marked Bryan's campaign march "from Nebraska to the sea" and back again quickly caught the attention of leading Republicans. William McKinley's chief political adviser, Mark Hanna, anxiously urged McKinley to take to the stump himself. The Republican candidate demurred, for good reason. He realized that he was no match on the open road with the Nebraskan. "I might just as well put up a trapeze on my front lawn and compete with some professional athlete as go out speaking against Bryan," he wisely decided. "I can't outdo him, and I am not going to try."[48]

Bryan, meanwhile, hoped that his energy and oratorical skills on the campaign trail would make up for what he lacked in terms of finances and organization. He pounded the rails from state to state, giving dozens of speeches each day and struggling to come up with enough money to pay his train fare. Eventually, the Democratic National Committee scraped together enough cash to provide him with a private car; but at first, working without any real staff or advance agents, he personally carried his own suitcases to and from hotels, checked railroad schedules at the depots, and bought his own tickets. At one point in the oppressive heat of a Delaware evening, he collapsed. The next morning, he was back on his feet, but observers increasingly worried about his health. He frantically pressed on, catnapping when he could, fighting off a terribly sore throat, and sponging his body with gin to reduce body odor. In a four-day period in Michigan, he covered a thousand miles and delivered sixty-six speeches. His resiliency during these agonizingly demanding weeks was simply astounding. Equally astonishing was the fervid response from densely packed audiences that were sometimes almost unmanageable. Nor was such enthusiasm altogether misleading.

On 3 November, William Jennings Bryan received more votes (6,509,052) than any previous presidential candidate in American history. He captured twenty-two states, including all of the South and most of the West. Approximately 80 percent of eligible voters showed up at the polls, a figure that subsequent elections over the next nine decades did not even approach.

The huge turnout and Bryan's record showing did not, however, produce victory. McKinley won by a margin of around six hundred thousand votes. Bryan and his followers tried to find some comfort in defeat by hailing the Nebraskan's unprecedented performance and by attributing McKinley's success to unfair methods. Donning martyr's robes, Bryan asserted after the election that at least he, unlike his opposition, had not coerced or bribed voters. However misleading such an interpretation was in explaining McKinley's victory, it nevertheless helped to create the legend that Bryan, the beleaguered people's candidate, had lost because of foul play. As Bryan himself said, he had nearly triumphed "in spite of the threats of money loaners at home and abroad; in spite of the coercion practiced by corporate employers; in spite of trusts and syndicates; in spite of an enormous Republican campaign fund."[49]

Like most legends, the one that portrayed the forces of privilege ganging up on Bryan in 1896 was not completely fabricated. The financial resources that McKinley drew upon for the campaign were staggering. Never before in American history had so much money gone into a political race. The Democrats were simply swamped in a sea of Republican dollars, and the Populists were not even in the competition. A letter to multimillionaire banker J. P. Morgan from James J. Hill, owner of the Union Pacific railroad, set the tone for the GOP's financial success. Convinced that "an epidemic craze" for free silver had infected most farmers and many laborers, Hill believed that it was time for McKinley's managers to "get to work *at once*. . . . I will do anything or everything in my power to further the end we all have in view." The five hundred thousand dollars in contributions from Morgan and Standard Oil alone exceeded the total Democratic fund. Other large corporations chipped in almost equally impressive amounts to the Republicans. Some of the money was used to send boxcar loads of slick campaign literature across the country, to pay expenses for huge teams of speakers to publicize McKinley and "sound" money from coast to coast, and to buy tickets home for college students who intended to vote for McKinley. As an alternative to sending the reluctant McKinley himself on the stump, the Republicans brought the people to him. The candidate conducted his famous front porch campaign, staying at his Canton, Ohio, home while some 750,000 individuals poured in from distant points to see and hear him. Careful advance preparations set an impressive stage for the throngs of visiting delegations. Bryan, in his account of the election, thus printed a letter from one observer indicating that only a miracle could have overcome Republican spending.[50]

Bryan also noted that during the campaign he had encountered evidence of employers trying to pressure their workers to vote for McKinley. His charges were not unfounded. Some businesses had warned employees that Bryan's election could very well cost them their jobs. "Men, vote as you please," advised one company, "but if Bryan is elected tomorrow the whistle will not blow Wednesday morning." Although the railroads were especially guilty of such tactics, other companies suggested that a Bryan victory might jeopardize insurance policies, loans, and mortgages. Bryan was convinced that such coercion had "exerted a most potent influence on election day," and he hoped for a time when "neither creditor nor employer can control the result" against the wishes of the majority.[51]

Such a conspiratorial interpretation of the election consoled Bryan and his supporters, but it faltered badly by suggesting that McKinley's victory represented a denial of democracy. Actually, the fifty-three-year-old Republican had conducted a shrewd campaign that effectively conveyed extremely popular messages to appreciative audiences, including workers and farmers. It was unfair and inaccurate to attribute his substantial political appeal simply to the machinations of privileged economic elites.

Whereas Bryan's rhetoric tended to polarize sides, McKinley's message was soothing, with an emphasis on unity rather than social or regional conflict. The Ohio governor declared that he offered the nation domestic peace rather than the class warfare that a Bryan victory might bring. "Instead of seeking to work the masses," which Bryan was allegedly doing, McKinley offered "to try to get work for the masses." The way in which to accomplish this, he argued, was not with free silver but with protective tariffs: "This great American doctrine of protection is associated with wages and work and linked with home, family, country, and prosperity." Striking a patriotic chord, McKinley described the American flag as "a holy banner," and promised "an industrial policy that is for America and Americans." He also avowed that he could receive no higher title than that of "the workingman's friend." His promise of "a full dinner pail" for all citizens was especially appealing in the depression-ridden 1890s. For good reason Bryan thus lamented, "I have borne the sins of Grover Cleveland."[52]

Given Bryan's handicaps—the Cleveland record, the resurgent GOP, the fierce opposition of the largest companies, and the divisions within his own party over silver and populism—the Nebraskan's performance in 1896 was amazing. Probably no one other than a Republican could have won. In terms of issues and strategy Bryan undoubtedly campaigned as well as any opponent of McKinley could have done. One man who had come fifty miles to listen to Bryan said, "By gum, if I wasn't a Republican I'd vote for you."[53]

That statement was laden with meaning, although Bryan could hardly have suspected how much. More had happened in 1896 than defeat for himself, for the silver cause, and for populism. A new political and economic consensus was taking shape—a Republican, corporate consensus. By successfully linking the GOP to values of stability, nationalism, business prosperity, and law and order, McKinley sketched out the formula with which his party would dominate national politics for more than thirty years.

So persuasive was the Republican appeal that Bryan failed to carry any of the states of the old Northwest (Minnesota, Michigan, Illinois, Indiana, and Wisconsin). Here, as opposed to the urban Northeast, he was on familiar turf; yet he lost the region, and by wide margins in Illinois and Wisconsin. A slight improvement in the prices of wheat, butter, and eggs just before the election may have encouraged some farmers to believe that better times were returning and that they needed McKinley-style prosperity more than Bryan and free silver. Unless they were deeply in debt, or had little to risk, bimetallism seemed a dangerous experiment, something upon which it was foolish to gamble the future. The warnings of Theodore Roosevelt and other GOP campaigners, that Bryan "would steal from the creditors of the nation half of what they saved," added to their nervousness.[54] Moreover, because many of these midwestern farmers had traditionally been rock-ribbed Republicans, Bryan had to convince them to leave the Grand Old

Party at a time when they were not blaming it for their problems. He did not do so.

Nor was he able to mobilize the new voters in the region. The coming of age of young males, along with a major influx of new immigrants in the 1890s, had swelled the electorate in Minnesota by 30 percent, and throughout the old Northwest generally by 25 percent. The success of the Republicans in attracting the new electoral participants may have cost Bryan the election. Here the substantial organizational and financial advantages of the McKinley forces were perhaps decisive.[55]

Equally harmful to Bryan's cause was his limited appeal to the urban working class. Management's ability to intimidate employees was probably less of a factor in this respect than was fear of the unknown—in this case, the impact of free silver on the economy. For workers concerned with creating more jobs, the issue of bimetallism held little appeal. Factory wage earners, for example, had more of a stake in the emerging urban, industrial system than in agrarian America. Free silver might boost the price of Kansas corn, but for urban laborers this would mean higher food bills. Bryan's reference in his Cross of Gold speech to "our farms" and "your cities" hardly helped. Indeed, here he opened himself to attack along ethno-cultural lines. His solidly Protestant, village background was virtually the same as McKinley's, but Republicans were able to suggest that it was Bryan who had little in common with most city residents. Ultimately, urban workers in Pittsburgh's immigrant steelyard districts or New York City's Lower East Side may not have voted for Bryan because of the cultural gap that separated them from the agrarian worlds of southern Illinois or Nebraska. Bryan, despite trying, fared no better than had the Populists in attracting eastern laborers. In fact, cities generally were disaster areas for him, something that was painfully evident when he carried only twelve of the eighty-two cities with populations exceeding forty-five thousand.

For the young, dynamic Nebraskan the year 1896 had thus brought both good and bad news. He had rescued the Democratic party from the Cleveland wing and had placed himself in a leadership role. With an enfeebled political organization and vastly limited resources, he had staged an impressive campaign—a genuine testament to his powerful charismatic appeal at the grass roots. Yet he had lost the election;

the cause of silver was in shambles; the Populist ranks, upon which he had drawn since he entered politics, were in terrible disarray and diminishing; and the voting patterns that provided McKinley's victory did not bode well for the Democrats. Typically, however, Bryan looked optimistically to the future. He entitled his account of the election, published shortly after the results were in, *The First Battle*. By implication, Bryan was not through fighting.

# 4

## STUMBLING
## TOWARD THE
## TWENTIETH CENTURY
### (1897–1900)

Soon after his 1896 defeat, William Jennings Bryan, like all Americans, found himself on the threshold of a rapidly changing environment. In 1897 the United States was moving quickly out of the terrible economic depression that had blanketed the nation in general since 1893, and the agrarian regions since the late 1880s. And in 1898, with the sudden involvement in a war with Spain, which John Hay dubbed "a splendid little war," millions of Americans focused their attention on the prospects for colonial expansion, empire, and being a world power. Bryan stumbled into this strange, new world of economic optimism and dreams of glory as ill prepared as everybody else. But he picked himself up from the 1896 defeat, remained the Democratic standard-bearer, and challenged William McKinley for the presidency once again. He did so while attacking American foreign policy as an imperialistic violation of the nation's republican and Christian principles, and while clinging tightly to free silver and all

that it symbolized to him as a critique of the emerging industrial economy. Although he did well in the 1900 election, the odds against him
were unbeatable: the returning prosperity with which McKinley identified his administration, the rush of jingoistic feelings following the
victory over Spain, and the legacy of free silver that to many Americans was a painful reminder of recent social conflict and radicalism.

Throughout 1897, Bryan was concerned mainly with fending off the
efforts of Grover Cleveland and other gold Democrats to recapture the
party leadership. The Nebraskan toured the country, urging state legislatures to restrict the power of corporations and to reform election
laws by limiting corporate donations and allowing for more direct democracy. Mostly he touted the virtues of bimetallism and tried to keep
the silver forces intact. In a speech at the beginning of the year he
restated his belief "that the gold standard is a conspiracy against the
welfare of the producing masses." Eleven months later, he was still
convinced that "free and unlimited coinage of silver at 16 to 1 is near-
er now than it was a year ago."[1]

Actually, economic developments were rapidly eroding the prospects of silver coinage. By the end of 1897 prosperity was definitely
returning to the United States, a result largely of events over which
the nation had no control. Europe had rebounded much more quickly
than the United States from the panic of 1893. When European factories could not meet demands, consumers turned to the United States
and other foreign markets. Huge European purchases of American
wheat boosted trade in the grain-growing states and brought additional gold into the United States. "Republican prosperity" was already
influencing American politics, despite Bryan's firm belief that bimetallism was the key to better times and Democratic hopes.

In 1898, he could hardly have guessed that American imperialism
would shortly be an issue, let alone one loaded with political meaning
for himself. That year he, like most Americans, rallied to the flag in
a war against empire. When war broke out in April between the
United States and Spain, he shared the broad popular sentiments that
America had a compelling opportunity to advance its democratic
ideals by liberating the Spanish colony of Cuba. After Cuba's ongoing
struggle against Spanish rule had exploded with renewed fury in 1895,
the Caribbean island attracted considerable attention and sympathy
within the United States. Certainly, reports of Spanish atrocities grat-

ed increasingly on American sensibilities. In Bryan's home state, for example, the populist *Nebraska Independent* called for saving "the Cubans from intolerable outrage and starvation."[2]

A series of events in early 1898—including the sinking of the battleship *Maine* in Havana harbor, killing 260 Americans—touched off a massive public outcry. "Patriotism," according to one observer, was "oozing out of every boy . . . old enough to pack feed to the pigs."[3] On 11 April President McKinley, influenced partly by advice from aides that the Democrats might make political headway in 1900 by campaigning for a free Cuba as well as for free silver, asked Congress for a declaration of war. Within two weeks, America and Spain were officially at war.

Although Bryan was sympathetic to the Cuban cause, he initially agreed with the Populist Tom Watson that war could undermine reform. As late as January 1898, he was still concerned primarily with free silver and contended that the annual number of American deaths due to the gold standard exceeded that of Cubans who died because of Spanish bullets. But events in Cuba and the swelling outcry to liberate the island from colonialism quickly swept him up. By March, with a small American flag in one hand and a small Cuban flag in the other, he was vigorously championing Cuban independence before enthusiastic crowds. At a press conference he asserted that "the time for intervention has arrived. Humanity demands that we shall act." Indeed an unwillingness to intervene would indicate sadly that "we, as a nation, have become so engrossed in money making as to be indifferent to distress."[4] On 25 April, immediately upon learning that Congress had declared war, he volunteered his services to the president in any capacity.

When McKinley dragged his feet, understandably reluctant to make a war hero of his chief political opponent, Bryan enlisted as a private in the Nebraska National Guard. The next day, however, the governor established the Third Regiment with the understanding that the men would elect Bryan as colonel. In mid-July, amid a rousing send-off, "Willie's Wonders," as critics dubbed them, were en route to Florida and, presumably, Cuba. Another Nebraska unit, the First Nebraska Volunteers, ended up in the Philippines—a Spanish colony, like Cuba, ripe with political unrest, and where Spain and the United States first exchanged gunfire.

By serving in a state volunteer unit, Bryan placed himself in an area of military service infused with symbolic meaning. Nebraska's Third Regiment was in the tradition of state National Guard organizations. Like the guard, its points of reference were not national but local, oriented toward small-town or neighborhood environments. Unlike the professional, regular army, which contained only twenty-eight thousand officers and men in early 1898, the guard and state volunteer units were anything but disciplined servants of a military bureaucracy. State units resembled separate, small armies. Even within them there was little uniformity or organization. Significantly, at a time when small towns across the United States seemed to be slipping in status and self-sufficiency, it was the National Guard and state volunteer units that stepped forward to help liberate the Spanish colonies. In the process, of course, such units also struck a psychological blow for the independence and worth of local America. The emotional claims of the guard and volunteers were thus substantial, especially among citizens who worried about impersonal, centralizing trends in the United States. Regular army people were far less inclined to celebrate the virtues of state units; indeed, they typically were aghast at the lack of discipline and casual familiarity that pervaded them. But from the perspective of the communities from which they came, local military organizations represented the best in American life: neighborhood and familial ties, along with the personal dignity and importance of individualism.

For guardsmen, and state volunteers who avoided federal service out of fear that they would have West Point graduates as their superiors, Colonel William Jennings Bryan posed no threat. He much preferred the nation's "citizen soldiery," which he viewed as "the sheet-anchor of a republic's defense," to the regular army.[5] Far from overbearing or strict, he personally felt uncomfortable in a spit-and-polish setting. He spurned military procedures as much as possible and refused to memorize commands that appeared in the army manual. Sometimes he asked his men to vote their preferences. In his opinion, privates were the equals of their officers. He was entirely comfortable with the "Hello, Billy" greetings from the corporal of the guard. This did not mean that he took his job lightly, however. He cared about the morale of his men and spent considerable time with them, counseling them and sometimes joining them in singing "Home, Sweet Home" and other favorites. He was also attentive to their health and personal rights.

He had good reason to worry about the health and future of the Third Regiment. By September, it was still in Florida, where a combination of heat, humidity, and disease were taking a terrible toll. Malaria and typhoid had put dozens in the hospital or in their quarters, and Bryan's own bout with typhoid sent his weight plummeting twenty-five pounds.

Adding to his concerns about his men was a major foreign policy development. On 12 August, after 113 days of military conflict, American and Spanish representatives signed a preliminary instrument of peace. The war, in effect, was over. Bryan assuredly had no quarrel with this, even though the Third Regiment regretted having had to leave the liberation of Cuba and the Philippines to units such as Leonard Wood's and Theodore Roosevelt's Rough Riders. His complaint was that the Third Regiment continued to languish in a snake-infested Florida camp despite the defeat of the Spanish. Suspicious that the McKinley administration was altering its foreign policy, he journeyed to the White House to protest. Greatly agitated, he reminded the president that troops had "volunteered to attempt to break the yoke of Spain in Cuba, and for nothing else." He feared that the administration had settled on another objective: that of annexing former Spanish colonies such as the Philippines, which Americans and local insurgents had just freed. Bryan had already warned against turning a war "for the sake of humanity . . . into a war of conquest." He feared now that the administration had swerved precisely in that direction. Make no doubt about it, he informed the president, the Third Regiment "did not volunteer to attempt to subjugate other peoples, or establish United States sovereignty elsewhere."[6]

Back in camp, frustrated and sick, in mid-October Bryan implored Mary to join him "at once." Uncertain about McKinley's foreign policy, and unsure about his own future in that swampy Florida setting, he lapsed into martyrdom. "I am not free to please myself," he wrote his wife. "I have consecrated whatever talents I may have to the service of my fellow men. To aid in making the government better and existence more tolerable to the producers of wealth is my only ambition."[7]

He seized upon the signing of the peace treaty on 10 December 1898 as an opportunity to resign from the military and hold a press conference in which he challenged the McKinley administration. By then the president had formally instructed his peace negotiators in

Paris to secure the Philippines for the United States. In a crowded Savannah, Georgia, hotel room, Bryan alerted reporters that the United States was in danger. Americans had just "defended Cuba against foreign arms." Now they faced a new threat. They needed to "defend themselves and their country against a foreign idea—the colonial idea of European nations." Within a month he was stumping the country in opposition to the "forcible annexation" of the Philippines. Such action would "not only be criminal aggression," he argued; it would also mean that "the whole people will pay the cost while a few will reap all the benefits."[8]

Suddenly, Bryan emerged as the nation's foremost political opponent of the administration's imperialist policy. And he did so at a time when, in the excitement of victory over Spain, public opinion appeared to be warming up to the idea of a colony in the Philippines. For the scattered groups to whom such a trend was alarming, Bryan offered a political rallying point. Even some people who had loathed him for his free silver campaign in 1896, but who now shuddered at the prospects of an American empire, began to see him as a potential ally.

In early 1899, however, he threw the anti-imperialist ranks into confusion by backing the administration's fight for senate approval of the peace treaty. Under the treaty, Spain relinquished its sovereignty over Cuba and ceded Puerto Rico, Guam, and the Philippines to the United States. To anti-imperialists such as Republican senator George Frisbie Hoar of Massachusetts, the gauntlet was down: "They cannot get through a treaty which commits us to imperialism." Only a treaty that guaranteed independence to the former Spanish colonies would be acceptable. Bryan jolted Hoar and the membership of the newly formed American Anti-Imperialist League, based largely in the Northeast, by endorsing the existing treaty. For one thing, he did not want the war to resume. Indeed, if the treaty failed, the McKinley administration would have "an excuse for military expenditures which cannot be justified after the conclusion of peace." He worried also about placing the fate of the Filipinos back into the hands of diplomats, and perhaps with Spain. He thus favored ratification in order to free the Philippines from Spain, after which the United States via a senate resolution could immediately set the islands on their way to independence. "Who will deny to our people the right to haul down the flag in the Philippines if they so desire?," he asked. Specifically, he endorsed Georgia senator Augustus Bacon's proposed resolution granting independence to the Filipinos once they had established a stable government.[9]

In Hoar's estimation, Bryan was now "worthless as an Anti-Imperialist." The Massachusetts senator suspected that the Nebraskan was playing politics with anti-imperialism, using it to advance free silver and other domestic reforms. Moreover, Hoar saw little difference between McKinley's policies and Bryan's plans to provide eventual independence for the Philippines. When the Senate subsequently consented to the treaty by a margin of one vote, Hoar blamed the Nebraskan. "We had the treaty all beaten," he seethed, until Bryan had descended on Washington: "His course was as if some influential General in our Revolutionary War had surrendered West Point to the British."[10]

Actually, despite Hoar's interpretation of Bryan's decisive influence on the final vote, the Nebraskan's role was unclear. He had indeed thrown himself into the fight, even though friends had warned him that treaty supporters would gladly accept his help and would then snub him when he pressed for Philippine independence. Stationing himself outside the Senate chambers, he had urged Democrats to vote for the treaty. He may not in fact have converted anyone to vote for consent, but he had denied the treaty's opponents whatever advantages they might have gained had he been on their side. More influential than Bryan for the outcome, however, was an exchange of gunfire between Filipinos and American troops the day before the Senate voted.

The outbreak of fighting between Filipinos and Americans may also have been a key reason the Senate two weeks later defeated the Bacon resolution guaranteeing future Philippine independence. With thirty-two senators choosing not even to vote, a tie resulted. The vice president broke the deadlock, leaving the future of the Philippines undecided. Bryan had calculated that Philippine independence would follow ratification of the treaty. Events had not followed his desired scenario, however. A permanent American colony in the Pacific seemed inevitable.

For Bryan, the results of these quickly breaking events were mixed. He had hoped to set aside the issue of empire so that in 1900 he could concentrate on issues of free silver and the trusts. His main concern was with keeping the agenda of 1896 alive, and he fretted that the question of Philippine independence would be a distraction. On the other hand, he recognized that the Philippine issue was not without political advantages. Anti-imperialism was a cause that might draw some of his former conservative enemies to his side, despite the anger of George Hoar and others at his role in the treaty ratification fight. And there was no doubt about it: Bryan still had presidential hopes.

Strong political overtones thus marked the Nebraskan's anti-imperialist position, even though he genuinely opposed colonialism and supported Philippine independence. During the spring of 1899 he encountered encouraging signs that public acceptance of McKinley's policy was wavering. Filipino resistance and rumors of American military atrocities raised questions about whether, as one individual phrased it, "we are doing in the Philippines what we made war upon Spain for doing in Cuba."[11] Such suspicions were notably evident among several important ethnic groups, particularly German-Americans, who had fled European militarism, and Irish-Americans, who associated colonialism with the hated English. Similarly alarmed were members of the newly formed Anti-Imperialist League—largely New England aristocrats who viewed McKinley's foreign policy as yet further proof of their declining influence and the nation's break from tradition.

Bryan's barnstorming tour across much of the country from February into autumn 1899 suggested that imperialism was very much a political issue. As he hit the McKinley administration again and again for shoving "old world imperialism" upon the United States, he attracted large, friendly audiences that sometimes listened for three hours. In Buffalo, New York, the crowd was reportedly the largest in the city's history. Back in Nebraska, J. Sterling Morton sniffed that "this soldier who never fired a gun or saw a battle" was "again in the saddle," peddling his usual recipes for disaster. Bryan had the last word, however. He dominated the state Democratic convention in August, obtaining strong anti-imperialist and antimilitarist planks. He also worked carefully with state Populists who adopted similar positions. That November, with anti-imperialism the major theme, a coalition of Populists and Democrats swept Nebraska's major offices. The hand of Bryan was undeniable. As Republican Charles Dawes, a McKinley henchman, put it, the results were "due to Bryan's personality."[12]

By March 1900, Bryan's use of the anti-imperialist issue was making McKinley's people nervous. In Indiana, which both parties had targeted as a pivotal state in the upcoming election, the administration had recently enjoyed a commanding position; citizens had appeared willing to accept McKinley's foreign policy as humanitarian and they attributed better economic times to him. But in the spring a burst of anti-imperialist sentiment in the Middle West sent Democratic hopes soaring. Some Democrats saw an opportunity to seal over their divisions of 1896 by attacking McKinley's foreign policy. Significantly, Indiana's state party platform (like those of Michigan, Ohio, Wisconsin, and Illinois) took dead aim at the "imperialism" of McKinley. But just as important, twenty-one of the twenty-two Indiana delegates destined for the Democratic national convention in Kansas City did something else: they opposed reiterating the 1896 plank calling for the free and unlimited coinage of silver at a ratio of sixteen to one.[13]

Here was a clear danger signal for Bryan. He was willing to fight against colonialism, but he had no intention of letting any issue push aside the unfinished agenda of 1896. As he wrote in a magazine on the eve of the Democratic convention, "The issue presented in the 1900 election is the issue between plutocracy and democracy. All the questions under discussion will . . . disclose the conflict between the dollar and the man." Imperialism was assuredly a manifestation of this conflict; but he specifically placed it behind issues involving silver and the trusts.[14]

His dedication to silver seemed misdirected in some respects. New discoveries of gold in the late 1890s and improved technology by which to reduce the gold from ore had dramatically increased the availability of the precious metal. In effect, the expansion of the money supply that Bryan had hoped to effect with silver at sixteen to one had become a reality—without silver.

Bryan's continuing allegiance to silver was perhaps due in part to what an ally described as "the love of a mother for her first-born." The issue had worked miracles for Bryan's political career, and he believed that his legions in the previous campaign counted on him not to let them down. But silver, to Bryan, invariably went beyond politics; he persisted in interpreting it as a matter of culture—a symbol of the confrontation between the producer classes and their corporate oppressors. Foes of silver, as he identified them before a New York City gathering in April 1899, were "those who have their hands in the pockets of their neighbors." Ultimately, first principles were at stake. And on this point no one could accuse him of hedging.[15]

In an impassioned, lengthy speech on 20 January 1900, in Baltimore, he applauded "that heroic band of Democrats who in 1896 rescued the Democratic party from the domination of plutocracy," and who continued to defend it against those who would deliver it back to "the money interests." He was proud that, despite pressures from large banks and corporations, "the plain people in the Democratic party have stood, and now stand, for the Chicago platform." Identifying the silver issue as "a righteous cause," he pledged, "I am not willing that a handful of English bankers shall control seventy millions of American people." When several individuals, including prominent anti-imperialists and conservative Democrats, subsequently begged him at least to play down the silver issue, his response was unyielding. Harking back to "every plank" in the 1896 Chicago platform—"including the silver plank"—he quoted emotionally from the Bible: " 'Intreat me not to leave thee . . . for whither thou goest, I will go; . . . Thy people shall be my people, and thy God my God.' "[16]

Conservative Democrats, to whom 1896 had been a nightmare, agreed with New York's Republican senator Chauncey Depew when he described Bryan as "a bodysnatcher, carrying a corpse in a coffin, the dead silver issue." Indiana's popular novelist and gold Democrat, Maurice Thompson, loathed the Nebraskan as "a terror. He stands for all that is bad in our political and social life." His supporters, according to Thompson, stood for everything reprehensible. They were "traitors, aliens, populists, anarchists, socialists of all shades, disgruntled office-holders, repudiators—whatever is vile is for him from Maine to Texas." Bryan's suspicions of those who urged him to drop "silverism" and to turn anti-imperialism into "the principal issue" were thus not unwarranted.[17]

Leaders of the New England-based Anti-Imperialist League, for example, most assuredly did not share his domestic political commitments. Typically fifth- or sixth-generation Americans with wealth, connections, college degrees, and socially conservative views, they were gold advocates who despised anything that smacked of populism. One of them dismissed the silver cause as "an intolerable fraud." Virtually the only thing they shared with Bryan was the conviction that imperialism violated America's heritage and threatened to destroy the nation's highest ideals.[18]

As in 1896, Bryan stood in a battle zone of social class in American life. Reactions to him throughout 1900 were almost visceral, reflecting again and again intensely felt emotions about the masses, social position, and privilege. A hostile Nebraska editor said that Bryan "reminds one of Uncle Josh Whitcomb, 'by gosh,' dressed in his old slouch hat. All he lacks is a pair of red top boots and a pair of overalls stuck therein to make the outfit complete." The influential New York *Tribune* described him as "the apostle of claptrap and appeals to ignorance"; and the Baltimore *Herald* asserted that only "the unthinking crowd" listened to him. Theodore Roosevelt, whose social pedigree was unassailable in elite circles, berated the Nebraskan for dispensing "the doctrine of envy, the doctrine of greed," and for appealing "to the worst, basest passions in mankind." Members of the Anti-Imperialist League broke with Roosevelt over foreign policy; but they remained with him—one of their own in terms of background and status—in their distaste for that "by gosh" Nebraskan with his old slouch hat.[19]

Bryan hoped that his opposition to colonialism would diminish such animosities enough to provide the margin of victory in 1900. No one needed to remind him that four years earlier he had barely lost. This time it just might be different.

But he was unwilling to seek victory by burying the ideals of 1896. In his opinion, in fact, it was impossible to separate anti-imperialism and domestic reforms. He believed that foreign policy and domestic issues alike pitted the people against the corporations. His interpretation of American imperialism resembled that of Kansas Populist John W. Breidenthal, candidate for governor in 1900, who believed that "the great corporations of this country" simply wanted "new fields to conquer." Bryan was unwilling to concede either America's internal or foreign affairs to the monied interests. "The gold standard financiers," he argued in the spring of 1900, "stand behind every abuse of government and we can not make peace with them on one thing without weakening our fight against other things."[20]

A grateful John Peter Altgeld, one of the era's most diligent opponents of privilege, cheered Bryan's "heroic stand," and described him as "the grandest figure in the civilized world." The former Illinois governor's praise was effusive, but the Nebraskan's steadfastness demonstrated genuine political courage. Despite the risks involved, Bryan stuck to his principles. He insisted that when it came to "the money question, the trust question and imperialism," he would "emphasize them all."[21]

Bryan's dogged commitment to the ideals of 1896 posed difficult problems for the Democrats as they gathered in Kansas City to select a platform and ticket for the 1900 election. The WELCOME sign that a local mortician had placed on his building set the scene all too well. Everything seemed to conspire against a cheerful gathering. The oppressive July heat discouraged delegates and reporters from touring the area, and accommodations were so limited that members of the press had to convert a hotel dining room into sleeping quarters, spreading their blankets on the floor. Many delegates found even greater discomfort in the heated debates that wracked the meetings of the platform committee and the proceedings within the sweltering convention hall.

One of the most explosive issues concerned the inclusion of a plank specifically endorsing silver at sixteen to one. Some Democrats, hoping to defuse the topic somewhat, favored a compromise plank that would merely reaffirm the 1896 platform "in letter and in spirit." Bryan balked, apparently because he simply was not yet able to rethink his views on the money question. His continuing suspicions of people who opposed silver prevented him from considering their opinions seriously. From Nebraska, where he kept close touch with the Kansas City deliberations, he thus rejected as inadequate any simple reaffirmation of the 1896 document. Refusing to disappoint his rank-and-file supporters of four years earlier, he drew the line: he would not accept the presidential nomination unless the Democrats specifically included the Chicago silver plank. He thus threw down the gauntlet to the likes of New York Democrat and newspaper editor James Creelman who stated unequivocally that "we cannot, cannot, cannot, and will not, will not take up '16 to 1' in the East." And Bryan refused to waver despite the fact that 75 percent of the delegates opposed repeating the silver plank. If necessary, he was prepared to race to Kansas City by special train to take his fight to the convention floor. According to Mary Bryan, her husband was more nervous than she had ever seen him as he awaited news of the delegates' decision.[22]

He eventually won both his party's nomination and the platform fight—although barely one-third of the delegates cheered for the silver plank, and even then for less than five minutes. Despite the torrid disagreements that had marked the convention, Bryan was unquestionably the master of the Democrats. His opponents had been unable to muster any kind of serious challenge to his nomination.

But his success also demonstrated that, within limits, he was willing to compromise. He finally consented to wording in the Democratic platform that made anti-imperialism the "dominant" issue. When South Carolina's Ben Tillman read the platform to the convention, he repeated the word *paramount* twice, shaking his manuscript in the air and bringing three-fourths of the delegates to their feet for a frantic twenty-minute demonstration.[23] Bryan also settled for silver's protected place in the platform, and agreed informally to downplay the money issue when he campaigned in the East. With his party delicately balanced between the issues of silver and anti-imperialism, he launched his second presidential race.

On 8 August he delivered one of his greatest speeches. He accepted the Democratic nomination of several weeks earlier, and deliberately picked Indianapolis as the place to do so. No one could deny the importance of Indiana to the election; nor was it coincidental that he concentrated almost exclusively on foreign policy. He was thinking, of course, of the politics within his own party. Moreover, the Republicans at their June convention had renominated President McKinley amid a torrent of grandiose rhetoric justifying annexation of the Philippines and blaming the Democrats for the continuing Filipino insurgency. The GOP's vice-presidential choice of Theodore Roosevelt, perhaps the most strident of the expansionists, suggested that McKinley was quite willing to go toe-to-toe with the Democrats on the issue of imperialism. "Is America a weakling?" Roosevelt had asked the Republicans. "No," he had answered. "The young giant of the West stands on a continent and clasps the crest of an ocean in either hand."[24] Now, some seven weeks after Roosevelt had declared that Republicans did not stand "cringing" in the face of world responsibilities, Bryan replied with some flourishes of his own. Standing outdoors in front of a densely packed and spirited crowd of at least forty thousand in a downtown park, he evoked continued cheers with a finely crafted address.

Seldom had his commitment to the republican values of the American revolutionary era been clearer. "A republic," he reminded his audience, "can have no subjects." It is based on self-government:

"Every citizen is a sovereign, but . . . no one cares to wear a crown." McKinley's colonial policy required "an army large enough to support the authority of a small fraction of people while they rule the natives." This not only violated the principle of self-rule for the Filipinos; it also threatened Americans at home because it necessitated a standing army—"ever a menace to a republican form of government." Jabbing sharply at McKinley, Bryan thundered that "the Republican party has accepted the European idea and planted itself on the ground taken by George III." Should Americans, he wondered, repudiate their republican ideals and revolutionary heritage? Answers to such questions rested entirely with the citizens themselves because, ultimately, "the destiny of this republic is in the hands of its people." Bryan made his own position clear. He vehemently opposed the suggestion "that the flag of this republic should become the flag of an empire."[25]

While the theme of republicanism dominated his speech, so too did the ideals of Christian love and sacrifice. The simple truth, he pointed out, was that the United States was strong enough to do virtually as it pleased. "It can substitute might for right; it can conquer weaker people; it can exploit their lands, appropriate their property and kill their people." But such power would violate "the moral law" and "the teachings of Christ." Turning angrily upon advocates of "forcible Christianity," he insisted that "imperialism finds no warrant in the Bible. The command, 'Go ye into all the world and preach the gospel to every creature,' has no gatling gun attachment." Against "the swaggering, bullying, brutal doctrine of imperialism," he advanced the Golden Rule and neighborly love.

As eloquent and impassioned as Bryan's attack on imperialism was, it nevertheless carried within it contradictory messages. He renounced forcible expansion but believed deeply in America's moral and political superiority, as well as the nation's responsibility to influence world events through trade and example. His quarrel was not with enlarging America's role in international affairs, but over the proper means by which to do so. In his estimation, the United States was a beacon of liberty, a model of republican virtue and ideals, and an agent of Christian duty. As such, it should never impose its will on other nations with bayonets and cannon. It should never go the way of the Old World of Europe, heavy with the blood of fallen victims and reeking of imperial greed and corruption. The United States, he believed passionately, was a model of gentle persuasion, speaking to the minds and hearts of other peoples. He eagerly hoped to spread the American way throughout the world, but through the power of example, not military force. Indeed, he warned, in early 1900, "if this nation enters upon a career of imperialism it ceases to be a moral factor in the world's progress."[26]

A fervent nationalist, Bryan had more in common with the gun-toting and militantly aggressive Theodore Roosevelt than he realized. Born less than two years apart, both were products of an age that celebrated American strength and virtue. The standard fare of childhood reading for their generation had included romantic tales of valor and the glories of battle, whether in the stories of *Ivanhoe*'s knights, or of pioneers conquering Indians. George Bancroft's history of the United States, which Bryan had so much enjoyed as a student, exuberantly traced the march of the flag, and the *McGuffey Reader* drew numerous moral lessons from the nation's triumphs. At the close of the nineteenth century, a powerful wave of nationalism had inspired an unprecedented number of patriotic organizations and unquestionably left an imprint upon Bryan as well as Roosevelt. It was not by accident that the Nebraskan talked approvingly of "America's mission" or that in 1898 he waved the flag while exhorting his nation to take up arms in behalf of humanity.[27]

Bryan, as much as anyone, reflected the era's patriotic mood. He filled his addresses with talk about the "triumphant march" of American ideals. Indeed, during the nineties he had tied part of his crusade for silver to strong nationalistic sentiments. Describing silver as "the money of the fathers," he had quoted George Washington's warnings "against the insidious wiles of foreign influence" and then claimed that advocates of the gold standard would sell out American independence. "Let me appeal to your patriotism," he had said in one campaign speech when insisting that England's commitment to the gold standard should not dictate American policy. "Are we an English colony or an independent people?" Stumping in Philadelphia, he had "preach[ed] financial independence in the city which saw the Declaration of Independence signed"; he saw no difference between "the American who takes his patriotism from Lombard street" in London's financial district and those who had resisted the revolution in 1776. He had also charged the Republican party with "attempting to surrender the right of the American people to legislate for themselves" by binding them "to a foreign monetary system" and "foreign creditors."

At one point he had gone so far as to assert that many citizens faced the choice of leaving the Republican party or delivering "their country into the hands of foreigners."[28]

Such patriotic appeals not only fit well with the emotions of the day but placed him close to the same jingoistic orbit as the imperialists whom he despised. He told an audience in 1899 that the United States had "exerted upon the human race an influence more potent for good than all the other nations of the earth combined." Comparing civilizations, he said proudly: "Great has been the Greek, the Latin, the Slav, the Celt, the Teuton and the Anglo-Saxon, but greater than any of these is the American in whom are blended the virtues of them all. . . . 'To American civilization all hail! Time's noblest offspring is the last.' " In this respect, Bryan merely echoed the opinions of Indiana's senator Albert J. Beveridge, who asserted that God had chosen Americans to regenerate the world. The perspectives of the two men were remarkably similar; Beveridge, however, used his words to justify annexation of the Philippines.[29]

Bryan in fact shared the imperialists' pride in American expansionism. When he stated that "this nation is a great nation, a conquering nation, it should conquer the world," he sounded much like Theodore Roosevelt or Massachusetts senator Henry Cabot Lodge—"those jingling jingoes," as one anti-imperialist critic labeled them. The 1900 Democratic platform, which bore Bryan's imprint throughout, applauded the expansion of American trade and territory. The Nebraskan believed that commerce was good not only for economic reasons but for bringing nations closer together. And he referred approvingly to America's historical acquisition of the Louisiana Purchase and other areas on the continent. With obvious satisfaction he emphasized the Democratic party's support for expansion that "enlarges the area of the Republic and incorporates land which can be settled by American citizens."[30]

Although Bryan tried to distinguish Democratic-style expansionism from Republican-style imperialism, Theodore Roosevelt showed that the Nebraskan was venturing on historical quicksand. In his letter accepting the GOP's vice-presidential nomination, Roosevelt offered some arresting interpretations of his own: the United States, whether driving the Spanish out of Florida earlier, or out of the Philippines later, had acted in opposition to imperialism; Jefferson's sending of troops to Louisiana was no different than McKinley's sending them to the Philippines; and "the reasoning which justifies our having made war against Sitting Bull also justifies our having checked the outbreaks of Aguinaldo and his followers."[31]

Although Bryan's views of American expansion could, as Roosevelt demonstrated, easily serve the cause of annexation, so too did his racial attitudes. His praise of American greatness was partially a racial judgment. He lauded America's racial superiority, contending "that by any standard—physical, material, intellectual, aesthetic, moral or spiritual—the average American is far superior to the average Chinaman." Such an assessment squared nicely with arguments that the inferiority of the Filipinos ("half-breed Chinese," according to Roosevelt, Lodge, and others) mandated the need for American supervision. In popular cartoons at the turn of the century, Americans typically portrayed the Filipinos as primitive savages and bloody cannibals. In contrast to "civilized" Caucasians, Filipinos supposedly needed guidance and instruction even in how to take care of themselves: "O, Aguinaldo leads a sloppy life, / He eats potatoes with his knife, / And once a year he takes a scrub, / And leaves the water in the tub." An allegedly handicapped race, they reportedly needed all the help they could get. And this was precisely what many American advocates of annexation hoped to provide.[32]

Ironically, although prejudice provided one of the arguments for subjugating the Filipinos, it also helped make the case for leaving them alone. Bryan opposed annexing the Philippines partially for racial reasons. The weight that such reasons carried in a blatantly racist era was perhaps a consideration. But he also believed personally in Anglo-Saxon superiority and wanted the United States to be "a homogenous nation." In his Indianapolis acceptance speech he contended that it would be impossible "to bring into the body politic eight or ten million Asiatics, so different from us in race and history that amalgamation is impossible." And he rejected the idea that the Filipinos could "share with us in making laws and shaping the destiny of this nation. . . . The Democratic platform describes the situation when it says that the Filipinos cannot be citizens without endangering our civilization." The question, as he had phrased it a year earlier, was "whether this nation shall remain a homogenous republic or become a heterogeneous empire." Bryan was not as virulently racist as Missouri congressman Champ Clark, who opposed annexing the Hawaiian

Islands on grounds that Americans would be ashamed to have some pigtailed Chinese senator debating in broken English with an orator such as George Frisbie Hoar. But the Nebraskan, like Clark and other anti-imperialists, accepted a premise that was basic to the imperialists: people were fundamentally unequal.[33]

In profound ways, Bryan thus joined the majority paean to American superiority; but if the song was the same, he sang it in a somewhat different key. While he granted America's expansionist role, he spurned coercion: "Other nations may dream of wars of conquest and of distant dependencies governed by external force; not so with the United States." While he favored enlarging the nation's trade, he emphasized that "it is not necessary to own people in order to trade with them." "Trade," he reasoned, "cannot be permanently profitable unless it is voluntary." While he perceived the Filipinos as inferior, he conceded considerably more to them than did many of his contemporaries: "God never made a race of people so low . . . that it would welcome a foreign master. . . . It is a reflection upon the Creator to say that he denied to any people the capacity for self-government." And while he applauded a law-abiding, orderly society, he was far more sympathetic to nationalistic revolutions than was Roosevelt: "Can it be our duty to kill those who, following the example of our forefathers, love liberty well enough to fight for it?"[34]

He had no doubts that the United States could subdue the Filipinos but only at its own peril. By concentrating on a foreign war, it would neglect its own "grave domestic problems." He suggested with grim humor that for America's farmers and laborers the much-celebrated "White Man's Burden" was all too suggestive a term: "Since it crushes the wealth-producer beneath an increasing weight of taxes, it might with more propriety be called The Poor Man's Load."[35]

Perhaps an important key to Bryan's sympathy for the cause of the Filipino insurgents, however much his racial opinions may have compromised his position, was that he spotted parallels between the attacks on them and on his supporters in 1896. Ever alert to elitist snobbishness, Bryan recalled the condescending portraits of protesting farmers in the last presidential election. "We are told that the Filipinos are not capable of self-government; that has a familiar ring," he said. "Only two years ago I heard the same argument made against a very respectable minority of the people of this country." Lest anyone miss his point, he spelled it out carefully: "The money lenders, who coerced borrowers, did it upon that theory; the employers who coerced their employees did it for the same reason."[36]

To Bryan, then, the fight against imperialism was closely related to his battles of 1896. He thus refused to substitute anti-imperialism for issues involving silver and the trusts, as the Anti-Imperialist League and many eastern Democrats wanted. Instead, he insisted that it was impossible to separate foreign and domestic matters. Whether the campaign was against gold or imperialism or monopoly, the enemy was the same—the monied, non-producing classes. An imperialist policy came at the expense of farmers and laborers whose small incomes would subsidize military expenses disproportionately. And who would benefit? Army contractors, "ship-owners, who would carry live soldiers to the Philippines and bring dead soldiers back," salaried officials, and franchise-builders. "It is not our duty to burden our people with increased taxes in order to give a few speculators an opportunity for exploitation."[37]

During the presidential campaign, of course, Bryan had to fight this domestic political war on different fronts and against an astute Republican foe with strategies and resources of his own. If the Nebraskan's tactics seemed uneven and contradictory, it was largely because his task was so formidable. His alliance with the eastern anti-imperialists was tenuous at best; he constantly faced desertions from the old Cleveland wing of the Democrats; his attacks on the American-Filipino war opened him to charges of being disloyal to the United States; and he faced an incumbent president whom many people credited with bringing better times and who, in the words of editor William Allen White, "combined the virtues of the serpent, the shark, and the cooing dove."[38]

Anti-imperialism as an issue might not have dominated the campaign anyhow, but McKinley shrewdly made sure that it did not. Deftly avoiding spread-eagle rhetoric about the glories of annexation, he emphasized themes of "honor and duty" in the Philippines. "No blow has been struck except for liberty and humanity and none will be," he reassured his audience. Indeed, he carefully noted that the GOP, "the party of liberty and emancipation" during the Civil War, was leading the way "in the liberation of 10,000,000 of the human family from the yoke of imperialism." He not only downplayed differences between himself and Bryan over imperialism, but he also skillfully diverted attention from foreign policy as much as possible. Striking a presidential pose—dignified, remote from the political fray, and responsible—he pointed to his accomplishments: "The public faith has been upheld; public order has been maintained. We have prosperity at home and prestige abroad." All this was in jeopardy, he warned, because "the menace of 16 to 1 . . . still hangs over us."[39]

Bryan quickly ended up on the defensive. For one thing, he had to deal with charges that his criticism of the administration's foreign policy was simply prolonging the war against the Filipinos. According to the *Republican Campaign Book* for 1900, Filipino insurgents—the killers of American soldiers—were toasting Bryan's health. Although it was true that Emilio Aguinaldo, the leader of the insurrectionaries, saw Bryan's candidacy as "a ray of hope," it hardly followed that the continuation of the war was the Nebraskan's responsibility. Yet the New York *Tribune* contended in October that Bryan was in fact the commander of the revolutionaries, "and every American soldier that is killed during these months can be laid directly at his door." A Chicago newspaper cartoon portrayed Bryan astride a Democratic donkey, galloping over American bodies toward the White House. Theodore Roosevelt, the Republican vice-presidential candidate, specialized in tarring Bryan for his lack of patriotism. Referring to the "gallant lads" who had died in the Philippines, Roosevelt pleaded that they "at least be spared the slights and sneers of our own people." As Josephus Daniels, who covered the election as a young reporter, later observed, "the American people could not be aroused by any wrongs done to people across the sea."[40]

While Bryan was discovering the pitfalls of trying to campaign on the issue of anti-imperialism, he learned that talking about silver in the West made him even more vulnerable to the Republicans. Indeed, had he not been willing to take the silver ground himself, the administration would have done everything possible to push him there. "The threat of 1896," as McKinley labeled it, was what the GOP really wanted as the centerpiece of the election. Bryanism, according to this interpretation, still loomed as irresponsible and dangerous. In Secretary of State John Hay's words, the Nebraskan stood for "the yelp and snarl of a cur from start to finish."[41]

Theodore Roosevelt, as usual, got directly to the point when he asked voters to "repudiate the populistic and communistic doctrines enunciated in the Kansas City platform exactly as they repudiated them in '96." Waving his arms and pounding his fists, he compared Bryan and his followers to "the leaders of the Terror of France in mental and moral attitude." The Nebraskan, he charged, "would mean terrible and widespread disaster" for agriculture, labor, and business. Other Republican speakers similarly denounced Bryan as representing disorder, "hooliganism," and a terrifying threat to Republican prosperity. Ohio senator Mark Hanna, directing McKinley's campaign with the same genius that he had four years earlier, summed up the GOP message with ringing clarity: "Let well enough alone."[42]

During the last two months or so of the campaign, Bryan for the most part gave up trying to juggle the issues of silver and anti-imperialism. He shifted his attention to the trusts, trying to show that McKinley-style prosperity did not necessarily bode well for common Americans. Arguing that corporate behemoths were "closing the door of opportunity against our young men and condemning the boys of this country to perpetual clerkship," he aligned his cause with the traditional American faith in hard work and upward mobility. His indictment of the trusts was relentless. As sprawling monopolies, they sought to eliminate competition and control the marketplace; they drove small industries into the domain of a wealthy few while condemning "the real producers of wealth" to "servitude"; and they replaced locally controlled businesses with absentee owners. Bryan pledged that, if elected president, he would exempt trusts altogether from tariff protection and would vigorously enforce federal laws prohibiting business practices in restraint of trade. But his assault on big business never sparked the interest that he intended. Within a few years, the trust issue would become a compelling political topic; in 1900, however, its time had not come. Instead, Bryan was left with the unenviable task of running against McKinley's "full dinner pail" prosperity.[43]

Mark Hanna's organizational talents and the massive GOP campaign fund did not make the task any easier. In a repeat of 1896, the Republicans (with perhaps ten times as much money as the Democrats) flooded the country with literature. The party's national committee estimated that on a single day its lecturers delivered seven thousand speeches, as compared to twenty-five hundred for the Democrats. At least two thousand small-town newspapers depended upon political news they received directly from GOP headquarters, courtesy of a special division within the campaign committee. There was even enough money to hire horses and men dressed up as Rough Riders in local parades that featured Roosevelt.

As before, Bryan depended upon his own stamina and voice to carry his campaign. He covered nineteen thousand miles and delivered 546 speeches. At age forty, carrying a solid two hundred pounds, he still looked impressive with his striking eyes, his lips pressed resolutely in a thin line, and his hair, thinning on top but flared slightly over his ears and along the back of his head. And, certainly, he was still robust, enthusiastic, and energetic. Journalist George Creel recalled how, in Missouri, "at the first note of his organ voice audiences reared back and bayed like coon dogs." His labors were sufficient to throw a scare into such key administration people as Secretary of State John Hay. On 31 October Hay nervously observed "that this last month of Bryan, roaring out his desperate appeals to hate and envy, is having its effect on the dangerous classes. Nothing so monstrous has as yet been seen in our history. . . . We have an awful handicap to overcome."[44]

Hay need not have worried. Bryan not only lost the election but was outdueled even on the political stump. Theodore Roosevelt, bothered by a sore throat but contending that he was "fit as a fighting cock," gave 673 speeches over a distance of twenty-one thousand miles. Often resembling a windmill in motion, and with a high, frantic voice, he lacked Bryan's majestic style; but his slashing, hard-hitting attacks were among the most effective weapons in the Republican arsenal. "Well, I drowned him out," Roosevelt later happily claimed. "I talked two words to his one. Maybe he was an oratorical cocktail, but I was his chaser."[45]

Roosevelt had reason to smile. The McKinley ticket captured six states that had belonged to Bryan in 1896—including Nebraska, where Bryan lost even his own city and precinct. Actually, the Democrat's defeat was less devastating than such results suggested. The president gained only 1 percent more of the popular vote than he had four years earlier. And, even though Bryan's electoral vote fell from 176 to 155, his showing in the East was surprisingly better, particularly in New York. McKinley had nevertheless strengthened the increasingly formidable Republican coalition, further identifying it with industry, prosperity, and national pride.

For the Democrats, badly bruised a second time, there would be less willingness to embrace anti-imperialism with any fervor again. Bryan's critics within the party also had additional ammunition to use in their fight to put aside the "Boy Orator of Platte" and everything for which he stood. Even fusion, Bryan's chief political tactic for a decade, had revealed serious limitations. Indeed, in 1900 the Populist ranks were in such disarray that some stalwarts (most notably, Mary Elizabeth Lease and Marion Butler, the party chair in 1896) bolted to the Republicans.

On election day the paramount issue was Republican prosperity, not the topics that Bryan had pushed. Following the turbulent depression years, the return of better times was welcome indeed. Some people, such as William Howard Taft's brother Charles, believed that Bryan would have brought about a revolution. Others simply saw little reason to vote for the Nebraskan. One of the most familiar and telling anecdotes about the 1900 campaign concerned a Missouri farmer who interrupted a Democratic attack on imperialism by saying, "Well, I guess we can stand it as long as hogs are twenty cents a hundred." A majority of voters simply agreed with Hanna to "let well enough alone."[46]

This hardly justified the lament of the reform-minded sociologist E. A. Ross that, with McKinley, "reaction was in the saddle and rode like a drunken bully."[47] Substantial signs of a reform mood were much in evidence, even in the McKinley foreign policy that so repelled Ross. Enthusiastic volunteers had signed up to fight Spain not simply because of nationalism, but also out of a sense of service and duty. Bryan himself had shared the desire to rescue Spanish colonists from their imperial oppressors. A spirit of reform had also marked the subsequent debates over annexation of the Philippines. Granted, the debates had contained conspicuous doses of talk about America's commercial advantages; and people such as Theodore Roosevelt and Albert J. Beveridge had emphasized great power rivalries, military strength, and heroic action. But McKinley himself had realized the popular limits of such appeals, and he—as well as the Republican platform—highlighted themes of humanitarianism. Many Americans who favored annexation of the Philippines did so out of a desire to uplift and civilize. American military officials who administered the city of Manila after the ouster of the Spanish excitedly hoped to alleviate social ills from that beleaguered city. They wanted to institute good government, to improve public health, sanitation, and education, and to teach "retarded" peoples the advantages of "civilization."

Reform perspectives were equally important to many within the anti-imperialist camp. Unanimity was, of course, no more a characteristic of the anti-imperialists than it was of the annexationists. The conservative, upper-class, eastern Anti-Imperialist League loathed Bryan's domestic proposals. But, especially in the Great Plains region, the driving force behind anti-imperialism came from Populists, silverites, and Bryanites, to whom annexation of the Philippines was a reprehensible boon to the hated corporate interests.

Although the Spanish-American War and its aftermath raised complicated issues with many sides, they drew upon the same optimism and idealism that also fueled social activism at home. Herbert Croly, one of the era's most astute observers, contended that the war had given "a tremendous impulse to the work of national reform."[48] Many imperialists and anti-imperialists shared that reform impulse, however much they disagreed over strategies. Not surprisingly, the same volatile mixture of emotions, ideals, motives, and values that led Bryan to join the crusade for Cuban liberation, and that convinced others to stay on in the Philippines in the name of justice and social uplift, produced domestic ferment as well. As American troops in the Pacific set out to alter the environment of the Filipino population, there was within the United States a flurry of reform activity—from campaigns to clean up government to battles against liquor, prostitution, and child labor.

Opponents of William Jennings Bryan thus prematurely assumed that his defeat in 1900 would relegate him to political obscurity. Barely forty and twice candidate for president, he still had a role to play. Clearly he did not see himself as ready for political retirement. And for Americans yet concerned about the shift toward large corporate influence and the power of big money, he remained appealing. Just before the 1900 election, a small group of former Populists, then socialists, including editor B. O. Flower and Frank Parsons, signed a statement that "a vote for Bryan is a vote for the first practicable step toward the cooperative commonwealth." This, they pointed out, was not because he himself advocated such a radical goal, but because his political instincts and sympathies were on the right side. Similarly, the old reform warhorse John Peter Altgeld, who had once again campaigned strenuously for the Nebraskan, argued that Bryan was "not necessarily radical to begin with," but his predilections were "with the great toiling masses" and he would "not be controlled by concentrated wealth." Insofar as a reform mood marked early twentieth-century American life, the era would still belong in large part to Bryan.[49]

William Jennings Bryan as a boy.

Bryan as a young congressman, 1892.

Mr. and Mrs. William Jennings Bryan, Ruth, and William. November, 1890.

A "stump" speech in a southern lumber camp, 1896.

A popular early campaign photograph.

Photograph of William Jennings
Bryan courtesy of the Library of
Congress.

Colonel Bryan and attaché shown during the Spanish-American War, 1898.

Bryan in front of the Commoner building, 1908.

Bryan sleeping on board a train on the Chautauqua circuit, 1919.

Campaign poster, 1908. Courtesy of the Chicago Historical Society.

Woodrow Wilson and Bryan, with the
son of Ruth Bryan Owen, 7 October 1912.

Bryan and niece Mary Louise Bryan in front of Fairview, 1910.

Secretary of State Bryan on his way to deliver Chautauqua address in Richmond, Virginia, 1913.

William Jennings Bryan viewing an eclipse of the sun, 24 January 1925.
Afterward he remarked that the Democratic party, like the sun, would "soon
shine again." Courtesy of the Library of Congress.

# 5

# PROGRESSIVE LEADER
## (1901–1908)

"At no time during a century have moral forces been more potent than they are in America today," a jubilant William Jennings Bryan wrote in 1906. "At no time has the conscience been more sensitive; at no time has a larger percentage of the people been engaged in altruistic work." True, he conceded, there were still many greedy and corrupt individuals who thought only of personal profits. And there were many desperate and exploited victims. "But between these classes there is a larger middle class—God fearing and God worshipping; a class composed of both men and women in whom the spiritual element predominates and who . . . yearn to be of real service to mankind."[1]

In a few words he captured vital aspects of a remarkable reform ethos, progressivism, that grew out of the crisis-ridden 1890s and dominated American politics for much of the first two decades of the twentieth century—optimistic, heavily religious, attentive to moral issues, committed to helping the disadvantaged, bent on elevating "service" over private gain, and mindful of the particular importance of the middle class as an agent for social change. Reformers of the era did not speak with one voice, but, in the continuing debate over the nature of the domestic reform agenda, no one was more active or vocal than the sturdily built, balding Nebraskan whom growing numbers of people knew affectionately as the Commoner.

Between 1900 and 1908, when he ran for President a third time, he more than anyone identified the Democratic party with the surging spirit of Progressive reform. And in doing so, he raised a powerful voice in behalf of the nation's democratic traditions, evoking the rights of "the people" against "the interests," among which he included the trusts, the arrogant rich, the panderers of vice, and the elite experts who seemed to place more faith in efficiency and organization than in the wisdom of the rank and file.

Progressivism meant many things to many people, yet one of its defining ingredients was a religious sensibility that Bryan reflected, as much as anyone. William Allen White, recalling the "profoundly spiritual" aspects of the era, described the commitment to reform as "an evangelical uprising." Lincoln Steffens, one of the leading journalists of the era, wore a gold cross on his watchchain and claimed that he wanted to be more dangerous than an anarchist; he wanted to be "a Christian." Frederic Howe, another Progressive reformer, also remembered the "evangelical-mindedness" of many of his contemporaries. "Early assumptions as to virtue and vice, goodness and evil remained in my mind long after I tried to discard them," wrote Howe. "This is, I think, the most characteristic influence of my generation." Bryan held firmly to such assumptions, never even questioning them, let alone trying to jettison them. He once warned a young attorney, for example, that taking unjust cases or trying to deceive a jury could place a "strain upon your morals."[2]

This religious outlook among Progressives was hardly surprising. Indeed, it had characterized American reform for generations. Whether the movement was that of American revolutionaries dedicated to republican virtue, abolitionists convinced that slavery violated God's laws, or union leaders such as Eugene Debs who saw the workers' movement as the means by which to establish God's Kingdom on earth, the goal had been to effect a moral transformation of individuals and institutions. Here, too, was "the new gospel" that sustained so much of the culture of Populism and that turned many Progressives into "Ministers of Reform." The social status of the various groups was often different. Populist-style evangelism, for example, typically came from rural outsiders angry at the new institutional insiders—the village churches and preachers who seemed cliquish, snobbish, and condescending toward those with manure on their boots. Progressive-style evangelism, in contrast, more often flowed from established and advantaged insiders who hoped to make their institutions more attractive and hospitable to outsiders. Hence, among the most conspicuous Progressives were those in the Social Gospel movement, who struggled to adapt their religion to the needs of workers and new immigrants. Although age and social class separated many reformers (and radicals as well), a common moral vision often inspired their critiques of American life. Many, perhaps most, would have agreed with socialist Upton Sinclair that "the world needs a Jesus more than it needs anything else."[3]

Bryan felt especially comfortable relating religion and reform. At age twenty, he had expressed a "great desire to honor God and please mankind." This included bringing "justice to every creature, whether he be rich or poor." Throughout his life, words such as *mission*, *righteousness*, and *moral duty* laced his rhetoric. In a series of public letters in 1906, he scorned any nation "crowded with missionless men and women, each one intent upon his own problems but unconcerned about the problems with which his fellows are struggling." It was not enough, he argued, simply to do no evil; instead, one should take "that active interest in others which our Gospels enjoin." Invoking Christ as a model of action, he asserted that "the man who does good is vastly superior to the merely harmless man." "Awake! Awake! Bestir yourself!" he entreated his audience; individuals were "under obligation to be helpful to the world." Certainly he had little regard for "the colorless, passionless, useless man who by a negative existence leaves the world no better than he found it." And he was confident that "whenever God is as faithfully served at the ballot box as He is in the church . . . the era of trusts, of imperialism, of spoliation and of corruption will be at an end."[4]

Themes of character ("habitual righteousness," as Bryan defined it), usefulness, and service were lodestones of the Progressive era. "Character," according to Bryan, shined "from every window of the soul, either as a beam of purity, or as a clouded ray that betrays the impurity within. The contest between light and darkness, right and wrong, goes on; day by day, hour by hour." Self-discipline and individual choice were thus the anvils upon which character took shape. On this topic the Nebraskan echoed wisdom that Americans were already hearing across the country, from pulpits and public platforms to the West Texas college catalog. The basic way to display one's character was by aiding society. "Service is the measure of greatness," as Bryan phrased it. In that spirit a host of youth organizations sallied forth in the early 1900s to perform good deeds: Boy Scouts, Girl Scouts, Campfire Girls, and Christian Endeavor groups. So too did their adult equivalents. Rotary emerged in 1905 with an emphasis on "Service, not Self"; the Lions organized in 1913, saying, "There is no progress without service"; the Kiwanis, founded in 1915, took as their motto, "We build"; and the Gideons, founded by traveling salesmen, began in 1908 to place Bibles in hotel rooms.[5]

"What an opportunity for service this age presents!" exulted Bryan in 1905. On the one hand, modern technology opened huge new possibilities for disseminating knowledge and resources. On the other hand, there was "vast work to be done." Poverty, corruption, class divisions, faltering consciences and flawed morals offered a veritable mission field for those who would become great by doing good. "The opportunity is here and the field inviting." He and Mary were both pleased when their daughter Ruth spent time at Jane Addams's Hull House, the famed social settlement in Chicago's slums.[6]

Insofar as progressivism constituted efforts to salvage traditional values in a rapidly changing industrial and urban world, Bryan thus held center stage. Insofar as it represented a summons to duty in the struggle against perceived injustices and inequities, he was undeniably one of its most effective advocates. And insofar as monopolies and trusts ("legalized grand larceny" was the definition that the Nebraskan preferred) emerged as a major issue, Bryan was primed for that battle.[7]

But while progressivism included all these elements, it was also much more. It was full of competing and contradictory impulses— some democratic, others exclusive and elitist; some aimed at solving problems through political processes, others by removing issues from politics. Bryan sometimes mirrored the contradictions; on other occasions, he more clearly represented one side of the reform dialogue.

On the issue of grass-roots, participatory democracy, he definitely was in the camp of Progressives who worked to open up the political process. He favored such reforms as the popular election of senators, direct primary laws, the initiative, referendum, recall, and woman suffrage. "Shall the people rule?" That, he believed, was the central question of the age, and his own answer was sharply affirmative.

A problem, however, as William Allen White later observed, was that the reform movement "passed from shirt sleeves and galluses into the high-hat stage."[8] There were substantial numbers of Progressives who felt genuinely uneasy about the masses. The Reverend Charles Sheldon's best-selling (and in many respects, quintessentially Progressive) novel, *In His Steps* (1897), illustrated such concerns. The story was about several quite different individuals who changed their lives by trying to respond to modern problems as Christ presumably would have done. On one level, certainly, the incredibly popular book dramatized the kind of practical Christianity for which Bryan and so many of his colleagues pleaded. Bryan no doubt also appreciated the author's criticism of the idle rich and corrupt corporations. But the Commoner could hardly have felt comfortable with the novel's portrait of working-class people as wild, brutal, ignorant animals.

Because many Progressives shared Sheldon's unflattering interpretation of the poor and lower classes, it was hardly surprising that they hoped to control such groups and diminish their political power, or at least guide them down appropriate paths. A highly significant aspect of progressivism thus emphasized the authority of trained experts. This was due in part to the emergence of a new middle class of college graduates, salaried professionals, and white-collar workers (a group that was eight times larger by 1910 than it had been in 1870). It was also due to a growing confidence in the natural sciences, engineering, and the new social sciences such as sociology. There was much excitement about scientific management, efficiency, and social engineering. "In the past," wrote the leading advocate of scientific management in 1911, "the man has been first; in the future the system must be first." In this context, an influential group of reformers favored "management" over "politics," and took steps to remove volatile issues from the streets to the conference rooms of educated professionals. "The golden rule will be put in practice through the slide rule," one enthusiast predicted in 1912.[9]

Bryan placed far more faith in the voting booth than in any slide rule, and he steadfastly resisted movements that would put "the system" ahead of people. Quoting from the Scriptures that "the common people heard Him gladly," he extolled the virtues of rank-and-file individuals. "The common people," he wrote, "form the industrious, intelligent and patriotic element of our population; they produce the nation's wealth in time of peace and fight the nation's battles in time of war." Self-reliance and independence characterized their behavior. And one other thing was certain: "the common people do not constitute an exclusive society—they are not of the four hundred" most socially prestigious and wealthy American families. One never heard the masses arguing that they lacked the capacity for self-government; that claim came from "upper-crust" people who considered themselves "the cultured"—people, in Bryan's opinion, "not nearly so important as they think they are." Bryan contended "that the farmer is entitled to as much respect as the factory owner," and that it was "arrogant and impudent" for any particular class to presume to speak for the masses. If the voice of the people was not the voice of God, it was nevertheless "the best expression of divine will to be found upon the earth." Bryan respected education but was cautious about the wisdom of so-called experts. Thomas Jefferson, he believed, had correctly observed that "the principles of right and wrong are so easily understood as to require not the aid of many counsellors."[10]

The condescension and fear with which many Progressives viewed the working class was remarkably absent in Bryan. His respect for "the dignity of labor," especially of struggling farmers, had suffused his political campaigns during the 1890s. But he always lauded other workers as well, and was a persistent champion of their right to organize, to bargain collectively, to strike, and to receive "an equitable distribution of the proceeds of toil" through a guaranteed minimum wage. In a Labor Day speech, he distinguished corporate trusts, in which "a few men attempt to control the product of others," from unions, where workers "unite for the protection of that which is their own, namely their own labor." In his opinion, labor organizations were part of a "great movement of the masses toward closer fellowship." Later, in 1919, he would attribute the growth of labor radicalism to business's "unpatriotic plundering" and pursuit of "conscienceless profits."[11]

It was little wonder, then, that Bryan stirred the sympathies of laborers, even though he often had difficulty getting their votes. Memories of the "Democratic" depression of the 1890s and the GOP's "full dinner pail" invariably proved insurmountable for him on election

day. Still, few politicians enjoyed the respect that he did among workers. On one summer day at the turn of the century, a throng of Utah
silver miners listened intently to him, as he told them from the balcony of a dingy wooden hotel that he would always fight for the little
folk. When he finished, there was a long moment during which the
workers stood silently, almost reverently, their caps off and their heads
bowed. Then the valley echoed with cheers as they pressed forward to
shake his hand and touch him. Few of his contemporaries received
such awe and admiration. Moreover, when Bryan looked down from
that hotel balcony, he saw workers who were endangering their lives
in unsafe mines in order to make a living. They were dignified members of the producer class—not the besotted, violent, ugly types that
inhabited the novel *In His Steps*.[12]

There was, nevertheless, a glaring exception to Bryan's democratic
sentiments. It was on the issue of race, especially regarding blacks.
The Jeffersonian phrase that he so fondly quoted—"Equal rights to all
and special privileges to none"—was in fact something that he applied
primarily to Caucasians. He did so with little intellectual discomfort.
Beliefs in white supremacy suffused his culture. As a child in Salem,
Illinois, he had encountered a world in which 25 percent of the white
adults were from slave states; and his own father had objected to Lincoln's turning the Civil War into "a free negro crusade." Between 1889
and 1903, years when Bryan was forging a national reputation as a
crusader for justice, he virtually ignored a grim statistic: on the average, every week white mobs lynched two blacks. The word *lynch* was
often a euphemism for burning at the stake and torturing to death.
Even when he condemned lynching in 1903, he helped to justify it
by speaking of "the hideous offenses which have led the white people"
to such misdeeds. When states such as Mississippi adopted various
legal devices to keep blacks from voting, Bryan hardly winced. In his
opinion, "when races of different degrees of civilization are thrown
together . . . then the more advanced race has always exercised the
right to impose conditions upon the less advanced." He was willing to
support Booker T. Washington's Tuskegee Institute with donations,
but he protested in 1901 when President Theodore Roosevelt invited
the black educator to the White House. "When Mr. Roosevelt sits
down with a negro," Bryan asserted, "he declares that the negro is a
social equal of the white man."[13]

Bryan's thoughts on majority rule and reform strategy partially accounted for the contradictions between his opposition to privilege and his defense of white supremacy. Convinced that the will of the people must always prevail, he advised reformers to go only "as fast and as far as public sentiment will permit." On the matter of racial tolerance at the turn of the century, that was not very far. Racial stereotypes, words such as *dago* and *pickaninny*, and romantic versions of the civilizing role of Anglo-Saxons were common coin. In some respects, Bryan was more open to diversity than were many of his contemporaries. He shunned anti-Semitism and anti-Catholicism. His tactfulness and congenial nature invariably made a good impression on foreigners wherever he traveled. And despite supporting the exclusion of Chinese and Japanese from the United States, in 1898 he accepted into his home for five years a Japanese youth whose family he had met when traveling, and who, through a misunderstanding, simply showed up to attend school in Nebraska. For the most part, however, Bryan, like the vast majority of his white contemporaries, was virtually blind when he confronted racial injustice. On the race issue he stayed well within the bounds of public sentiment—choosing, as he described the reformer's role, "to fight with the army . . . instead of being a scout."[14]

On other issues, he was more willing to take a position in advance of that "army" of public opinion. Again and again, he stressed that it was not popularity but principle that counted. Independence, moral courage, fighting the good fight, and arousing the conscience of the people—these were critical virtues that he consistently applauded. It was he, after all, who had told the Chicago convention in 1896 that "all the hosts of error" were nothing compared to the individual "clad in the armor of a righteous cause." Placing himself at the forefront of what he called "the radical element" at the turn of the century, he was determined to make sure that the Democrats stood for "habitual righteousness." Thus, a little over a year after his 1900 defeat, he issued a public pledge: "The party will never go back to the odious and odorous days of 1892–1896."[15]

At first glance, however, it seemed that his second loss to McKinley might push him to the political sidelines. In March 1902, he and his family moved to a thirty-five-acre farm some three miles southeast of Lincoln. The Bryans had purchased the first five acres almost ten years earlier, had gradually added additional land, and had planted orchard and shade trees. The spacious, four-story brick house, completed by the end of 1902, featured cornices, gables, stained-glass windows, electricity and running water (conveniences that many farms still did not have), and was very nicely furnished. Perched on a knoll, it provided a pleasant view of the area. Critics were quick to note that such luxury attested more to Republican prosperity than to Bryan's status as a "commoner." Bryan countered that proceeds from his publications, especially *The First Battle*, had supplied the necessary funds. By 1908 the farm had grown to 160 acres. It was repose, not agriculture, that made the place so attractive to Bryan. Hired hands, whom he paid well, did most of the work, while he spent time writing and relaxing on horseback. "Fairview," as the Bryans called it, initially seemed primarily to offer a place of retreat from the hurly-burly of public life. Additional evidence that he intended to be less politically active appeared in his announcement, immediately after losing in 1900, that he had no interest in his party's nomination in the next election. Indeed, from the spring of 1902 into 1904, he seemed particularly drawn to international travel, making extensive trips to Latin America and Europe.

But the pronouncement after the 1900 election that Bryan was "dead and buried beyond hopes of resurrection" was far from true. At the least, he quickly proved to be the world's most active political corpse. With a newly founded newspaper in 1901 and a staggering number of speaking engagements, he continued to take his reform message to the public. By the time the Democratic national convention adjourned in 1904, it was emphatically clear that he was far from ready for any political funeral.

He launched his weekly newspaper, the *Commoner*, in January 1901 as a mouthpiece for "Jeffersonian democracy." This was, of course, not his first experiment in journalism. He had been political editor of the Omaha *World-Herald* for two years, until just before the 1896 election. But he had actually spent little time on that job. The *Commoner*, in contrast, would be a serious and long-lasting venture; until 1923, it provided the most consistent forum for his political views. Although he was out of the office much of the time, the editorials and selection of news very much reflected his thinking. His younger brother Charles was business manager and sometimes did some of the writing—along with Mary Bryan. The little publication, selling for five cents a copy or one dollar per year, started off with seventeen thousand subscriptions and a printing of seventy-five thousand. Within a year, subscriptions were up to one hundred forty thousand. Included in each issue were brief summaries of national and international news, editorials from other newspapers, a section on home living, and a few advertisements (typically for patent medicines, but none for any large corporation, liquor, or tobacco).

The newspaper's chief objective was "to aid the common people in the protection of their rights, the advancement of their interests and the realizations of their aspirations." If this seemed vague, the tone and contents of the first issue left few doubts about the *Commoner's* political orientation. Big business, bankers, and Wall Street speculators had most assuredly not found a new voice. One story indicated how difficult it would be "to fix the amount which a man must steal before becoming a Napoleon of finance instead of a common embezzler." There were also clear signals that Bryan had no plans to stand by quietly while the antireform wing of his party tried to reorganize it. His advice to the opposition was to "spend more time opposing Republican policies and less time denouncing the populists."[16]

However much Bryan hoped to use the *Commoner* as a forum, he still relied primarily on his effectiveness as a speaker. No lecturer was in greater demand as the twentieth century opened; and none would be so for more than two decades. Even on the Chautauqua circuit, where he usually avoided specific mention of politics, his very presence made him a political force. The name Bryan could summon audiences from hundreds of miles away, allowing him to tap grass-roots emotions as no one else could do.

By the early 1900s, the Chautauqua was one of the most familiar forms of popular culture in small towns throughout the nation. Its intellectual ancestry went back to the organized public lectures and debates during the several decades before the Civil War. Its institutionalization had occurred in the 1870s when summer religious gatherings on Chautauqua Lake in western New York had been transformed into permanent educational meetings. Across the nation, small towns came up with their own versions of "Chautauqua week," usually trying to bring in famous people to give a series of lectures or performances. Chautauqua became a large business; agencies organized tours by which orators, musicians, singers, and other entertainers took "culture" to the provinces. The main purpose was ostensibly to educate and uplift. For local people, Chautauqua could be an unforgettable experience, offering the opportunity to see and hear nationally known people, including former presidents, popular writers, and other celebrities. It also helped to call attention to host towns and to give local businesses a boost. In some cases, community bands waited at railroad depots to welcome the Big Chautauqua Special, packed with crowds arriving for the momentous event.

For many Chautauqua performers, life on the circuit was not very pleasant, because of the tedium and discomfort of constant travel to remote communities in what some described as "the Bed Bug Belt, the Cyclone Belt, the Broiling Belt, and the Hellish Hotel Belt." Sometimes, as one lecturer recalled, the day would be so hot that "paint peeled off the tent poles"; at night, swarms of mosquitoes attacked audiences and speakers alike. In the Great Plains and Midwest especially, severe electrical storms and tornadoes could make untimely appearances. Once when the reform journalist Charles Edward Russell was speaking in Ohio, a furious storm collapsed the tent, temporarily imprisoning six hundred people and killing one. To Russell, Chautauqua represented a "painful story"; glory be to the radio, he wrote in 1933, "for it killed Chautauqua."[17]

Bryan, in contrast, loved the Chautauqua; to him, it was anything but a painful story, partly because he enjoyed some advantages that other performers did not. For example, he had the luxury of selecting towns and dates, and he did not have to arrange his schedule far in advance. If Bryan's desired schedule conflicted with another's, he prevailed. According to Charles Edward Russell, less well known speakers regarded the Commoner "with loathing." After such a person "had been ditched" several times in one season, left sitting "in a horrible hotel room while he heard of Mr. Bryan's wondrous success," it was easy enough to resent the Nebraskan. Still, even the unhappy Russell could never forget watching a massive crowd in Ashland, Oregon, "waiting to hear Mr. Bryan for the nineteenth time." Some told Russell that they had traveled a hundred miles to be there to hear the great man. It was a sight, Russell recalled in the 1930s, that "has not been equalled in our day." The Nebraskan had sufficient reason to bask in such moments. He was, according to Russell, "the incomparable Chautauqua pet and favorite."[18]

There was still the question why, in the words of another Chautauqua performer, "summer after summer, in heat, rain, wind or dust, immense crowds clogged the roads and nearly tore down the tents to listen to Bryan." Apparently "this simple, kindly man spoke to their hearts." Like them, he knew disappointment. And even "if he had never shared their muddy struggles, he could imagine them." Certainly he felt close to his audience. He claimed that he could make a million dollars annually as a New York attorney or championing the special interests, but preferred to pick up his "two grips and go out to the chautauquas." Not only was "every penny . . . clean," he said, but "these are the people who believe in me and stick by me."[19]

In many respects, the Chautauqua brought out the best in Bryan. Even though he enjoyed more advantages than did a Russell or other lesser-known lecturers, his routine could still be strenuous and demanding. He bore up under the strain with remarkable equanimity. The "crew boys," who set up tents, chairs, and platforms, reportedly liked him. Unlike many performers, he was not snobbish or demanding. During his free time he would often chat with them, collecting little details about their lives that he never seemed to forget. When he needed some rest, he did the same as the crew—he stretched out on a roll of extra canvas, even though he could have gone to more comfortable surroundings. Once he had to borrow a quarter to pay a carriage driver; a year later, when he next encountered the individual who had lent him the money, he quickly approached the person: "Here's the quarter. Many thanks." No matter what unexpected delays or difficulties arose, he refused to complain or lose his temper. Invariably, he cared about his audience and spent hours after lectures talking with people, never seeming to notice shabby clothing and grizzled appearances. He insisted that children pay no admission and that adult tickets be cheap. Although he was important enough to have received a guaranteed minimum payment for each performance, he relied upon a percentage of the gate. He preferred constantly to test his power to draw an audience, rather than take for granted any stipulated sum.[20]

No matter how many thousands of times he had given a particular lecture, he was always enthusiastic. Audiences never encountered a jaded Bryan, simply going through the motions. Standing before them in his oversized coat and baggy, wrinkled trousers, flicking his famous palm-leaf fan to keep cool, and consuming huge quantities of ice water, he spoke with a simple eloquence. One individual remembered "the slow way he smiled, with crinkles in the corners of his kindly eyes, or if he mentioned injustice the way he angrily snapped shut his thin lips." The images he drew upon were familiar, often homely. According to an Iowa editor, "Words flow from Bryan's lips like water over Niagara." When he finished his talks, he stood with endless patience, shaking hands as people lined up to meet him. For the Nebraskan, the Chautauqua was thus always more than a source of considerable income. The Chautauqua sites—towns whose average population was less than five thousand—helped to keep him in touch with what his wife described as "the mind of America." This was his turf, far more than a Madison Square Garden. The people who showed up to hear him—as did some thirty thousand in Shelbyville, Illinois—were those with whom he felt a particular kinship. They were, as one person recalled, "plain people of the broad, flat midlands, the far-west cattle ranges, the poor southern cotton fields"—people who, like him, "had been scorned by the sophisticated east." He spoke to them and for them; he articulated their thoughts. "He belonged to them; he knew it and they knew it."[21]

On one level, Bryan's Chautauqua addresses were indeed intellectually thin, so full of cultural bromides that some critics called him "the boy orator of the platitude." His messages were typically inspirational, aimed at soothing and uplifting rather than probing or questioning. They included the kinds of packaged clichés that increasingly marked twentieth-century American greeting cards. The Commoner of lecturing fame could be painfully shallow, using oratorical flights to obscure what William Allen White thought was "a stunted mind." "He appeared," White wrote, "with snake-charmers, tumblers, bell ringers, elocutionists, singers, freaks, magicians, and notoriety seekers." To White, he sometimes resembled "a squatting Buddha," with a "smile rather fatuously spread upon the moon-face" of his amply jowled countenance.[22]

On another level, however, Bryan's lectures evoked much of the tone of progressivism. His message resembled that of the muckraking *American Magazine*, which in 1910 printed a prayer of Social Gospel minister Walter Rauschenbusch, asking God to purge corruption from the nation and fill it with "a new spirit." The journal was the creation of leading reform journalists such as Ida Tarbell and Lincoln Steffens, who hoped to portray "a happy, struggling, fighting world, in which, as we believe, good people are coming out on top." In the same spirit, a professor of social economics at Columbia University compared misery to tuberculosis; both were "communicable, curable, and preventable." Similarly, editor George Creel proclaimed that the fight for equal justice was "the Great Adventure which has ever enlisted all that was best and truest in the American heart. For the People! Say that word over. People! *People!* Why, it grows electric! It thrills!" A prevalent assumption of the era, as Frederic Howe recalled, was that "through the truth we would redeem the world." Sermons and politics blended imperceptibly in the Progressive mind. Thus muckraking journalists tried to evoke from readers a sense of shame at urban corruption and squalor, and wrote essays about such topics as the "Fall and Redemption of Minneapolis."[23]

In this context, Bryan's Chautauqua lectures were charged with political content. He asked his listeners to "purify politics" and "to scrutinize the methods of money-making." He urged placing America's "awakened conscience against the overflowing tide of corruption." Heralding the virtues of service, he called attention specifically to Jane Addams and others who volunteered for benevolent work. "We must go about doing good," he said. To Bryan's critics, such idealistic sentimentality and optimism may have seemed mere fluff. But, in fact, there were few better examples of the moral and religious sensibilities of progressivism. Once those sensibilities began to flag, the news would be bad not just for Bryan, but for the Progressive reform crusades in general.[24]

In the early twentieth century, however, enthusiasm for reform was rising, not ebbing—buoying up Bryan's career at the very time that he might have become a beached political whale. His opponents were certainly anxious to consign him to political oblivion. Convinced that "Populism and Bryanism" had led the Democratic party to another defeat in 1900, a group of "reorganizers" set out to find a "sensible candidate," draft "a good old-fashioned platform," and "repress the Wild People."[25] The reorganizers drew most of their support from the Grover Cleveland, "goldbug" wing of the party; socially conservative and business-oriented, their loathing of the Commoner was almost instinctive.

At the state and local level in 1901 and 1902, heated confrontations occurred as the reorganizers tried to regain control of the party and restore its pre-1896 identity. When Bryan's followers in St. Louis lost control of the local party to the gold Democrats, they bolted, running their own candidate on a "public ownership platform." In Illinois, Michigan, Pennsylvania, Ohio, and elsewhere, the battle was on; at some state conventions Bryan's name elicited catcalls, and even displaying his picture was an issue. Midway through the 1902 elections, as the Republican juggernaut continued to dominate American politics, an Ohio Democratic congressman agonized that his party was doomed unless "it gets rid of Bryan. He is a millstone around its neck."[26]

The Commoner fought back. From 1901 to 1904, in his newspaper and in numerous speeches, he hammered out his opinions. Standing on a twelve-foot-high, wooden platform in Telluride, Colorado, in October 1902, he lambasted the trusts. Leaning slightly forward, his black hat shading his eyes, his fingers outspread and pressing the railing, he struck one reporter as being "in good voice" and still possessing "his old power." Elsewhere, he contended that Grover Cleveland had wreaked more havoc upon the Democratic party than had any Republican president. Indeed, Cleveland had "stabbed his party to prevent its return to virtue" and had led it into "the mire." The former executive represented "the plutocratic element of the party," spoke for "the waterlogged enterprisers of the trust promoters," and had saddled Bryan with "his sins in two national campaigns." Enough was enough. If these were harsh words for the former leader of his own party, Bryan showed that he was willing to take aim as well at the likes of the multimillionaire oil baron John D. Rockefeller. "No criminal now incarcerated . . . for larceny," he angrily asserted, "has shown more indifference to human rights and property rights." According to the Nebraskan, the primary objective of government was to protect human rights from such people. In communities across the country, Bryan unleashed steady volleys at his opposition. As the 1904 election year opened, he outlined a kind of Democratic litmus test to a banquet gathering in Lincoln: "We want the trust magnates against us, not for us." This reportedly pleased the GOP more than it did "crestfallen" Democrats, according to Republican John H. Flagg. The Wall Street investor observed happily that it would be impossible to effect a truce within the Democratic party unless Bryan "should turn tail, and he does not appear to know enough to do that."[27]

At the 1904 Democratic national convention, in the steaming July heat of St. Louis, the Bryanites and reorganizers slugged it out. Surprisingly, considering that Bryan was a two-time loser in presidential races and faced stalwart opposition, he exerted considerable influence. Reorganizers arrived in St. Louis intending to "Bury Bryan."

One, in fact, predicted "a slaughterhouse job. The first duty of this convention is to kill Bryanism, root and branch." To journalist George Creel, who felt pity for the Nebraskan as he watched Democrats ganging up on him, the gathering resembled "an undertaking parlor."[28]

Bryan refused to play dead. He led what was in effect a guerrilla movement, continually harassing the reorganizers and letting them claim no ground without a fight. At the outset, he challenged the seating of the Illinois delegation, under the command of the fiercely anti-Bryan John P. Hopkins. Although he lost this early contest, he emphatically registered his presence at the convention.

Subsequently, a sixteen-hour meeting of the platform committee was, according to one reorganizer, "taken up in contests with Mr. Bryan." Suffering from a severe cold, he at one point wore a mustard plaster over his chest. When the resolutions committee by a seven-to-three vote endorsed a gold plank, he strenuously demanded a reaffirmation of the platforms of 1896 and 1900. Shouting and waving his fingers in the face of one of his strongest foes, he forced a compromise: the 1904 document would mention neither silver nor gold. By keeping the platform completely silent on the money issue, Bryan made sure that the reorganizers could claim no more of a victory than he could. He also pressed for an income tax plank, "bellowing like a mad bull," in the words of one witness, and relenting only when the reorganizers agreed to accept the antitrust plank of 1900. Looking back some twenty years later, Bryan described the platform struggle as "the most memorable contest through which I have ever passed." He conceded that he had not gotten all that he wanted, but he had kept out "everything" that he opposed. Indeed, he believed in retrospect that he had never rendered his "party more service than . . . during this fight over the platform." One reorganizer, Charles S. Hamlin of Massachusetts, reported that he and others had "begged Bryan almost with tears" to keep quiet in order to unify the party. But the Nebraskan refused. "He insulted almost everyone and seemed more like an insane man."[29]

Although the 1904 Democratic platform very much bore the imprint of Bryan, the party's presidential nominee did not. The nomination went to Alton B. Parker, chief judge of the New York State Court of Appeals and a gold Democrat who had avoided lining up too openly with any faction. He was so bland that, according to one newspaper, he had all "the salient qualities of a sphere." Bryan was less kind. He had already dismissed Parker as "the muzzled candidate of Wall Street." Now, at 4:30 in the morning of 9 July, he pleaded with the exhausted delegates not to choose the judge. Worn down himself because of lack of sleep, and with his cold verging on pneumonia, he spoke for twenty minutes. "You cannot deny," he told the twenty thousand present, "that I have kept the faith." Taking a jab at the reorganizers, he reminded the convention that he had lost in previous presidential elections—despite receiving a million votes more than any other Democrat—because of those who had abandoned their party. Now, he said, the greatest issue facing the nation was whether the people or "the moneyed element of the country" would control the government. Even though he did not mention Parker by name, the audience had no difficulty understanding in what camp Bryan placed him. Gasping for breath, he urged the delegates to find a candidate who would provide "positive, aggressive, democratic reform, something to hope for, something to fight for." The speech was so moving that, incredibly, given the reorganizers' strength, he was interrupted forty-seven times by applause and received a huge ovation. Near collapse, only with help could he stagger from the auditorium.[30]

Around midnight the next day, he was back unexpectedly. Despite Bryan's speech, Parker had received the nomination, but then he shocked the convention by sending a telegram that he would not accept unless the platform specifically endorsed gold. A joyful Grover Cleveland lauded Parker for "beating back the wild hordes of Bryanism." Bryan, with pneumonia settling in one lung and with a high fever, forced himself out of bed while his doctor was absent, and returned to the auditorium. He walked into the hall with the support of his brother as cries of "Bryan, Bryan" poured forth. His voice, raspy and weak, was at first inaudible to some of the audience. In retrospect, he described his speech as his "last stand against the Parker element."[31]

Eventually, the delegates answered Parker simply by declaring that there was no need to discuss money in the platform. The judge did not press the matter. In his *Memoirs*, Bryan offered a significant admission. The reply to Parker was unimportant, he said, because it stated a recognized fact: "the money question was not an issue any longer." Not long after the election, he would state this publicly.

For Bryan, who had suffered physically and emotionally through several harsh days, the convention had produced better results than he had expected. "I went to the convention expecting to be disregarded by a hostile majority," he later wrote. But instead of enduring humiliation, he had "found victory. . . . I think the victory at St. Louis was really a greater personal triumph than the victory at Chicago, and did more to strengthen me in the party." Events subsequently helped to confirm such an interpretation. At the end of the convention, it was nevertheless still possible to reach a different verdict. Newspapers speculated upon Bryan's "downfall" and "political suicide"; and William Allen White, covering the convention for *Collier's*, believed the Commoner at the end was "surrendering his power. . . . He seemed bidding farewell—a long farewell." The Kansas journalist, who had been so critical of Bryan in 1896, even felt some admiration for "the pluck which he showed at the last."[32]

Reorganizers who believed they had won the battle at St. Louis realized subsequently that Bryan had won the war. Parker not only lost badly in November to Theodore Roosevelt; he received a million fewer votes than Bryan had in the previous elections and failed to carry even one state outside the South. Although Bryan finally gave Parker lukewarm support, it was not until after the Commoner had lamented that the Democrats were "under the control of the Wall Street element." During the last weeks of the campaign, in fact, his speeches in effect kicked off his own candidacy for 1908. Calling for "radical" reforms, he advocated such things as abolition of monopolies, government ownership of the railroads, and a federal income tax. And he candidly declared his intentions to rebuild the Democratic party along Progressive lines, aligning it with "the plain, common people," not the "plutocracy." After the election, one pro-Parker newspaper admitted that Bryan had "the reorganizers on the hip."[33]

Convinced that the Democrats had "passed through the Valley of the Shadow of Death," Bryan now hoped to make them into "a real reform party." This time "the logic of events," which had been so important to his career in 1896, seemed even more promising. Across the entire country there were unmistakable signs of the growing popularity of reform ideas and causes. Indeed, in five northern states, reform-minded Democrats won gubernatorial races by impressive margins. Voting aside, in little Emporia, Kansas, William Allen White noted "the towering piles" of reform literature that accumulated monthly at the local bookstore. "Reform was in the air," wrote White. "Universally the people began to understand what slums were, what sweatshops were, what exploited labor was." Books carried such titles as *Shame of the Cities*, *Poverty*, and *The Bitter Cry of the Children*. "The strongest impression" that a visiting German journalist had of America at the time was that there was great interest in social reform, especially among middle-class people. "I have gone to many meetings and clubs," he wrote, "and always somebody says something serious and earnest about social matters—about child labor, about strikes, about insurgency—something." The German firmly believed that every magazine had "at least one muckraking article in it."[34]

The expanding reform mood attracted many individuals in both major parties who, less than a decade earlier, had panicked at the specter of populism and Bryanism. Among them were Wisconsin's "Fighting Bob" La Follette, Albert J. Beveridge of Indiana, Nebraska's George Norris, noted attorney Louis Brandeis, Woodrow Wilson, the president of Princeton University, and William Allen White. In 1896, White had feared Bryan as "the apotheosis of riot," and had dismissed the Populists as "gibbering idiots" who gave "the prosperous man the dickens" while whooping "it up for the ragged trousers." By 1906, however, he was apologizing for his earlier judgment and aligning himself on the side of "the poor and the under dog." Indeed, within a few more years he would develop a "great respect for Bryan" and feel ashamed for having excoriated him in the nineties.[35]

Bryan's nemesis of 1900, Theodore Roosevelt, especially symbolized the shifting reform climate. In the 1890s, he had favored lining Populists up against a wall and shooting them, and had viewed the Nebraskan as a demagogue. But after he succeeded the assassinated McKinley as president in 1901, he embraced reform as a means of undercutting more radical, even revolutionary, responses to the nation's economic and social problems. Encountering opposition from the large business elements within his own party, he concluded that "the criminal rich and the fool rich will do all they can to beat me." In 1904, he campaigned as a Progressive reformer against Judge Parker, arguing that the nation could not "afford to sit supine on the plea . . . that we are helpless in the presence of new conditions." And by 1907 he was even willing to concede that "about half of Bryan's views are right."[36]

115

After the 1904 election, the Commoner could reasonably speculate that maybe—just maybe—the political pendulum and his career were finally synchronized. According to a Portland, Oregon, newspaper on 9 November, he more than anyone spoke for the "hopes and aspirations of the common people . . . in the ceaseless, never ending, fundamental struggle between the House of Have and the House of Want." Wasting no time, Bryan in December urged Democrats to "appeal to the moral sense of the Nation," and to bring "the plutocratic tendencies of the Republican party before the bar of public conscience." In March 1905 he looked ahead to the next presidential election with special interest. "It must be plain to everyone," he wrote in the *Commoner*, "that the greatest political contest in history will be waged in 1908." More immediately, just before leaving on a world tour in September 1905, he felt good enough to tweak Roosevelt, asking whether the president had "the courage to be a reformer."[37]

When Bryan returned in August 1906, after traveling around the world for almost a year, he received a hero's welcome in New York City. Influential Democrats hosted a huge reception that included sending some two hundred tugs, whistles blowing, to greet his ship. Reformers such as Missouri's governor Joseph W. Folk and Cleveland's mayor Tom Johnson were on hand. The next evening, Bryan, fighting back tears, walked into Madison Square Garden, packed with twelve thousand cheering people. When the audience finally quieted, he delivered a major political address.

Speaking for sixty minutes, he pulled the curtain down on the silver issue. He did so, not because the cause had been wrong, but because it was no longer necessary. The unexpected increase in gold production had achieved, however belatedly, what Bryan had sought a decade earlier: an expanded currency supply. This meant that the Democrats could now put the divisive money debates aside and "present a united front" on other goals. According to Bryan, these included a graduated income tax that would apportion the costs of government in an equitable way; the direct election of senators, thereby making Congress less a "bulwark of predatory wealth"; and—a shocker—federal control of the railroads, except for local lines, which would be the jurisdiction of state governments. "The overshadowing evil of the day," he insisted, was that of the corporate trusts and their "plutocratic tendencies." He concluded with hard-hitting accusations that the nation was drifting into the hands of the rich, a trend that was "vulgarizing social life and making a mockery of morals." Now was the time "for the overthrow of this giant wrong."[38]

There was no doubt about it. The Commoner was back, only this time when he addressed the issue of the trusts, he found a greater public interest in the topic than ever before. Fears of concentrated wealth and its corrupting influence on politics had, of course, marked the American imagination for years. The muckraking Progressive journalist Charles Russell was convinced that no "hideous demon of destruction" had "so great a power to shake us with alarm as . . . Monopoly."[39] For much of the nineteenth century, however, the extraordinary size of the huge national pie had helped to focus attention on the process of distribution rather than on its fairness. Many communities had been willing to temper their uneasiness as long as big business seemed to aid local prosperity or to supply services that would otherwise depend upon taxes. Apprehension over corporate combinations had nevertheless been strong enough to effect the Sherman Antitrust Act of 1890, a vague law that made illegal any business in restraint of trade. Such fears had also given rise to various movements, especially among farmers, whose experiences with banks and railroads provided direct evidence of the dangers of a distant money power. For the Populists, certainly, the evils of corporate monopoly had been readily apparent. And during the depression of the 1890s, many towns had learned firsthand how risky it could be to rely on corporations to provide such things as electricity, water, and transportation. But it was around 1904 that a shocking series of journalistic and investigatory disclosures jolted the public. Detailed, systematic descriptions of politico-business corruption poured forth as never before. Through muckraking news stories and a wave of legislative investigations, shocked citizens confronted mounting evidence of business domination of American politics.

"We have got our eyes open now," wrote one Kansas resident about these revelations. Many citizens agreed with him that it was time for a "new politics" dedicated to "the general welfare." Suddenly, the state platforms of both major parties and political debates jumped with references to the "pernicious ends" and "undue influence" of large corporations. As anxious citizens sought ways to protect "the public interest" from corrupt "private interests," support grew dramatically for government supervision and regulation—or in some cases, municipal ownership. Even Theodore Roosevelt, privately attributing some of his ideas to Bryan, had started hammering on the trust issue during his first administration.[40]

No better political script could have existed for Bryan. The Nebraskan's animosity toward the trusts had been clear at least since his first presidential campaign. In 1899, he had plunged into Arkansas during angry debates over the state's new antitrust act. When several large insurance companies had threatened to leave the state unless the legislature repealed the law, Bryan had given a fiery, hour-long pep talk to a massive crowd in a Little Rock park, urging Arkansas residents not to give in to the trusts. Before the Arkansas Supreme Court finally overturned the law, the state's attorney general Jeff Davis, one of Bryan's most ardent disciples, had slapped antitrust suits against sixty-three out-of-state fire insurance companies, as well as other businesses. Davis, claiming to speak for the people "in the fields and hollows" against "this mighty combine of wealth," drew his inspiration directly from Bryan—"the grandest and truest man the world ever knew." A year later, Bryan had concentrated the last part of his presidential campaign on the antitrust issue. By 1906, when he pledged his "desire to see the trusts exterminated, root and branch," he was echoing his own words from the past decade; but, this time, more people than before were willing to listen. With the 1908 election approaching, one magazine observed that "Mr. Bryan seems now just come to the day of his real public strength."[41]

There was no doubt of his prominence once again within the Democratic party. The much-chastened reorganizers were in retreat. As what Bryan affectionately called "the radical element of the party" reasserted itself, the party tilted decidedly toward reform. After 1904, Theodore Roosevelt found himself in the embarrassing position of having to depend upon Progressive Democrats for his strongest support.

While Bryan basked in renewed popularity and influence, he still had to watch his steps carefully. In his ringing 1906 Madison Square Garden speech, for example, he had caught many people off guard with his ideas about federal ownership of railroads. Although the Progressive intellectual Herbert Croly believed that Bryan's "advocacy of public ownership was the most courageous act of his political career," the general response was far less enthusiastic. Especially unhappy were those Democrats who had specifically advised him not to mention the railroads at all. The next day, eastern newspapers carried head-lines, "BRYAN OUT FOR GOVERNMENT OWNERSHIP." The unfriendly New York *World*, noting that Bryan had again split his par-ty, snickered, "That was indeed peerless leadership." White southern Democrats stirred nervously at the prospects that government own-ership might jeopardize segregated facilities. Bryan bridled at this, ex-pressing anger at Democrats whose "personal objections to riding with Negroes" would block their support for "a great national reform." In the White House, a delighted Roosevelt "drew a sigh of relief after reading Bryan's speech." In the president's opinion, the Nebraskan had "helped us, as he came a bad cropper in his much heralded great speech."[42]

A few days later, in Louisville, Kentucky, Bryan backed away from the issue. He suggested that he would not press for government own-ership, even though he firmly believed in it. He admitted that he himself had been slow in realizing that government regulation of the roads was an insufficient response to corruption: "I can therefore be patient with those who stand now where I stood for years." He pre-dicted that eventually regulation would have to give way to public ownership. "The corrupting influence of the railroad on politics" re-quired this. But having made his point, he settled for leaving the issue of public ownership to the future. Over the next few months, he care-fully moved toward a less controversial way of framing the issues, and even seemed to hedge on the future. On several occasions, for exam-ple, he put distance between himself and the socialists. While he cred-ited them with "honestly seeking a remedy" to corporate crimes, he argued that ironically they resembled the trusts in their disdain for competition. Whereas socialists would give the public just another kind of monopoly, one in the hands of the government, Bryan favored individualism and competition. Indeed, he suggested that he was a more effective opponent of socialism than were conservative Repub-licans. His kind of progressivism, he believed, would eliminate the abuses that spurred socialist complaints and solutions. The enlarged socialist vote in recent elections, in his opinion, flowed directly from Republican hostility to reform.[43]

Bryan also tried to mend southern fences, which were shaky following his talk of an enlarged federal economic role. His message was that white Southerners need not worry about him regarding local racial policies. In April 1907 he argued that race was an issue that should remain with state and local governments. Indeed, he went so far as to say that "even a winter's stay in the South" would make a northerner more sympathetic to the concerns of white southerners. Several months later, he added that suffrage restrictions were "a matter of self-preservation" to allow the white South "to protect its civilization."[44]

By 1908, Bryan was organizing his third push for the White House around the question "Shall the People Rule?"—which allowed for local as well as national expression of democracy. In the *Commoner*, in speeches across the country, and when stumping for local Democrats, he spoke to that issue. Through his brother Charles, he also effectively utilized a national mailing list of Progressive Democrats that his family had been putting together since 1896. The list reportedly made it possible to flood a congressional district with some three thousand letters at any time. As 1908 arrived, Charles had approximately six hundred thousand letters in the mail asking Progressive Democrats to establish Bryan Clubs. According to one reporter, "To be suspected of disloyalty to Bryan in those days was almost like buying a ticket to private life."[45]

Long before the Democrats convened at Denver in July, it was certain that Bryan would once again have their nomination for president. He was in such a commanding position that he virtually dictated the platform. To make sure there were no misunderstandings, he spent forty hours on the telegraph line to the resolutions committee and also relied upon Charles as his personal representative.

Chosen easily on the first ballot, he was truly confident about his prospects of winning the election. For one thing, the Democrats were more united than they had been since the early nineties. To achieve this, Bryan had made concessions. He had placated some political bosses by agreeing not to press for the initiative and referendum, and agreed to keep quiet on government ownership of the railroads. He had even wired the platform committee that "any mention of government ownership would be a mistake."[46] If the resulting Democratic truce enhanced his chances of victory in November, so too did the fact that the genuinely charismatic Roosevelt had chosen not to seek another term. Bryan thus faced a much more vulnerable opponent:

William Howard Taft. Although Taft was Roosevelt's personal choice, he was a political giant in size only. Weighing over three hundred pounds, he certainly appeared imposing enough; but there was no indication that he enjoyed anything like the president's popularity.

Bryan's acceptance speech, which he delivered in Lincoln on 12 August, was a masterful effort—upbeat and conveying a sense that, this time, the Democrats spoke for the majority. Placing his party unequivocally in the reform camp, he scorned predatory wealth and Republican ties to it. At his partisan best, he quoted from Roosevelt and Taft to indict their own party. And with splendid effectiveness, he repeatedly asked, "Shall the people rule?" They could not, he answered, as long as corporations secretly controlled elections. To remedy this, he and his party favored a campaign disclosure law by which all donations over one hundred dollars would be a matter of public record prior to an election, and no one could contribute more than ten thousand dollars. To give the voters more power, the Democrats also endorsed popular election of senators. Both proposals had just met defeat at the Republican National Convention. Turning his attention to the corrupting influence of the trusts, Bryan championed government control that would "not permit any corporation to convert itself into a monopoly."[47]

Over the next few weeks, the Nebraskan ran an impressive campaign. It was impressive partly because of the exuberance and energy that he brought to it. Once again he resorted to an exhausting schedule, traveling thousands of miles and giving between twenty and thirty speeches a day. According to one campaign aide, "We would throw cold water on his face to wake him, and he would get up, go out on the platform, and give 'em hell, then tumble back into bed to sleep until the next performance."[48]

The campaign was memorable as well because of Bryan's discussion of issues. He did not simply harangue the opposition nor engage in rhetorical fluff. His major speeches generally shunned bombast in favor of serious, detailed assessments of the nature of problems and of proposed solutions. Despite publisher Arthur Brisbane's complaint that "Bryan is a mouth," the Commoner raised fundamental questions and issues. His main question—"Shall the people rule?"—was in itself vital. It had been and would remain the paramount issue in American political history. In 1909, Progressive theoretician Herbert Croly asserted that in many respects, Bryan was "an advanced contemporary radical . . . indeed, more of a radical than any other political leader of similar prominence." Years later, William Allen White concluded that "he was a twelve-year-old boy in many things, yet a prophet far more discerning of the structure of the world . . . than were many of us."[49]

"I would make it a crime for men to organize monopolies," Bryan had once told Cleveland's reform mayor Tom Johnson.[50] During the 1908 campaign, he made this goal a centerpiece for discussion. Most important, he favored a federal licensing law for corporations. The idea was not new. He himself had advocated it at least as early as 1899; and Kansas Populist Edwin R. Ridgely had introduced a bill in 1900 that would have established licensing procedures. Like many Progressives, the Nebraskan still found appealing the historic America of small units—shopkeepers, farmers, and laborers. But like many reformers, he also recognized that larger and more concentrated businesses were a fact of life. Licensing, as he conceived it, would not preclude large businesses. Its purpose was to abolish monopolies, thereby keeping the field open for smaller companies.

On 25 August 1908, Bryan, speaking in Indianapolis, outlined a plan that was strikingly direct and simple. Any business that controlled 25 percent of a product would have to apply for a license, and no corporation could control more than 50 percent. A corporation that already controlled more than half of the market would have to divest itself of enough holdings to bring it within that percentage. Under this arrangement, small businesses would not even have to worry about licenses; and, at the other end of the economic spectrum, a large, licensed company could operate legally—as long as it did not exceed 50 percent of production. Bryan favored other antitrust policies as well (such as removing tariffs that protected "trust-made goods"), but the licensing law was the linchpin in his plan to restore competition to American industry, revitalizing it and protecting consumers. It would also reduce corruption. "Mr. Rockefeller's corporation is the most notorious lawbreaker in the United States," he told one audience.[51]

In Topeka, on a torrid 27 August, Bryan devoted an entire speech to another problem, that of how to shield "the common people" from banks that failed. His closely argued solution would insure deposits through a tax on banks. Simple justice to the depositors dictated this, but he also tried to convince skeptical bankers that they too would benefit. If people knew their deposits were guaranteed, they would be more willing to entrust their money to the banks. And as confidence in private banks returned, there would be less demand for a government savings bank. In any event, he emphasized that, in any conflict between the twenty thousand banks and fifteen million depositors, it was imperative that "the depositors have a prior claim to consideration."[52]

In his efforts to show that the Democrats sought relief for "the average man," Bryan threw his support strongly behind the labor movement. After the Democratic convention, he checked personally with Samuel Gompers, president of the American Federation of Labor, for his approval of the labor plank. The plank called for the creation of a Department of Labor within the president's cabinet, and opposed the use of court injunctions in industrial disputes. Gompers, in turn, broke from his usual political neutrality and campaigned for Bryan. When Josephus Daniels, a member of the Democratic National Committee, observed Gompers firing up a crowd of workers in Bryan's behalf, he was convinced that the Commoner would win the labor vote.[53]

"Bryan is making a wonderful campaign, and the Republicans are very anxious," observed Roosevelt's military aide Archie Butt. A worried Roosevelt advised Taft to be more aggressive and to go after Bryan: "Don't let *him* make the issues. . . . Hit them hard, old man!" Taft, who had hoped for a front porch campaign, bestirred himself, observing that "the subordinates in the ranks are not liable to tear their shirts" unless he also did some work. And although the huge man did not much like campaigning, his amiable personality served him well on the stump. Roosevelt, still wishing that Taft "would put more energy and fight into the matter," injected "a little vim" of his own by using the White House as a kind of propaganda machine for the candidate.[54]

Bryan, confident in early October that "things are looking well," must have felt subsequently as if the massive Taft had fallen on him. The Republican crushed the Commoner in the electoral college 321 to 162, and at the polls by more than a million votes. Bryan's third bid for the presidency, which had seemed so promising, ended in his worst defeat. Outside the solidly Democratic South, he had carried only Kentucky, Oklahoma, Nebraska, Colorado, and Nevada. Terribly disappointed and baffled at the outcome, the Nebraskan "could not understand how we were so badly beaten."[55]

The past, it turned out, was not really past. Memories of the "Democratic" depression of the 1890s still lingered. In that sense, Bryan continued to pay for the "sins" of Grover Cleveland, and some of his own as well. To many people, even some who traveled miles to hear him, he was still suspect—the person who, as the Progressive journalist Harold Ickes recalled, "sent goose pimples running up and down tough hides that had long been immune to apprehensions."[56]

Most important, insofar as the election was primarily a judgment on the previous administration, there seemed little reason to "throw the rascals out." The exceptionally popular Roosevelt had boosted the GOP's public stock and, in effect, given Taft a head start at the polls. Bryan needed to breach the ascendant Republican coalition and was unable to do so. He had given the Democrats new life by helping to align them with the swelling reform mood of the day, but Roosevelt had aided the Republicans in the same way. Indeed, Roosevelt had shrewdly used the Commoner as a radical foil. Just as Bryan had warned that a failure to deal with corporate abuses aided the socialists, the president had increased his own attack on corporate irresponsibility by pointing to the specter of Bryan's "socialistic" ideas about the railroads. Ultimately, the election demonstrated what Harold Ickes described as "a truism that while Bryan got the crowds, the Republicans would have the votes."[57] This was certainly the case among laborers who, despite Gompers's prodding, failed to mark their ballots for the Commoner.

Ironically, if the past helped to account for Bryan's defeat, he had significantly prepared his party for the future. The Democrats as a whole seemed on the rebound, gaining eight seats in the House and capturing governorships in states such as Minnesota, Indiana, and Ohio. In Nebraska, for the first time they won control of the legislature and the governor's mansion. Collier's magazine believed that the election indicated "plainly the country's discontent with the Republican Congress." Ohio's newly elected representative, James Cox, had no doubts about the Commoner's role in all this: "Bryan's return to leadership was very inspiring to the Democrats. It was a factor in our carrying Ohio for the state ticket." In 1908, the evidence seemed to confirm what Bryan later stated as a kind of political axiom: "The Democratic Party must be progressive if it is to be an important factor in national politics." His role in shaping the party into an instrument for reform had been substantial. In that sense it was far readier than before to take advantage of fissures that might develop within the Republican coalition.[58]

# 6

## POLITICAL MISSIONARY

### (1909–1914)

After listening to William Jennings Bryan in the early 1900s discuss the trust issue over dinner at Cleveland mayor Tom Johnson's home, Frederic Howe concluded that "more than anyone I have ever known, he represented the moralist in politics. He wanted to change men. He was a missionary." While Bryan's politics had always been profoundly moralistic, the missionary tendency became even more noticeable following the disappointment of his 1908 defeat. During the next few years, he identified himself more directly than before with the Prohibition forces, and his battle to keep the Democratic party on the side of virtue assumed special intensity, especially at the 1912 convention. When newly elected president Woodrow Wilson appointed the Nebraskan as secretary of state in 1913, Bryan helped to inject a strong moral tone into the nation's foreign policy. Throughout Bryan exhibited what Frederic Howe characterized as a "self-righteous missionary mind."[1]

In this sense, the Commoner exemplified contradictions within progressivism. Progressive reformers, including Bryan, were in many respects tolerant and generous; they hoped to liberate people from restrictive political and social environments, and to make the American dream of opportunity and democracy meaningful to immigrant and working-class groups. Hence they campaigned to open up the political process through such devices as the direct election of senators; they idealized the inclusive concept of the "public" interest; and they struggled to improve working, living, and institutional environments in order to rescue individuals from stunted and exploitative conditions. By rehabilitating the settings in which people lived, they hoped also to uplift and transform the people. But such open, humanitarian sentiments could assume coercive, intolerant forms. "It is a dreary, old truth," said the reform journalist Jacob Riis, "that those who would fight *for* the poor must *fight* the poor to do it."[2] Here was the rationale for turning some Progressive programs into social shoehorns to ease the beneficiaries of reform into desired places. The strong moral predilections of many Progressives often inclined them to turn their causes into crusades against sin and evil. And insofar as such crusades encouraged self-righteousness, progressivism typically wavered between offering a helping hand or a push.

Bryan by nature was not sympathetic to coercion, whether between individuals, groups, or nations. "The chief duty of governments, in so far as they are coercive," he believed, "is to restrain those who would interfere with the inalienable rights of the individual." And he himself was always reluctant to force his personal habits or beliefs on anyone. For one thing, he had enough confidence in the ultimate superiority of his own beliefs that he saw no reason for any strategy other than educating and informing individuals about moral and intellectual absolutes. For another, he liked people and did not want to offend. Mary Bryan knew "him to repeat mistakes in English rather than hurt the feelings of some old man who had had no early opportunities." His disposition was tolerant and magnanimous. This was initially evident in his views on Prohibition.[3]

Although Bryan did not himself drink liquor, he long avoided a judgmental stance toward those who did. Partly, this was a matter of temperament. As a twelve-year-old he had taken the abstainers' pledge, and as a young man he had delivered temperance lectures, so there was never any doubt about his personal preferences. He nevertheless refused to let his own opinions about liquor slide into bigotry and intolerance. One of his Nebraska acquaintances "drank with some regularity," but Bryan firmly believed that "little differences like that" should not destroy friendships. When Bryan learned that the Reverend Sam Small, a noted evangelist, had gotten intoxicated, he urged critics to be "charitable toward his recent lapse" and not to let "an unguarded moment" detract from the minister's otherwise exemplary life. On another occasion, Bryan was on the Chautauqua circuit, talking in a hotel lobby to some members of the Women's Christian Temperance Union. He happened to notice in the nearby, noisy bar another speaker, author Opie Read, who was drinking in violation of the Chautauqua rules. The Commoner "said nothing," according to one individual who was present; "instead, he moved just enough to cut off the view, so the ladies would not be shocked at the sight of their other lecture-hero, and the next morning, affable as ever, Bryan joined Read and me at breakfast."[4]

Initially it also made good political sense for Bryan to avoid the liquor issue. His silence on the matter when he first entered politics squared with the Democrats' traditional aversion to governmental interference in private lives. It attested as well to the nature of Bryan's home district in Nebraska, which included the third largest distillery in the United States and large numbers of recent European immigrants who were "wets." In the 1890s, he thus voted against statewide prohibition and courted wet votes by asserting that "it is unjust for any one man to say that another must 'live like I.' "[5] In 1902, when teetotaler Carry Nation tried to close Nebraska's saloons, she received no encouragement from the Commoner, whom she angrily dismissed as a man who looked out strictly for his own political interests.

Mary Bryan had another explanation for her husband's tardy enlistment in the Prohibition cause: "He did not want to confuse the mind of the voter with too many issues and was unwilling to approve this reform until it was ripe for action."[6] Although in 1904 he endorsed local option laws on grounds that communities had the right to decide whether they would have saloons, he carefully kept the issue out of his 1908 campaign. He continued to keep quiet a year later when temperance advocates in Nebraska pushed unsuccessfully for a county option law.

In 1910, however, he decided that it was time for action. For one thing, he believed that in the last presidential election liquor interests might have cost him at least four states. Such personal grievances aside, he, like many Progressives, was more and more inclined to judge the liquor industry as an enemy of reform. The fact that brewers in 1908 had blocked direct legislation bills in Nebraska seemed proof enough that democratic processes were falling hostage to the saloon.

By the time that Bryan unequivocally threw his support to the antiliquor movement, the temperance cause had constituted a major aspect of American reform for more than three-quarters of a century. In the early 1800s, drinking alcoholic beverages had been an accepted part of most people's daily routine. Warding off the "bad humours" and "grog time" had been so familiar that Abraham Lincoln described the culture of his youth as one in which "we found intoxicating liquor . . . used by everybody, repudiated by nobody." This changed dramatically during the several decades preceding the Civil War. Growing problems of crime, poverty, idleness, and civil disturbance prompted anxious efforts to encourage self-discipline and build a web of voluntary and institutional restraints. The American Bible Society, for example, distributed hundreds of thousands of tracts or small booklets, packed with vivid moral lessons. In the 1850s, one former drunkard's wife, pointing to her neat home and happy family, reportedly stated, "O, the Tract—the Tract—the Tract has got all these nice things! My husband never drank after you gave him the Tract." Many antebellum reformers, especially the abolitionists, detested liquor, seeing in it another example of enslavement. The taverns, from this view, were in the "whore-making, criminal-making, madman-making business." Powerful antisaloon messages painted the drunkard as a slave to drink, sitting stupefied in a barroom, his family shivering and hungry in a back alley slum: "Shoeless, over frozen ground / His wretched children go." The astoundingly popular melodrama *Ten Nights in a Barroom* thrilled audiences in the 1850s and after, with its emotionally wrenching scenes, including one in which the small, angelic daughter tearfully implores her father to leave the tavern and come home.[7]

For many nineteenth-century Americans, the tavern nevertheless represented something far more benign. In the rapidly expanding cities of the late 1800s, for example, large numbers of working-class men found a genuinely useful social institution behind the swinging barroom doors. Neighborhood taverns served as ethnic and communications centers in immigrant, tenement districts where illiteracy rates ranged over 60 percent. They also provided a host of varying services: public toilet facilities; locations for political and labor union meetings in areas where public halls were nonexistent; places much closer and less formidable than downtown banks where workers could cash their paychecks (one tavern near Chicago's Union Stockyards cashed forty thousand dollars worth of checks monthly in the early 1900s); shelters for the transient and the homeless; free lunches; settings in which to pass the hat to help local families; locations from which to make telephone calls; and a respite from crowded and monotonous living conditions. Although temperance enthusiasts were sometimes correct in judging saloons as threats to family life, in other cases the tavern may have provided a kind of social safety valve for the release of domestic tensions. The fact that taverns proliferated in the tenement neighborhoods was due to many factors, including efforts on the part of authorities to segregate vice from "proper" districts; but it also testified to the lack of privacy in most tenements, whose residents tumbled into the streets to find recreation and escape. A miner insisted in 1912 that the saloon "supplies a want—a need. It offers a common meeting place. It dispenses good cheer."[8]

Some Progressive reformers, such as Jane Addams, the founder of Chicago's famed Hull House settlement, and Raymond Robins, director of Chicago's Municipal Lodging House, recognized the saloon's social role and tried to build alternative institutions. They thus championed such innovations as organized recreational activities, public drinking fountains and restrooms, and coffee houses in immigrant neighborhoods (for example, the Episcopal Church's "Boozeless Bar" in Denver). In their opinion, the detrimental effects of taverns far exceeded any utilitarian value. While seeming to benefit the poor, saloons actually drove families further into poverty and unhappiness, feeding off them in order to line the pockets of "the liquor interests."

As Progressives mounted their campaigns for urban political reform and for improving the lives of what Jacob Riis called "the other half," they saw the saloon as forming one of the strongest links in a chain of corruption, exploitation, and social "waste." It was, Robins said, "the enemy of the home and the church and of the school—a stench in the nostrils of all decent folks."[9]

Bryan, agreeing that the liquor industry represented a conspiracy "against the home and everything good," also increasingly spotted connections between taverns and the worst in American life. "The saloon is next-of-kin to the brothel and the gambling hall," he wrote in late 1909; "it is a rendezvous for the criminal element and the willing tool of the corrupt politician." As a young man he had tolerated barrooms, even though he had usually stayed away from them. On the several occasions that he had been in taverns, he had ordered milk or sarsaparilla. Like many Progressives, however, he tended more and more to see Prohibition as an essential reform. At a time when statistics showed that thirty-five thousand of the two hundred thousand annual industrial deaths were alcohol-related, banning liquor seemed crucial for public safety. Like Raymond Robins, who argued that "the old right, if there ever was one, of personal liberty to get drunk" had disappeared along with the "12-mile-an-hour world" of the nineteenth century, Bryan championed society's right to defend itself. Surely, he argued, neighbors could protect themselves against the drunkard, who jeopardized life and property and whose family members could end up as wards of the community.[10]

Economic changes added a disturbing new element to the liquor business. Independent neighborhood taverns were falling under the control of multimillion-dollar, consolidated breweries bent on eliminating competition. Bryan conceded that the old-fashioned neighborhood tavern, "owned by a resident and amenable, to some extent at least, to the sentiment of the community," may have had some legitimacy. But such saloons had given way to "the evils of the trust system." Communities that had traditionally dealt with liquor problems simply by working with local merchants now faced what Bryan described as the equivalent of "a war with a foreign power." For the Commoner and many reformers, the time had indeed arrived to close permanently the swinging barroom doors. And when such a powerful moral issue was involved, Bryan sensed that "the rising wrath of a determined people" was on his side.[11]

In 1910, when he threw himself wholeheartedly into the antisaloon ranks, he told the old Populist James B. Weaver, now a Democrat, that "the fight against evil is always an uphill one, and the hill is never steeper than when you fight the liquor interests." In his opinion, this was "the biggest fight" he had yet undertaken, but he was convinced that he was "right and that is enough." Taking to the stump in favor of county option laws in Nebraska, he apologized for his earlier silence. He now believed that communities needed help in barring taverns from within their borders. By 1908, 450 Nebraska communities had outlawed saloons only to find that alcohol was still available just outside their boundaries. Bryan reasoned that they could protect themselves somewhat more if they could banish liquor sales from entire counties. "This is a moral question," he argued. "There is but one side to a moral question. Which side do you take?" He contended that he had "never espoused a more righteous cause," and, now that he was in the battle, he would not sound retreat: "I shall not do it—never, never, never!"[12]

While Bryan and other drys were not wrong in seeing connections between liquor and such social maladies as poverty, poor health, family abuse, and crime, their perspectives on the saloon were nevertheless far from unbiased. And while they drew upon familiar and time-honored aspects of a rich American reform tradition that hoped to protect innocent and disadvantaged victims from corrupt and exploitative liquor interests, that tradition reflected class, ethnic, and religious preferences.

At its roots, the battle over the bottle was a matter of culture. The Anti-Saloon League's description of itself as "the Protestant Church in action" aptly characterized the entire history of America's Prohibition movement. Prohibition had invariably found its greatest support among the major Protestant denominations, such as the Methodists, Congregationalists, Presbyterians, and Baptists, which emphasized personal conversion and correct behavior. To Catholics and Jews, however, the Prohibitionists' efforts to legislate morality impinged upon the role of religion. From their perspectives, rituals and traditions—not the state—should guide individual conduct. Indeed, laws that tried to impose moral standards amounted to religious tyranny on the part of the nation's dominant groups. Because so many newer immigrants and laborers in America were Catholics and Jews, religious beliefs were typically also laden with class and ethnic meanings. Many working-class people who were crowded into congested neighborhoods in the major cities looked upon the saloon as one of the few easily accessible places to which they could escape for relaxation and conviviality. Understandably, when blue-collar workers had the chance, they voted overwhelmingly against Prohibition laws. In their estimation, the drys were little more than blue-nosed "do-gooders" trying to impose their values on other people. And in a sense, of course, such a judgment was quite defensible.

Ironically, Bryan believed strongly that "religion and politics suffer by a union of the church and the state. . . . When prejudice enters a contest," he warned, "reason retires from the field."[13] He strenuously resisted any insinuation that his support for Prohibition was an example of religious bigotry or coercion. The dry issue, to him as well as many other Progressives, was something upon which all good and decent people could agree. It went beyond particular denominational preferences to universal standards of morality. Who, after all, could really defend the befouled saloon once it stood exposed for what it was: the tool of irresponsible profit-seekers and a terrible agency of human misery and suffering? Surely the righteous could never retreat from such clear-cut moral issues, even if principled steadfastness involved political risk.

Declaring in 1910 that he did not want the Democrats to "die of delirium tremens," Bryan put his leadership of the state party on the line. When he introduced a minority report favoring county option at the state Democratic convention that year, he not only lost badly but was booed. He also ended up at odds with two popular members of the party, Governor Ashton C. Shallenberger and Jim Dahlman. In 1908 Shallenberger had established himself as a bright Democratic star by receiving more Nebraska votes for governor than Bryan had won in the presidential race. In April 1909 Shallenberger persuaded the legislature to pass a daylight saloon bill, forcing taverns to close by 8:00 P.M. Within a year, however, Bryan judged the law inadequate and urged the governor to call the legislature into special session to establish county option. Shallenberger, who had hoped to defuse the liquor issue with the daylight law, refused to do more, thereby incurring the Commoner's anger and eventually losing Nebraska's first open primary election to Dahlman by a mere five hundred votes. "Cowboy Jim," one of Bryan's most loyal backers, had served five terms as mayor of Omaha. A colorful figure who in his forties still participated in rodeos, he had once driven some gamblers out of Omaha by firing bullets into a saloon chandelier. He was also a stalwart wet who had promised to sponsor a free beer party if elected governor. Bryan, unable to accept his old friend's position on the liquor issue, declared publicly that Dahlman had no "moral right to the Democratic nomination of the state." Dahlman subsequently lost the governor's race.[14]

During these stormy political months, Bryan's family provided comfort and stability. In October 1909 he and Mary celebrated the twenty-fifth anniversary of what had been a remarkably rewarding marriage. Her abilities and energy were considerable, and she shared his opinions on religion and reform. From the start, they had both been active in local church and civic groups. Because he relied on her more than others for advice and support, she correctly viewed herself as his "confidante" and "mental safety valve." Although she proudly described him as "my hero," she was no fragile, clinging vine. Instead, her personality was as strong as his, and she served as his critic, adviser, and sounding board. According to William Allen White, who first met her in 1900, she was very protective of her husband and viewed people who approached him "with a fishy eye of distrust" until they had demonstrated their friendship. "She was," White recalled, "exactly the kind of woman he needed." In order to work closely with him, she too had earned a law degree and in 1888 had been admitted to the Nebraska bar. As much as possible she accompanied him during political campaigns and speaking tours. Her role in the *Commoner's* success was substantial, and she handled a great deal of William's correspondence. Their silver wedding anniversary, to which they invited some six hundred guests, was a happy affair, marking an admirable relationship that was mutually satisfying.[15]

At approximately the same time that the Bryans commemorated their wedding, all three of their children also married. William, Jr., who had graduated from the University of Nebraska, married in 1909 and moved to Arizona to study and practice law. Grace, the youngest and a victim of health problems for years, wed in 1911. But, in its eventual resolution, perhaps their most gratifying relationship was with Ruth, the eldest child. Her marriage in 1902 to an artist substantially older than she had infuriated her parents, so much that Mary had stayed away from the wedding. Within six years the marriage had ended in an emotionally wrenching divorce. For a brief period, starting in 1908, Ruth and her two children lived with Mary and William, allowing daughter and parents a chance to rebuild their relationship. By the time Ruth remarried in 1910 at her parents' home, and prepared to embark on a career of her own as a lecturer, writer, and politician, the family reconciliation was complete.

While the period immediately following Bryan's political disappointments of 1908 provided some particularly pleasant family moments, so too it allowed him to "make hay," as he put it, on the lecture circuit. No other speaker in the nation could match his income per lecture, although he often spoke without compensation to religious and civic groups. Already wealthy, Bryan, according to a close acquaintance, Colonel Edward House, was worth at least two hundred thousand dollars, and could earn a hundred thousand annually from Chautauqua tours, where "Bryan Day" was the highlight. But it was not simply money that lured him back to the podium. He loved contact with his audiences and relished the opportunity to discuss a variety of issues with them, including such matters as conservation, peace, and public service. Even vacation trips that he made in 1910 to Central and South America and Scotland were jammed full of speeches. For a man who had just lost his third presidential election, such continuing popularity in front of crowds was particularly welcome.

Barely fifty, he must have wondered about his political future. The hostile reaction of many Nebraska Democrats to his endorsement of county option raised questions about his influence in his own state. In 1910, he had longingly eyed a position in the Senate, but the anticipated draft fizzled when a drive to collect fifteen thousand signatures turned up only two thousand. His old ally and former employer at the Omaha *World-Herald*, Gilbert Hitchcock, was elected, heightening the growing rivalry between them.

When Bryan turned his attention to party matters outside Nebraska, he worried that the reorganizers would try, as they had in 1904, to prune the party of reform. "The privileged classes never sleep; their agents are always at work," he warned.[16] To make sure that "Bryanism" prevailed, he spent two weeks meeting with members of the new Congress in early 1911, urging Progressive legislation and leadership.

Back on the road again, he carefully kept abreast of the fight on Capitol Hill over tariff reform. The previous year, President Taft, caught between warring factions in the increasingly divided Republican party, had ended up endorsing the Payne-Aldrich tariff as a reform measure. He had clumsily done so despite the tariff's excessively high schedules, the howls of unhappy GOP Progressive "insurgents," and strong sectional complaints—such as a Florida newspaper's claim that "the South was the victim, the East took the money, and the West got nothing." In the spring of 1911, the Democrats, sensing that steadily rising prices might be turning the tariff issue to their advantage, renewed their pressure for lower rates. Oklahoma's Democratic senator Thomas P. Gore sketched out what he believed was a winning political formula: "less tariff, more trade, free ships, no trusts, no graft, no Taft."[17]

After alerting readers of the *Commoner* to machinations of high tariff "predatory interests," on 30 May Bryan presumptuously instructed Speaker of the House Champ Clark of Missouri to be more of a fighter. This was especially necessary, he advised, to effect the removal of the tariff on wool, which at the time enjoyed a 44 percent duty. "Don't be afraid," Bryan lectured him. "A leader must *lead*." The irritated Clark, who had respectable Progressive credentials of his own and was a strong contender for the Democratic presidential nomination, much resented Bryan's effort to pull him "around by the nose." But from Bryan's viewpoint, if a "few shop owners" could send panic into the Democrats, the clout of large protectionist manufacturers would be enormous. The Democrats in the House eventually compromised on a 20 percent tariff rate on wool, while pledging to place it on the free list at a later date. When a joint congressional committee in early June edged the rate up to 29 percent, Bryan turned his wrath on Democratic majority leader Oscar Underwood of Alabama, claiming that he was a closet protectionist. Infuriated, Underwood, with the support of North Carolina's Claude Kitchin, took the floor of Congress to deny Bryan's charges. The enthusiastic applause and cheers from Democrats in the House suggested that the Commoner's ranks were thinning within his party on Capitol Hill as well as in his home state.[18]

Bryan gave no indication that his recent setbacks had in any way chastened him. Turning his attention to the Democratic National Convention, still a year in the future, he stated emphatically, "When the time comes to name the man for the candidacy, I will not be silent." Indeed, he had no intention of being quiet until the convention either. On 4 August 1911, he addressed thirteen questions in the *Commoner* to potential candidates, and he continued to offer a running commentary on the virtues and errors of leading Democrats.[19]

Between the emerging front-runners—Champ Clark and New Jersey's governor Woodrow Wilson—Bryan initially leaned toward the congressman from Missouri. In fact, in early 1911 he gave his political blessings to Clark by inviting him to speak at his birthday banquet. Subsequently, however, Bryan began to doubt Clark's reform sentiments and turned to Wilson, who he believed "was becoming more radical" and battering the party's "reactionary element."[20]

Few people could have predicted that there was any chance of an alliance between Wilson and Bryan. In 1896, Wilson, then a distinguished scholar at Princeton, had backed the Cleveland wing of the party and had detested the Commoner. Over the next dozen years, he had been a conspicuous member of the anti-Bryan faction, describing the Commoner as "foolish and dangerous," a demagogue without "mental rudder," someone who needed to be knocked "once and for all into a cocked hat," and a person full of "errors and heresies." In 1908, he had refused at least twice to sit at the same table as the Nebraskan. Bryan, in turn, had little regard for Wilson and after 1910 initially viewed with skepticism the new governor's apparently sudden conversion to progressivism. But Bryan increasingly warmed to Wilson, as the governor compiled an impressive reform record and welcomed his advice. Wilson, meanwhile, dropped his early aversion to Bryan. Politics was certainly a factor. One Wilson aide, William G. McAdoo, predicted that "Bryan will be a power in the next National Convention. . . . He will hold the 'balance of power' absolutely." But Wilson also liked Bryan as he got to know him better. After listening in March 1911 to the Commoner deliver one of his best-known Chautauqua addresses, "Faith," the governor had "a very different impression of him" and judged him "truly captivating." In early 1912 Bryan told his brother Charles that he still had not made up his mind between Wilson and Clark, but obviously his opinion of the governor had changed substantially over the preceding year.[21]

When Bryan went to the Democratic convention in Baltimore in late June as both a reporter and a Nebraska delegate-at-large, it was less to champion any particular candidate than to prevent "turning the party over to Wall Street." He was convinced that the prevailing mood across the country was overwhelmingly Progressive. The Republican convention, which he had just observed firsthand for the press in Chicago, had badly fractured the GOP. Theodore Roosevelt, now a bitter opponent of Taft, had come to the convention as his party's popular choice after compiling impressive primary election victories. But the incumbent president had controlled the convention and the nomination, spurring Roosevelt to bolt and form a third party. In Bryan's opinion, the Republicans were undergoing the same "con-

vulsions" that the Democrats had experienced in 1896, "when progressive Democracy was born." Because Taft's GOP stood for "stand-
patism," many Progressive-minded Republicans were in search of a
new home. Whether they found it in a Roosevelt-led movement or
with the Democrats depended on what transpired at Baltimore. It was
thus imperative that the Democratic party not "disappoint the hopes
of the progressives of the country and surrender itself to the service of
Wall Street."[22]

Bryan later claimed that he had "expected to play a minor part" at
Baltimore but had been "forced into a fight at the very outset." In
fact, he arrived in that sweltering city with almost messianic fervor,
spoiling for battle. He was determined to make sure the Democrats
did not "take sides with the reactionaries." In this sense he was what
William Allen White described as "the embodiment of a cause."
White, who attended the convention as a member of the press,
viewed him as at once "ridiculous" and yet possessing "tremendous
power." He was ridiculous in appearance—heavy "in jowl and belly,"
looking somewhat "frowzy" in his two-button alpaca "deacon's" coat,
white vest, and rumpled trousers. He was powerful in terms of his
ability to influence the convention with speeches that evoked
"howling approval." White, who by this time was thoroughly in the
Progressive camp, watched with amazement "the formation of a left-
wing group led on the floor unofficially by Bryan, who even in victory
looked like an adorable rag baby, but who had steel at the core."[23]

Once again, Bryan virtually dictated the Democratic platform,
which resembled a Progressive reform list. It called for downward re-
vision of tariff duties on grounds that existing rates made "the rich
richer and the poor poorer," and accounted for "the high cost of living" that plagued American families. It endorsed legislation to make
private monopolies illegal. It urged the ratification of the pending
constitutional amendments for an income tax and popular election of
senators. It recommended publicizing campaign contributions prior to
elections and imposing maximum limits on what corporations or individuals could give. For labor, it supported unionization, an eight-
hour work day, and a cabinet position. The Democrats might not have
Bryan as their candidate in 1912, but he ensured that at least their
platform bore his stamp.

On the convention floor, in interviews, and in daily articles, the
Commoner unleashed a steady barrage against "the Money Trust,"

"the despotic power of organized greed," and "the wicked schemes of the privileged few." "Down with the bosses!" he asserted at one point, and on another occasion he invoked "the moral power of the people." He tried unsuccessfully to block the choice of Alton B. Parker as the convention's temporary chair, charging that the judge was "the most conspicuous representative of the reactionary element of the party" and would deliver a keynote speech that would "be an offense" to Democrats.[24]

His strategy was not simply to sway delegates with his rhetoric but to mobilize public opinion outside the convention hall. As he told Indiana's John W. Kern, who had been his vice-presidential running mate four years earlier, "There is a manifest necessity of putting the rank and file of every cross roads on guard." If "the reaction of the folks at home" could reach the delegates, it would "put the fear of the Lord into their hearts." Subsequently, an estimated 110,000 messages—some bearing many signatures—cascaded upon the delegates during the proceedings. Bryan said later that he "had simply turned the faucet and allowed public sentiment to flow in upon the convention."[25]

On the fourth day, he electrified the delegates with what he called "a moral issue." As the band played "See the Conquering Hero Comes," he moved toward the podium. Ellen Maury Sladen of Texas observed that "W.J.B. is much changed. His head is a shining bald crown with a fringe of dull, lank hair, and the fine, strong features that made him so handsome twenty years ago have hardened and grown coarse." His jaw, however, she believed had taken on "an iron rigidity," and it was firmly set as he readied, in his words, "to throw down the gauntlet to the predatory interests."[26]

The stunned delegates listened while Bryan dropped what he later described as his "bombshell"—a resolution that "the party of Jefferson and Jackson" not nominate "any candidate for President who is a representative of, or under any obligation to, J. Pierpont Morgan, Thomas F. Ryan, August Belmont, or any other member of the privilege-hunting and favor-seeking class." He explained that these three people were "connected with the great money trust now under investigation" and would bring only "disgrace" upon the Democratic party. The party's presidential candidate simply had to "be free from alliance with them." When he claimed that an effort was under way "to sell the Democratic party into bondage to the predatory interests of this country," he snapped the word "bondage" in such a way that, according to one listener, "You could almost see the great money power of this country reaching out its tentacles around the throats of the people." Bryan's resolution had a second clause that demanded the removal of any delegates to the convention who represented Morgan, Belmont, and Ryan. But Bryan eventually dropped this part, sticking with his first request and citing the Bible, "If thy right hand offend thee, cut it off." As bedlam broke out on the convention floor, he moved to the back of the platform, picked up his familiar palm-leaf fan and told a friend, "There, that'll fix 'em."[27]

Ohio congressman James Cox doubted that "any national convention ever witnessed anything comparable to Bryan's dramatic speech against the alleged power of Wall Street interests. . . . It was a bitter invective" that suddenly threatened to shatter the Democratic party. "The convention was in an uproar," Bryan recalled. People were cursing him, shaking fists at him, and even threatening him with bodily harm. Hours of heated debate followed. Eventually, after another barrage of telegrams from across the country had descended on the convention, the delegates overwhelmingly approved the resolution by a four-to-one margin. A jubilant Bryan told reporters as he left the hall that the convention was now "absolutely in the hands of the progressives."[28]

Over the next several days, as the Democrats labored through forty-six ballots in search of a presidential nominee, Bryan may even have flirted with thoughts that he might again be his party's choice. He had earlier said that he had no chance of a fourth nomination because of, among other things, his recent stand on Prohibition and because some people considered him "a hoodoo to the party."[29] But it was clear from the convention's outset that he was still a powerful force—indeed, that no other individual at Baltimore matched his influence. Mary and his brother Charles became increasingly hopeful about his chances for another nomination, and Woodrow Wilson's supporters suspected nervously that the Commoner was maneuvering himself toward victory.

However tantalizing the prospects of another nomination may have been to Bryan as he worked in the convention's spotlight, it was Wilson who got the nomination. And it was the Nebraskan who helped to prepare the way. When the New York delegation shifted its support to front-runner Champ Clark on the tenth ballot, it appeared that the

Missouri congressman might gain the momentum to win. Bryan squelched this. On the fourteenth ballot he took the floor to explain why he was switching his ballot, even though the Nebraska delegation was pledged to Clark. He insisted that no candidate whose nomination hinged upon the New York delegation was acceptable. Any such person would be obligated to the Tammany Hall political machine that controlled New York's delegation, as well as to the Morgan-Ryan-Belmont "privilege-seeking, favor-hunting class" that the convention had just repudiated. For this reason the Nebraskan shifted his vote from the now-sullied Clark to Wilson.

Bryan's move did not throw the nomination to the New Jersey governor, but it effectively undermined Clark's candidacy. Wilson's prediction of more than a year earlier proved true: "No Democrat can win whom Mr. Bryan does *not* approve." When Wilson eventually got the nomination, Bryan, according to one reporter, rose quietly but with a "frozen" expression and the appearance of having aged ten years. Some saw in his face "the emotions of hope lost and a lifetime ambition again defeated."[30]

Bryan's reaction indicated his realization that the reins of party leadership were slipping into new hands. Wilson had shrewdly conducted his own candidacy, but at least Bryan could take satisfaction in knowing that the overwhelmingly Progressive nature of the convention was due substantially to his labors over some sixteen years. Insofar as the party was ready to take advantage of the Progressive mood of the nation in 1912, it was certainly the Commoner who had helped to prepare it for victory.

During the campaign, he stumped every day for seven weeks in behalf of the Democratic ticket. The train in which he traveled was jammed with passengers anxious simply to see and hear him. They alighted whenever Bryan delivered a speech at some crossroads and then hastened back to their seats as the train moved out. All day long they did this. Even the baggage man ran the length of the train each time to listen to the Commoner. While such attention certainly gratified Bryan, it hardly compared with his joy in November when Wilson won the election. With the Republican party split between Taft's candidacy and Theodore Roosevelt's new Progressive party, and with Wilson building an impressive reform coalition of his own, the Democrats for the first time in sixteen years captured the White House.

Several weeks after the election, Wilson asked Bryan to be his secretary of state. The choice at the time reflected political realities more than enthusiasm or confidence. "If I am elected," Wilson had asked a friend in October, "what in the world am I going to do with W. J. Bryan?"[31] Because the Commoner had a huge popular following and spoke for a still powerful faction within the party, it made sense to incorporate him in the administration rather than leave him a disgruntled outsider and potential critic.

Actually, for almost two years, the appointment worked out exceptionally well. This was partly because Bryan and Wilson agreed on a legislative program, but also because Bryan did not challenge the president's leadership. The Nebraskan was genuinely delighted that the Democrats were finally in power; and he was, according to Wilson's close adviser Colonel House, "as pleased with his new place as a child with a new toy." He said sincerely during one cabinet meeting, "I am here solely to help and carry my part of the burden."[32]

Certainly no one in the cabinet proved more instrumental in helping to push Wilson's "New Freedom" reform legislation through Congress. This included laws reducing tariff rates, instituting a graduated income tax (the first under the recently ratified Sixteenth Amendment), and establishing closer scrutiny of big business. The new Federal Trade Commission, for example, was supposed to serve as a watchdog over unfair business practices. And the Clayton Anti-Trust Act of 1914 legitimized peaceful strikes and exempted labor and farm organizations from prosecution as illegal combinations in restraint of trade—a measure for which the secretary-treasurer of the American Federation of Labor, Frank Morrison, gave Bryan special credit.

Bryan's role in the passage of the Federal Reserve Act was particularly important. By the time the new administration assumed office, economists and business groups agreed overwhelmingly that the nation's antiquated banking and money systems desperately needed reorganizing. The seven thousand banks across the country lacked the means of coordinating their actions, particularly of mobilizing sufficient bank reserves during financial crises. Bankers and their allies wanted a privately controlled central bank, with geographical branches, that could issue currency during periodic money shortages. Bryan objected. He viewed the bankers' plan as a blatant maneuver to deliver the nation's finances to the "money trust." Along with outspoken Progressives in Congress, he insisted that government must control the reserve system and the issuance of currency. "Banks exist for the accommodation of the public, not for the control of business," he declared in a 9 September 1913 speech. Financial groups responded angrily to the specter of government intervention in what had been virtually a wide-open private sphere. To a San Antonio banker such intervention smacked of communism, while a Wall Street representative loathed it as "the slime of Bryanism."[33]

The Federal Reserve Act that went into effect in early 1914 owed much to the Nebraskan. He helped convince Wilson to endorse public authority over the banking and currency systems, stumped the country in behalf of the idea, and saved the plan when it encountered trouble in Congress. Southern and western Progressives were not altogether satisfied with the proposal but generally relented because of their respect for Bryan, who, in turn, persuaded the administration to approve the addition of short-term agricultural loans to the law. At a cabinet meeting when none other than the secretary of agriculture claimed that the farm credit amendment was "class legislation," Bryan furiously retorted that farmers as well as bankers deserved consideration. The act that Wilson signed into law on 23 December created a publicly controlled federal reserve system. Although the twelve regional branches were privately owned, they were under the supervision of the government-operated Federal Reserve Board, which set the nation's general monetary and credit policies. The act also allowed for a more flexible currency system, a change Bryan had long advocated. It established a new form of government-backed money, federal reserve notes, that required only 40 percent gold backing.

On down the line, of course, the Federal Reserve Board's role would depend on the nature of the appointments to it. For the moment, however, Bryan apparently gave little thought to the possibility that the board might become the servant of the bankers. He was delighted that the bankers' plan to make the board a private entity had failed. And, like many Progressives, he was confident that governmental regulatory agencies would protect the public interest. Within a few years, disappointed Progressives would protest that the Federal Reserve Board, the Federal Trade Commission, and other regulatory bodies were falling into the hands of those whom they were supposed to regulate. Insofar as that happened, the results were quite different from what they, and certainly Bryan, had intended. In 1913 and 1914, he was swept up in the excitement that accompanied the remarkable burst of reform legislation with which the Wilson administration made its debut. A grateful president acknowledged that he had "relied greatly on Bryan," especially during the battle over the federal reserve system.[34]

As important as the Nebraskan's loyalty and deference were to a good working relationship between him and the president, another factor pulled them together. Despite their obvious differences in temperament and training, their perspectives on the world were remarkably alike. Both men were Presbyterian elders with relentlessly moralistic outlooks. They both rejected William Howard Taft's "Dollar Diplomacy," with its goal of protecting private investments in Latin America and the Far East, on grounds that it turned American foreign policy into a tool of the corporations. Bryan, of course, had been warning for years that the trusts not only bred corruption at home but also pushed the government toward interventionist actions abroad in order to enlarge their profits. By 1913, other influential Progressives, including Republican senators such as Wisconsin's "Fighting Bob" La Follette and Idaho's William E. Borah, also identified industrial monopoly with gunboat diplomacy and "financial imperialism." An identifiable reform constituency toward America's international role was thus emerging as Wilson and Bryan tried to construct a foreign policy to advance the ideals of democracy, freedom, and Christian example.

The president and his secretary of state were also both suspicious of a foreign service with aristocratic personnel and pretensions. Wilson, for example, fretted that those making foreign policy increasingly resembled "a caste, class, or order," and Bryan had long made clear his distrust of civil service laws that encouraged an undemocratic, permanent, office-holding clique. The Commoner, true to his nickname, believed that rank-and-file citizens in a democracy should serve in governmental positions and had the innate wisdom to do well. He had no quarrel with the traditional nineteenth-century "spoils system," by which supporters of the party in power reaped the rewards of victory. He thus relished the opportunity to sweep Republicans out of appointive positions and to replace them with loyal Democrats.

A long line of office-seekers—"the boys of '96," as the *New Republic* magazine called them—thus awaited interviews with the new secretary of state. Bryan, dragging a chair, moved down the line, intently giving each applicant serious attention. One cartoonist portrayed the interviewees as aging, portly men, seated under the sign "Applicants must file their 1896 credentials."[35]

State Department officials viewed this with disgust and alarm. The department for several years had been in the early phases of transition from its previously small, informal, and amateurish setting to one of bureaucratic growth, organizational continuity, and professional expertise. Insofar as this shift represented the work of Progressive reformers who celebrated "efficiency" and "scientific management," Bryan's ascendancy promised to be a kind of horror story. He had never paid much attention to administrative duties or organizational details. His hopelessly littered desk, the telegrams stuffed randomly in his pockets, and his willingness to scratch out official memoranda on the backs of old envelopes attested to this. Ambassadors and ministers abroad sometimes waited weeks for replies to routine questions, and occasionally they received none.

But pressures for a more streamlined, trained State Department also came from another direction—from genteel individuals who had long shuddered at the "menace of Bryanism." Wealthy, socially privileged, and politically conservative people, they talked much of the "respectable classes," "good breeding," "homes with tradition," and "culture." To some of them, the State Department beckoned as a kind of preserve, an adventurous alternative to prestigious but unexciting family businesses in which they had little interest. Working initially in the middle echelons of the department, some of them gravitated toward a bachelors' mess on H Street and viewed themselves as part of "a pretty good club." To such people, Bryan at a distance had been offensive enough; as the new boss of the State Department, he was appalling. One of them noted incredulously that he spoke "not of efficiency, fitness or long service, but merely places for Democrats." Equally shocked, another observed that "it never occurred to him for a moment that the slightest training was necessary." And one Harvard graduate with impeccable social credentials angrily resigned, convinced that Bryan's appointments had "debauched and weakened" the department.[36]

Bryan's disregard of diplomatic formalities hardly helped his image as a hapless amateur. After thumbing halfheartedly through a document on protocol, he dismissed it as material he could not remember. The lunch box that he brought daily to work and his habit of snacking on radishes unquestionably seemed undignified to some observers. His badly wrinkled suits and his carelessness about shaving gave him such a dumpy demeanor that one individual characterized him as "a Hottentot chief on his tropical throne." What Mary Bryan proudly characterized as her husband's "extreme simplicity of taste" struck more fastidious individuals as hick mannerisms that lacked sophistication.[37]

A marked lack of understanding and tolerance prompted that criticism, echoing the slurs that had plagued Bryan since 1896. His decision not to serve alcoholic beverages at State Department functions thus received much ridicule as "grape-juice diplomacy" and a social embarrassment. Actually, he and Mary had not wanted to make a major issue of their unwillingness to serve liquor. At the first state dinner he briefly explained to the guests that the Bryans would not be serving liquor because they did not believe in drinking it. He hoped that the evening's hospitality would more than compensate for the missing wine. "It was rather an embarrassing occasion to us," he later wrote, "because we had no desire to emphasize our views on this subject and I felt quite relieved when the explanation was finished."[38]

Just as Bryan's critics used his wineless dinners as an example of gauche provincialism, so too they lampooned his speaking on the Chautauqua circuit in 1913—or as the *Nation* magazine condescendingly put it, "dashing off again for a wild night ride . . . to some obscure hamlet." It seemed ridiculous for him to appear, as journalist Mark Sullivan later caustically wrote, with "jugglers, female impersonators, and swiss yodelers." Such comments were unfair. Many government officials delivered paid public lectures, and Bryan often discussed the cause of world peace in those "little hamlets," keeping the secretary of state in touch with grass-roots America. Nevertheless, it was not long before Ambassador Walter Hines Page moaned from Great Britain, "They now laugh at him over here." Page feared that it would take years for American ambassadors to recover from "the embarrassment of having the secretary appear as spokesman for his country."[39]

Complaints about Bryan's conduct were not without some justification, however. His appointees typically brought little to their jobs except political loyalty. He wondered, for example, about finding "a good Democrat who would like a winter's stay in Greece." Manton Wyvell, his personal secretary, had so little tact that he once referred to the Japanese ambassador, who was within hearing distance, as "the little Jap." An appointee to the office of foreign trade described Bryan as "the greatest man on earth since Christ," but admittedly did not "know a damned thing" about his new assignment. An appointee to a Nicaraguan post could not find his assigned country on the map. Unlike their predecessors, the new ministers to Latin American countries could not speak Spanish; and those in Haiti and the Dominican Republic were white, breaking a tradition of Republican appointments who had been black. Bryan opposed the nomination of Harvard's ex-president Charles W. Eliot as ambassador to China on grounds that the dignified Eliot, a Unitarian, was an inappropriate choice for such an important Christian missionary field; he need not have worried because Eliot refused to serve anywhere under Bryan.[40]

However flawed was Bryan's record of appointments, he deserved far better than the "eminent fathead" label that one reporter applied to him. The appointments that he actually controlled were few in number, and his concerns about the political affiliation of department officials were certainly not unique. Although some of his appointments were disastrous, others proved willing and able to learn. William Fleming, an elderly judge who came to the office of foreign trade conceding that he "didn't know what foreign trade was," turned out to be exceptionally capable.[41]

Perhaps most important, many of the socially advantaged men, who belonged to the "pretty good club" and looked with such disdain upon Bryan, brought serious limitations of their own to America's foreign policy. Temperamentally unsympathetic to social upheaval, they were typically insensitive to the revolutionary turbulence that was increasingly shaking the world. Just as Bryan and the boys of '96 stirred their fears, so too did popular, grass-roots movements in other countries.

In this respect, Bryan had more insight. He, like Wilson, was sensitive to the worldwide movements for social change, and often sympathized with them. In 1913, for example, the United States became the first nation to recognize China's new republican government. In 1899 Bryan had observed that revolution feeds upon misrule. "No nation can afford to make its people miserable," he had warned. If rulers "robbed life of joy and hope," they could expect angry subjects: "if a nation sows the wind it must reap the whirlwind." As secretary of state, Bryan also shrewdly realized that foreign financial interests, including those of his own country, were gaining an insidious power over the Latin American nations. Such monied agencies were rendering the people of Central and South America "as helpless as if a foreign army had landed on their shore." His proposed solution was a series of low-interest loans from the United States government that would, he told the president, aid countries "who have fallen among thieves." Wilson, however, rejected the proposal as too radical for the public to accept.[42]

Bryan's weakness as secretary of state resulted not from a lack of awareness of the massive social changes at home and abroad, even if he was often naive about the politics of other nations. (On his world tour in 1906, for example, he had discussed free speech with the czar of Russia—"Yes, free speech. I thought he needed to hear about it, and he seemed quite interested.") Instead his foreign policy was flawed largely because of his difficulty in understanding different cultural values. In this respect, he revealed his own kind of arrogance. He assumed, as he had said at the turn of the century, that America should "teach the natives to live as we do." American foreign policy, in his opinion, rested on a bedrock of good intentions, the altruistic spirit of Christianity, and a selfless desire to uplift. He could not even begin to suspect that America's moral principles and interests could be in conflict with those of another nation. To him, "teaching the natives" was not only an expression of America's beneficent nature; it was also an effort the natives themselves would appreciate. Like Wilson, he believed that serving humanity produced its own rewards. Unselfishness and a lack of commercial greed would in fact "prove profitable in the end, for friends are better customers than enemies." In God's benign universe, good deeds benefited the doer as well as the recipient.[43]

Bryan's perception of the world embraced a vibrant nationalism reflective of the most potent beliefs and myths in American history. From the Puritan settlements in colonial New England, when John Winthrop had described Massachusetts Bay as a "City upon a Hill," to George Washington's talk of America's "destiny," Thomas Jefferson's description of the United States as a "chosen country," and the references of John Quincy Adams and countless others to the sway of America's example, the belief had grown that the nation was indeed special. A dominant assumption persisted that the United States could conquer the planet with the strength of its purity, its morality, and its idealism. No one felt or articulated the power of this national belief more than William Jennings Bryan, or the president under whom he had agreed to serve as secretary of state.

Bryan talked incessantly of America's mission "to liberate those who are in bondage" and to champion human rights and peace. "I know of no limitation that can be placed on a moral principle," he asserted just before Wilson's election. He brought this point of view to the State Department. During an early cabinet meeting, he "flared up" when army and navy officers suggested that they were experts on military matters. As Secretary of Agriculture David Houston recalled, Bryan "got red in the face" and "thundered" that they "could not be trusted to say what we should or should not do." Clearly, he had not changed his mind that the military was purely a vehicle of physical force: "it does not reason, it shoots."[44]

Ironically, despite Bryan's distrust of the military and his aversion to physical force, he helped to preside over a series of interventions in Latin America. The most notable example involved the sending of troops to the Mexican city of Veracruz, which seventeen years earlier had affectionately awarded him an eleven-gun salute. He had visited Mexico in 1897 and in 1904, making an excellent impression upon his hosts and coming away with fond feelings about their hospitality and courtesy. In 1911, revolution broke out against Mexico's military dictatorship and the nation seemed on its way to establishing a constitutional democracy under Francisco Madero. But two years later Victoriano Huerta staged a military coup, assassinating Madero and establishing his own iron rule. Wilson and Bryan refused to grant diplomatic recognition to what the president described as a government of butchers. According to Bryan, the administration could not separate public questions, such as the status of Huerta's government, from "morals and the principle of popular government." The administration placed its sympathies with the "Constitutionalists" who took up arms against the Mexican dictator. Bryan looked with particular favor upon the revolutionary Pancho Villa, who—unlike the reported alcoholic Huerta—neither smoked nor drank. To the secretary of state, Villa was a "Sir Galahad"; Villa, in turn, respected the American.[45]

Emotionally supportive of the revolutionary movement, Bryan and the president opposed European intervention in Mexico, as well as the efforts of American investors to aid the counterrevolutionaries. When Wilson said in 1914, "We shall have no right at any time to intervene in Mexico to determine the way in which the Mexicans are to settle their own affairs," he echoed Bryan's words to him several months earlier. "We must," the secretary had advised, "protect the people of these republics in their right to attend to their own business, free from external coercion, no matter what form that external coercion may take.[46]

Yet, when Bryan had offered such advice, he left the door open "to go into" any Latin American nation as long as America's motives were good: the people of that country must "know that we do not seek their territory or ourselves desire to exercise political authority over them." Indeed, he advised Wilson that the United States should "rescue" the Latin American nations by increasing its influence, especially through low-interest government loans. By doing so, "we could prevent revolutions, promote education, and advance stable and just government." Like Wilson, Bryan defined America's role as that of a liberator, sweeping aside aristocratic and undemocratic systems to make way for independence and self-government. By acting as a modern Good Samaritan, moreover, the United States could also advance its own interests. Appreciative Latin American nations would pose no military threat and would be excellent trading partners. "Why should they not look upon the United States as the great clearing house of their national wealth?" he asked. According to the Wilson-Bryan formula, self-interest and universal service balanced out perfectly. Thus it was that the stridently anti-imperialistic Bryan could say, with no sense of hypocrisy or contradiction, that he wanted to "make absolutely sure our domination" of Mexico, Nicaragua, El Salvador, and other Caribbean nations.[47]

Wilson's decision on 21 April 1914 to send one thousand American marines into the city of Veracruz, hoping to tip the scales against Huerta, had Bryan's support. Several weeks earlier, the Nebraskan had advised against military intervention, but news of a German ship en route to Veracruz with weapons for Huerta jolted him into sanctioning troops. The invasion was a disaster, resulting in the deaths of 126 Mexicans, 19 Americans, and occupation of the city for seven months. Cries of "Death to the Gringos" echoed across Mexico as Constitutionalist rebels now prepared to "fight the invaders" as well as Huerta. Mexican newspapers carried headlines demanding vengeance, and anti-American riots broke out in at least five Latin American countries. Despite hostility to the United States throughout much of the Caribbean, the Wilson administration felt triumphant in mid-July when Huerta resigned. Bryan was so happy at the news that he embraced Secretary of the Treasury William Gibbs McAdoo and, as Mary recalled, they "danced about like a pair of boys."[48] Almost eleven months later, however, as civil conflict continued to rip Mexico, Bryan at a cabinet meeting suggested American military intervention once again.

By then, the Nebraskan's approach to Latin America had grown increasingly interventionist and less restrained. His frustrations in 1914 with trying to guide the Dominican Republic toward democracy finally ended with his advising Wilson to use American force to make the Dominicans hold United States–supervised elections. Indeed, with the President's approval, he dispatched the navy with orders to bombard the island if necessary. Following the elections and the establishment of a new government, he notified the Dominicans imperiously in early 1915 that "no more revolutions will be permitted." And he recommended "forcible interference" to solve Haiti's economic and political disorder. Despite the best of intentions, he pushed events toward the eventual landing of American troops in the summer of 1915 and the commencement of some twenty years of American control of the island.[49]

From the perspective of 1925, he was still convinced that "what we did was for the benefit of the people." Since it "was not dictated by any pecuniary advantage to us or to any of our citizens," it was morally defensible. Although he believed that intervention in Caribbean nations such as the Dominican Republic was in the service of "our altruistic values," Latin Americans undoubtedly had difficulty distinguishing between the consequences of the Wilson-Bryan moralistic foreign policy and the imperialism that both men deplored. Ironically, when the Commoner dealt with the Caribbean countries, he resembled "a saint with a gun"—a description that English writer D. H. Lawrence used in a different context when trying to assess the character of the United States.[50]

Before America's forcible intrusions into Latin America, Bryan had said that he wanted his country to be "the supreme moral factor in the world's progress" and "a republic whose flag is loved while other flags are only feared." Events, however, had not followed the desired script.[51]

Departures from Bryan's preferred scenario became even more painfully evident in Europe. Wilson, Bryan, and other members of the new administration increasingly faced the unenviable task of dealing with a world in which revolutions and war converged with cataclysmic results. On 9 May 1913, Bryan had optimistically predicted that "the world is advancing in morals" and that "there is a greater sense of kinship among men than there ever was before."[52] Slightly over a year later, the Continent tumbled into savage conflict. As dreams of peace collapsed in the bloodshed and ruins of the Great War, Bryan and other Americans confronted the problem of determining what morality dictated.

# 7

## PEACE, WAR, AND REFORM

### (1914–1920)

On 2 August 1914, William Jennings Bryan missed Sunday church services for the first time in years. All day, he stayed in his State Department office, keeping watch over the dreary stream of cables describing ominously the developing war in Europe. On his desk rested a small paperweight in the shape of a miniature plowshare, made according to his instructions from a melted-down sword. As a symbol of his hopes for world peace, it perhaps buoyed his thoughts somewhat when he looked at it. Those hopes competed, however, with feelings of apprehension when he turned his attention to the discouraging cables.

Like so many Americans, and especially the Progressive reformers, he was inherently optimistic about the future and America's role in the world. But tugging at such optimism were growing doubts. At home the "interests" remained strong and resilient while, abroad, corrupt Old World influences threatened to ensnare the United States. A counterpoint for years to Bryan's celebration of America's mission had been his continual warnings against the trap of "the European plan" of monarchy, imperialism, and militarism.

Now, as he sat anxiously in his office on that humid August day in 1914, with the Washington Monument visible out one window and the large grandfather clock near his desk marking the passage of time, he wondered how America could exert its leadership without tumbling into the European conflict. Earlier that year, he had written the president about extending "the sphere of American influence beyond what we have before exercised."[1] By late summer such happy prospects contended with the specter of an expanding war that threatened to involve the United States. Before he left his office late on 2 August, he and the State Department's counselor, Robert Lansing, drafted statements of American neutrality for the president to consider. But the problem of America's mission in a world at war pressed relentlessly on him for several more years, keeping him on an emotional roller coaster of hope and fear, imperiling his public reputation, and raising questions about the fate of domestic reforms.

The miniature plowshare on Bryan's desk contained the guidelines of his foreign policy. During the summer of 1914, he had ordered the recasting of many of the small paperweights from surplus swords at the State Department. He then distributed them to various ambassadors, foreign ministers, and State Department personnel. Each little plowshare bore three inscriptions.

"Nothing is final between friends," read one of them, reflecting Bryan's attitude about personal relationships as well as a tenet of his diplomacy. He had first made the comment in 1913, in the midst of a crisis with Japan over a California law denying the right of the Japanese to own land in the state. Woodrow Wilson had sent Bryan to California to try to temper the legislation and mollify the irate Japanese. It was an impossible assignment. For one thing, Bryan's own views of the Japanese resembled those of the nativist California legislators. Indeed, some seven years earlier, when the San Francisco Board of Education segregated Oriental children, he had urged the federal government not to interfere because the states had "the right to protect themselves and their people in matters purely local." It was not fair, he had argued, for any locality to bear "a special burden . . . for the benefit of the rest of the country." Later, as secretary of state, he was perhaps more alert to the larger consequences of "purely local" events. In any case, in 1913 he had asked California not to enact the ban on landowning that was so offensive to Japan. Although he had been unsuccessful, his remark to Ambassador Sutemi Chinda that "nothing is final between friends" exuded a spirit of good will and compromise that Chinda apparently appreciated and that may have eased bad feelings between Japan and the United States.[2]

"Diplomacy is the art of keeping cool," read another inscription on Bryan's paperweight. The maxim pointed up his faith in human reasonability and his confidence in the soothing power of amiability and patience. He hoped to put such advice into practice with arbitration—or "cooling-off"—treaties, which he saw as procedural instruments for settling international disputes. As early as 1905 in the *Commoner*, he had pushed for conciliation agreements by which nations would agree to submit arguments to an international commission for investigation and recommendation. During the period of fact-finding, which could last up to a year, the nations were not to go to war nor increase their armaments. Bryan, as an orator whose career attested to the power of words, believed that periods of "cooling off" would allow sensible, peaceful attitudes to prevail. In his opinion, fights broke out during the heat of the moment, when passions ran high. If people, or nations, had time to think and talk, they could avoid violence. Bryan's ideas were far from new, but they placed him at the forefront of a growing international peace movement in the early twentieth century. President William Howard Taft, noting Bryan's influence on him, attempted to work out arbitration treaties but ran into congressional obstacles.

When Bryan became secretary of state, he negotiated conciliation agreements between the United States and thirty countries. By mid-August of 1914, he had secured ratification of twenty of them. Theodore Roosevelt snorted that these "little arbitration treaties which promise impossibilities" simply demonstrated Bryan's role as "a professional yodeler, a human trombone." Generally, however, the agreements received praise. Even the usually critical *New York Times* conceded that Bryan's "prescription of endless conversation" as a cure for disagreements seemed to be working. The "cooling-off" treaties were the secretary of state's proudest accomplishments. He had them in mind when he chose the third inscription on the paperweights he distributed during the summer of 1914—the scriptural quotation "They shall beat their swords into plowshares."[3]

In that context, the rapid spread of war throughout Europe in the late summer of 1914 stunned him. Just a year earlier, he had optimistically predicted that there would be no more wars in his lifetime. But now, as the fires abroad reduced that prophecy to ashes, he was determined that the United States should help bring an end to the conflict while maintaining a policy of strict neutrality. On 19 September he scrawled out a letter to Woodrow Wilson, urging that the United States serve as a mediator to the embattled nations. "The world looks to us to lead the way," he wrote.[4]

Bryan's conviction that the United States had a particular responsibility to "lead the way" tapped one of America's deepest cultural wellsprings. Americans for generations had typically contrasted the promise and innocence of their nation with the antiquated and scarred European continent that most of their ancestors had left behind. While America was to be a model for the rest of the world, it also needed to be ever on guard against the corrupting, alien influences outside its borders. Bryan had sounded this theme again and again at the turn of the century when he opposed annexation of the Philippines. Then and later he had feared that the United States might somehow shed its ideals of freedom, liberty, self-government, and peace for European-style aristocracy, militarism, colonialism, and war. "The false philosophy upon which the European nations have acted," he wrote in 1915, threatened "the New World doctrine"—namely, "the new system of the Prince of Peace" that rested on the ideal of brotherhood. America's power, he stated once again, rested with its moral example and righteousness. It must never, he pleaded, become "tired of being good."[5]

"Being good" meant avoiding corrupting entanglements with the Old World. This traditional axiom of American foreign policy took on special urgency in the summer of 1914 as war in Europe threatened to involve the United States. The possibility that American soldiers might die across the Atlantic Ocean, in a conflict between dynastic and colonial rivals, was abhorrent, not just to Bryan, but to most Americans.

Bryan and many Progressives worried that American involvement would undercut their efforts to achieve social justice at home. As early as 1899 Bryan had argued that war was an enemy of domestic reform. He predicted that, once American soldiers began to die on distant shores, the public would ignore the question of "who will uproot the trusts at home." When that happened, monopolies would flourish. According to former Populist Tom Watson, this had in fact happened during the conflict with Spain. "The Spanish war finished us," he believed. "The blare of the bugle drowned the voice of the reformer."[6]

Progressives as a whole were slower than Bryan and Watson to spot the implications of foreign policy for their domestic goals. William Howard Taft's Dollar Diplomacy had finally alerted many reformers to relationships between the hated trusts and America's international role, sensitizing them to ways in which "the jingle of the bloody dollar," as Iowa's senator William S. Kenyon described it, made America's foreign relations a tool of the "interests."[7] When war broke out in Europe in mid-1914, Progressives like Kenyon became even more aware of the possible effects of foreign policy upon domestic issues. By 1916, Wisconsin's senator Robert La Follette was echoing Bryan's thesis of seventeen years earlier that war would divert public attention from festering domestic problems. Bryan, seeking desperately to keep America out of the spreading conflict, increasingly found some of his staunchest allies in the reform wing of the Republican party, which included senators such as La Follette, Kenyon, and Nebraska's George Norris.

Woodrow Wilson was at first equally wary of American involvement in the war, except as a peacemaker. Like Bryan he wanted to avoid choosing sides between Old World rivals whose fight seemed to have nothing to do with idealistic principles such as democracy. Both men interpreted the grim conflict as the lamentable result of European militarism, bitter nationalism, and imperialistic rivalry. In 1914 the president thus asked Americans to be impartial in "thought as well as deed." He also listened closely to Bryan's advice advocating policies to keep the United States neutral.

Despite the secretary's determined efforts, the United States nevertheless moved, crablike, toward military involvement. This was not due to any administrative design, nor to a diminished commitment to peace on Wilson's part. Instead, events and pressures forced choices that were often equally unacceptable to virtually every citizen. Within the United States it proved difficult to strike a satisfactory balance between the overwhelming popular desire to stay clear of the terrible carnage across the sea, the concern of producers and exporters to keep trade open, and the demand to protect American citizens abroad. It was also impossible for the administration to make decisions that were absolutely neutral, simply because specific policies invariably benefited or hurt some belligerents more than others.

In this context, Bryan suggested early in the war, on 10 August 1914, that Americans should not lend money to belligerent governments. His recommendation came in response to a proposed loan to the French by J. P. Morgan and others. The secretary believed that such loans would be unneutral acts. Money, in his opinion, was "the worst of all contrabands because it commands everything else." Ever suspicious of bankers and financiers, he also suspected that "the powerful financial interests which would be connected with these loans" would attempt to influence national policy in order to protect their investments. Initially, Wilson agreed not to sanction loans to belligerents, but the administration gradually eased away from such a position.[8]

While the administration tried to define America's neutrality, the belligerents themselves continually threatened to reduce its range of options. The British, whose powerful navy controlled the seas, sought to block shipments of goods and materials to Germany. To do so they slowly tried to control America's shipping without precipitating a hostile reaction from the United States. Germany, meanwhile, desperately needed to cut off supplies to Britain. No match for the British navy on the surface, the Germans, starting in early 1915, turned more and more to the use of submarines. Inevitably, these battles over the seas and trade raised perilous questions about what products America could trade and with whom. The British, for example, declared in 1915 that food destined for Germany was contraband, because it aided the enemy as surely as ammunition.

Ultimately, questions over the rights of American vessels, and of American passengers on belligerent ships, pushed the Wilson administration toward war and drove Bryan from the cabinet. The death of an American passenger on 28 March 1915, when a German submarine sank the British ship *Falaba*, starkly posed issues regarding the rights and honor of the United States. What was the nation to do? Some of Wilson's advisers argued compellingly that such wanton slaughter of an American citizen required a formal protest. Bryan countered that it was unfair to hold the lives of millions of Americans hostage to the decision of a single individual to travel in a war zone. This time, the Commoner prevailed, and Wilson ignored the incident.

The 7 May sinking of the *Lusitania*, killing 1200 people, including 128 Americans, was quite another matter. All but two English-language newspapers in the entire United States castigated the Germans. From London, Ambassador Page told Wilson "that the United States must declare war or forfeit European respect." Bryan, predictably, was far more cautious. When he first learned of the tragedy, he wondered immediately "if that ship carried munitions of war. . . . If she did carry them, it puts a different phase on the whole matter! England has been using our citizens to protect her ammunition!" Again, he desperately tried to convince Wilson that some sacrifice of neutral rights was necessary to keep the nation from the larger horror of war. Over the next several weeks, he advocated placing the *Lusitania* incident up for arbitration, warning American citizens to stay out of the war zone, and combining any protest against German violations of neutral rights with a similar one against the British.[9]

On 11 May Wilson stunned Bryan with the draft of a vigorous protest note to Germany. Although the president avoided specific threats and set no deadlines, he demanded that Germany disavow the sinking, pay for damages, and end submarine warfare against unarmed ships. Bryan, fearing that the message would plunge the United States into war, tried unsuccessfully to soften it. Eventually, "with a heavy heart," he signed the note, but only because he believed he had convinced Wilson also to protest English violations of American neutrality and to indicate that the United States still desired a peaceful solution to disputes. When the Germans subsequently indicated a willingness to discuss the *Lusitania* incident, Wilson suspected that they were simply hoping to buy time. On 1 June the president read to his cabinet the draft of another note to Germany charging that surprise submarine attacks violated the "principles of humanity." Bryan, extremely depressed at Wilson's rejection of his proposal to ban Americans from travel in the war zone, believed the note would make war inevitable. On 4 June the Nebraskan threatened to resign if the president sent it.

Three days later, after considerable thought, little sleep, and a long talk with Wilson, Bryan prepared his resignation. That afternoon, flushed with fever, he stretched out weakly on a couch at home and discussed his decision with Mary and their daughter Grace. "The President does not seem to realize that a great part of America lives on the other side of the Allegheny Mountains," he said. "I would not be true to the trust that thousands of Americans have imposed in me if I joined in any action that might lead to the loss of life and property when they are so greatly opposed to it." Mary Bryan broke into tears, sobbing hysterically for the first time ever in Grace's presence. The Commoner, near collapse, then sent his resignation to the president, explaining that he could not stay in office "without violating what I deem to be an obligation to my country." A few hours earlier, he had told treasury secretary McAdoo, "I think this will destroy me; but whether it does or not, I must do my duty according to my conscience."[10]

At his last cabinet meeting the next morning, Bryan, exhausted and emotionally drained, sat quietly with his eyes closed. Afterward, he told six cabinet members who joined him for lunch that he could more effectively oppose war on the stump than in the government. "I can work to control popular opinion so that it will not exert pressure for extreme action which the President does not want." As tears gathered in his eyes he explained, "I must act according to my conscience. I go out into the dark. The President has the Prestige and the Power on his side." Overcome by emotion, Bryan stopped momentarily before adding quietly, "I have many friends who would die for me."[11]

At age fifty-five, beginning to suffer from diabetes and deeply worried that American soldiers would soon be dying in the bloody trenches of Europe, he left public office. Theodore Roosevelt had already judged him "the most contemptible figure we have ever had as Secretary of State," while Wilson's more sympathetic secretary of the interior, Franklin K. Lane, sadly concluded that the Commoner was "too good a Christian to run a naughty world." What Secretary McAdoo described as a "hurricane of abuse" descended upon Bryan following his resignation. Eastern newspapers charged him with "unspeakable treachery" and of stabbing his country in the back. One cartoonist turned him into a preening peacock, saying as he strutted, "I want to be a neutral and with the neutrals stand, / A smile upon my ego, the German vote at hand."[12]

In the White House, however, Wilson astutely recognized that the Nebraskan was far from a beaten figure. Hostile reactions to the resignation, especially in the eastern press, did not fool the president. "The newspapers do not express the real feeling of the country for that strange man," Wilson observed privately. By now respectful of Bryan's "high motives" and dedication to public service, Wilson sensed why the Nebraskan was such a formidable adversary. "He is *absolutely* sincere," the president told his brother-in-law. "That is what makes him dangerous." Wilson thus anticipated that "there are deeper waters than ever ahead of us." He was not exaggerating. Several thousand supportive telegrams to the Commoner, mainly from small towns, suggested that Bryan could still marshall his legions. And Bryan's pledge "to direct public opinion" underlined his determination to be a watchdog on the administration.[13]

Within two weeks after his last cabinet meeting, the Commoner was in New York City, delivering two major addresses to ensure "THAT THE DEMAND FOR PEACE DROWNS THE DEMAND FOR WAR." Speaking to a standing-room-only labor audience in Carnegie Hall, he urged Americans to recall "the ideals of the fathers," especially George Washington's advice to avoid foreign alliances. Bryan hoped that the United States would remain faithful to its traditions, using "the uplifting power of that which is good and pure and noble," rather than sinking into "the quarrels of Europe." Five days later, with some fifteen thousand applauding people jammed into Madison Square Garden and another fifty-five thousand trying to get in, he spurned "WAR WITH ANY OF THE BELLIGERENT NATIONS." Describing some of the modern weapons that were wreaking havoc across the oceans, such as cannon that shelled targets fifteen miles away, he contended that individuals who wanted to immerse America in such carnage did not speak for the masses. The reaction of the large newspapers in the Northeast was fiercely critical. "When Sedition Is Afoot," read one editorial headline.[14]

Back in Nebraska on 29 June, Bryan spoke from the balcony of a Lincoln hotel to a crowd of around five thousand. Still stinging from the response of the eastern press to his resignation and recent speeches, he complimented his audience for living "a thirty-six hours' journey from the New York newspapers"—far enough to protect them somewhat from "the journalistic mosquitoes" bearing war germs. He pressed on, suggesting that the New York publishers knew more about Europe, where they often lived and traveled, than about the United States. "The Allegheny mountains are a god-send to the Mississippi valley," he thundered; "they serve as a sort of a dike; they protect it from being inundated by the prejudice and intolerance of that portion of the eastern press which affects a foreign accent."[15]

Bryan's words on that hot summer day in Lincoln contained loud echoes of his 1896 campaign. Still hostile to the conspiratorial mach-inations of "predatory wealth" headquartered in the big-city East, he insisted that advocates of war did not speak for 80 percent of the population—farmers, laborers, and the small businesses that served them. Farmers and other "PRODUCERS OF WEALTH," as opposed to "PRODUCERS OF TROUBLE," opposed war because "upon them would fall the burden of conducting it." As the Commoner had done at Chi-cago in 1896, when he praised people who lived "out there" in the West, he again spoke fondly of farmers, close to nature, "uncorrupted by that fierce struggle for wealth which makes men forget God and the duty which they owe to their fellow men." They were people, he said, who felt the strong ties of neighborhood and family. Because they had "no pecuniary interest in the industries which thrive on war," and because they valued their children so much, they were not bent on sacrificing their offspring "to gratify someone's military ambition or to purchase markets." Noting that some two million people had already died in the horrible conflict abroad, and that the recently constructed battleship *Arizona* cost only eight million dollars less than the De-partment of Agriculture had spent over the entire preceding year, he indicated that it was no wonder "the farmer's interest in peace" was unyielding.[16]

The themes of 1896 surfaced again and again over the next few months as Bryan took to the road on an exhausting antiwar speaking tour. In San Francisco, under a blazing sun, interrupted by rain show-ers, he addressed one hundred thousand people. He then went to Or-egon and Washington, before returning to the Midwest and plunging into the South. The issue, as he defined it, was one of "the people vs. the special interests." The ongoing people's fight against "the tariff barons," "the trust magnates," and "the real money power" of Wall Street now needed to include "the preparers of preparedness—the bat-tleship builders and manufacturers of munitions." These powerful in-terest groups hoped to turn the United States into "a pistol-toting nation" in order to make a profit. If they succeeded in immersing the nation in war, they would themselves, of course, be too busy negoti-ating army contracts and loans to go to the front lines.[17]

Bryan did not construct out of pure fantasy his conspiratorial fears of the links between profit seeking and war making. Throughout 1915 the war trade sharply boosted the revenues of major American cor-porations. As a war-induced boom inflated the American economy,

U.S. Steel's profits jumped from $24 million in 1914 to $76 million in 1915; a year later they soared to $272 million. Between 1914 and 1916, the profits of the Armour meat-packing corporation tripled. In 1916, largely because of the war, the number of millionaires in the United States increased by more than 50 percent. While these developments did not necessarily add up to a plot among various industries to involve America in the conflict, they at least demonstrated that war could indeed be good for the health of certain businesses. This was why a Progressive such as Nebraska's Senator George Norris, sounding much like Bryan, soon warned against "going to war upon the command of gold."[18]

Toward the end of that hectic summer of 1915, Mary Bryan wrote wearily in her diary, "These days are full of trains and changing cars and small hotels and crowds and shouts and rain and wind and auto rides across country. He has been making two speeches daily. It is hard work." Bryan told her one evening, "Maybe it is a good thing that I make my living this way. I believe I do good and it needs the spur of necessity to keep me at it."[19]

At one point, the Bryans took a much-needed, short break, visiting journalist William Allen White at his summer cabin in Colorado's Rocky Mountains. By this time White had developed "great respect for Bryan," the man he had feared so much in 1896. He observed that the Commoner had grown paunchy, "baldish and heavy-jowled. But his voice was fresh and his eyes were keen." As the two men sat on the porch for an hour, viewing spectacular Long's Peak, Bryan's mind was not on the scenery. Instead he talked obsessively about Woodrow Wilson's drift from neutrality toward war. White believed he had "never met a man with a kindlier face, with a gentler, more persuasive voice," and he listened appreciatively to the Nebraskan's "rhetoric full of biblical metaphors and similes." In retrospect, the journalist was convinced that "he was as honest and as brave a man as I ever met, with a vast capacity for friendship." Bryan had about him a kind of innocence that reminded White of "a child in a garden who loved its beauty, enjoyed its perfume, and never crushed a bud."[20]

An idea that Bryan began to push in July 1915 was that of a popular referendum prior to any American involvement in war, except in the case of invasion. In the *Commoner* he printed with delight the results of a recent informal referendum on war that a newspaper conducted in a small Pennsylvania town. By a vote of 203 to 0, citizens opposed

America's going to war with anyone. Convinced that this was indicative of grass-roots opinion across the country, Bryan spoke increasingly for a referendum on war and peace, reasoning that "the people who do the dying should also do the deciding." Invariably, "the masses are never consulted by the special interests." He also told journalist John Reed that, if indeed the majority wanted war, those voting for it "should enlist first, together with the jingo newspaper editors." On 18 October the *New York Times* asserted that the referendum proposal was silly, showing that "Mr. Bryan's mind is the Happy Valley, the Fortunate Isles." To Bryan, who had declared publicly several months earlier that the New York press had never taken "the side of the people on any question," the *Times* editorial could only have been a bracing reminder that he was on the right side. [21]

Meanwhile, over the tense summer of 1915 President Wilson moved reluctantly toward a military preparedness program. Convinced, especially after the *Lusitania* crisis, that the United States must be ready for any contingency, he had instructed his cabinet to draft armament plans. He also advocated the formation of a new ready reserve force that would bear the patriotic title of the Continental Army. On 4 November he described publicly a defense program that Americans had been learning about piecemeal for several months. Speaking at New York City's Manhattan Club, he called for substantial increases in the army and navy.

The president's speech galvanized a powerful antipreparedness reaction, and Bryan again took to the road. "The real question," he contended, "is whether, under the guise of preparing for defense, we shall load ourselves down with unnecessary taxes, stir up a war spirit in the country, create a military class among us," and depart from traditional ideals. He recommended adopting the same approach to international affairs that one would use when trying to keep "peace in a neighborhood"—the use of friendship, not bellicose threats and swagger. [22]

When Progressives such as Charles Lindbergh, Sr., a Minnesota congressman, argued that "true" preparedness started at home with an equitable economic system and justice, they picked up a theme that Bryan had addressed years earlier. In 1892 the Nebraskan had told Congress, "We cannot put our safety in a great navy" nor "in a great standing army." Indeed, the nation should concentrate on building a fair and just society, resting its defense on "happy and contented citizens," not armaments and fortifications[23] Now, twenty-three years later, others in Congress—especially Progressive Republicans and Bryan Democrats—dug in against preparedness on grounds that the domestic price was too high.

Wilson, on the defensive, took his case to the people. In January and February 1916 he spoke to groups from New York to Topeka, Kansas, saying at one point that America needed "incomparably the greatest navy in the world." Storming along behind the president was Bryan, attacking the president's plan and accusing him of following "the wishes of the manufacturers of munitions" and "joyriding with the jingoes."[24]

On Capitol Hill, a development took place that seemed to give Bryan additional leverage. After he had talked with them, Senator Thomas Gore of Oklahoma and Representative Jeff McLemore of Texas in February introduced resolutions in Congress that would prevent Americans from traveling on armed belligerent ships. An alarmed Wilson learned that the resolutions would probably secure congressional approval, perhaps by a two-to-one margin in the House.

The president and Bryan now squared off in a furious struggle to influence Congress. According to the *New York Times*, Bryan, "the smiler with the knife," was stirring up trouble: "The explosion in Congress is in great part the effect of his mines."[25] On 4 March, after sending a flurry of letters and telegrams to senators and representatives, Bryan descended on Washington. The day before, Wilson had successfully convinced the Senate to table Gore's proposal. Trying to offset the president's offensive against the McLemore resolution, Bryan met with representatives individually and in groups. But on 7 March he sadly watched the House stand by Wilson, 276 to 142.

Events were not treating Bryan well. Wilson, by working adroitly with Congress and the public, had dampened the antipreparedness fire. As a major concession to preparedness opponents who voiced traditional American fears of a standing army, he dropped the Continental Army proposal. And during his midwinter speaking tour through the Northeast and Midwest, he had argued that military readiness was essential to protect the nation's defense and honor, and to preserve the peace. In Kansas City he had led a packed crowd of eighteen thousand in singing "America," and he had told an approving St. Louis audience that only through strength could the United States protect its neutrality from attack. Bryan was alarmed that such "slush" might frighten the public and precipitate America's entry into the war. But the Commoner's credibility was shrinking. He had been warning of impending war for a number of months, but America was still at peace. Moreover, the major newspapers, with whom he had battled for years, rebuked him unflaggingly. On 19 April, when Wilson informed Congress that he had threatened to break diplomatic relations with Germany following the injury of several Americans on the recently torpedoed French ship *Sussex*, Bryan rushed again to Capitol Hill. But his conferences with Democrats were so discouraging that he left after only thirty hours. "He came. He failed. He went," snickered the *New York Times*.[26] Perhaps the worst blow came in Nebraska in April when Bryan, after campaigning in forty-four counties, failed in his bid to become a delegate-at-large to the upcoming national Democratic convention. The Commoner, who three times had run for president, ended up no better than fifth in the primary election's slate of delegates.

At the Democratic convention in June, however, it became clear that Bryan's defeat in Nebraska related to local politics and not to a collapse of the peace issue that he had been pressing so hard. Indeed, surprisingly, on 16 June the usually hostile *New York Times* declared him "the outstanding figure of the Convention." This was genuinely remarkable, given the fact that Bryan was not a delegate and, for the first time since 1896, did not personally help to write the platform. He attended only as a reporter for a nationwide newspaper syndicate. But from the moment he arrived in St. Louis, he was the center of attention. A stream of visitors stopped by his room and his appearance in the convention hall evoked resounding cheers and applause.

Insofar as the convention belonged to Bryan, it was because the antiwar feelings that he had articulated for months prevailed there. This was particularly evident during the keynote address of New York's ex-governor Martin Glynn. His initial references to Woodrow Wilson elicited only a mild response, but when he turned his attention to the subject of peace, the huge audience suddenly came to life. At first surprised and nonplussed, Glynn responded to the moment, soon saying again and again that, despite the ongoing horrors in Europe, "We didn't go to war." Bryan, sitting in the press gallery, wept unabashedly. On the evening of 15 June, shouts for "Bryan! Bryan!" were so loud and persistent that Wilson's floor managers had no choice but to allow

the Commoner the floor. They watched nervously as he took the podium amid resounding cheers. Their worries quickly dissipated, however, when Bryan praised Wilson unequivocally for enacting the
greatest domestic reform program in American history. The clincher
came when, with the exuberant audience on its feet, he thanked "God
that we still have a President who does not want this nation plunged
into this war." Shortly thereafter, the convention by thunderous ac-
clamation renominated Wilson. The incumbent retained his party's
support, but it was Bryan and the powerful mood for peace that dominated the convention and set the theme "He kept us out of war" for
Wilson's campaign.

Bryan subsequently stumped for the president in nineteen states. In
Chicago, in mid-June, he made clear his continuing objective—
namely one of preventing "a single American mother's son" from
being "shipped across an ocean 3,000 miles wide to bleed and die in
the settlement of some King's dispute." Averaging four or five speeches
per day from September into November, he campaigned before record-
setting crowds, especially in the West, applauding Wilson's domestic
reforms and chastising "the REACTIONARY members of the Republican
party." When Wilson defeated Republican Charles Evans Hughes in
November, Bryan interpreted the results as a victory for peace and
progressivism.[27]

But Germany's announcement in February 1917 that its submarines
would attack all ships—belligerent and neutral—in broadly defined
war zones suddenly pushed the nation toward military engagement.
On 3 February Wilson told Congress that he was breaking diplomatic
relations with Germany. Bryan had just finished delivering a peace
speech in New York City when he heard the news. Stunned, and
convinced that 90 percent of the American public opposed war, he
hurried to Washington where he met with Wisconsin senator Robert
M. La Follette and others to discuss strategy. For two days they tried
unsuccessfully to organize congressional support for an antiwar
resolution.

The prospects for peace quickly deteriorated. On 26 February, with
goods piling up on the nation's docks, Wilson went before Congress
to ask for authority to place naval gun crews on American merchant
ships and, even more ominously, to "employ any other instrumental-
ities or methods that may be necessary to protect our ships and our

people."[28] La Follette, recognizing that such authority would give the president a virtual blank check to make war, began organizing a filibuster. Bryan again hastened to Washington to help rally opposition to the president. Throughout the day on 28 February, he pleaded with Wilson and members of Congress that some neutral rights were not worth fighting for. This included, he repeated, the right to travel on armed merchant ships. Already he had on numerous times drawn an analogy that the government had the same responsibility for keeping citizens out of a dangerous war zone as did a city mayor for closing off a riot area. The next day, however, the president made public the interception of a note in which the Germans were prodding Mexico to go to war with the United States.

As the sensational news broke across the nation, Bryan retreated to Florida, where he and Mary had established a winter residence. By then he was receiving threats on his life for alleged disloyalty to his country, and a Baltimore mob was singing, "We'll hang Bill Bryan on a sour apple tree." Meanwhile in the Senate, La Follette, George Norris, and what Wilson described as "a little group of willful men" filibustered in a chaotic setting marked by rage and bitterness. One cartoonist portrayed La Follette and his ten colleagues receiving the German Iron Cross. A discouraged Bryan followed the debates at a distance.

On 29 March, the Commoner made a last desperate effort for peace. He sent a message to all members of Congress, insisting that the United States was in no danger of invasion and still had at its disposal the "cooling-off" conciliation process by which to investigate disputes. If the government were bent on signing "the death warrant of thousands, even millions," of Americans, it should at least be willing to hold a national referendum in order to consult those who would do the dying. His appeal was in vain. On 4 April, at the president's request, the Senate passed a resolution of war—introduced in the Senate by Bryan's Nebraska adversary, Gilbert Hitchcock. Nebraska's other senator, George Norris, objected strenuously. He believed the decision placed "the dollar sign on the American flag"; it exchanged mothers' tears of grief for the prosperity of those "in their palatial palaces on Wall Street." La Follette, likewise voting against the resolution, resented the lack of a referendum. The nation's poor, he stated bitterly, "the ones called upon to rot in the trenches," had no chance "to voice their will upon the question of peace or war." On 5 April, the House also approved the war resolution, and the next day the president signed it.[29]

The fight of Bryan, La Follette, Norris, and others was over. There would be no referendum, and there would be no peace. "God forbid that we shall ever entangle ourselves in the quarrels of the Old World," Bryan had told an audience less than two months earlier. He had added that, if he could have his way, not "one single mother's son shall be carried across an ocean to march under the banner of any European monarch or die on European soil, in the settlement of European quarrels." But he had not prevailed. The United States was now a combatant in the bloodiest war the world had yet seen. Much distressed and looking much older, Bryan told his wife, "I have done everything one man can do." Noting that "the blood of our young men" was now Congress's responsibility, he could at least say, "My hands are clean."[30]

"The thing has been done" said one disconsolate opponent of military intervention, Charles Lindbergh, Sr. But "however foolish it has been," he continued, "we must all be foolish and unwise together, and fight for our country." Lindbergh expressed Bryan's sentiments perfectly. The Nebraskan loathed Congress's decision, but on the same day that it passed the declaration of war he sent a telegram to Wilson, volunteering to serve in any capacity. Now that the nation had taken up arms, he advised citizens to unite behind the president. Indeed, he asserted that "whatever the government does is right and I shall support it to the uppermost. . . . There should be no division or dissension."[31]

For the duration of the war, Bryan closed ranks behind the administration. He deplored antiwar dissent on grounds that it would simply prolong the fighting and add to the suffering. Unity and respect for the law were essential, in his opinion, to avoid anarchy and help the nation win the war. With his usual energy, he threw himself behind fund-raising drives for the Red Cross, Liberty bonds, and other patriotic causes. Soldiers from Nebraska, en route to training camps, often sat in a Lincoln auditorium where Bryan lectured them on the great privilege of fighting for democracy. For years, the Commoner and other reformers had been championing the cause of democracy against conspiratorial foes such as the trusts, "the Beast," "the Octopus," and the "interests"; now their crusading energies could focus on leading the embattled public against a tangible foreign enemy that epitomized Old World corruption, imperial power, and lack of democracy.

Like many Progressives, who had initially been suspicious of any distraction from the battles for justice at home, Bryan decided that the war in fact provided rich opportunities for reform. He experienced what the Progressive intellectual John Dewey described as an "immense moral wrench," discovering that the madness of the reprehensible European bloodbath could, ironically, open up "social possibilities." Familiar exhortations about sacrifice and serving society now produced astonishing results. Hence Edward T. Devine, the general secretary of the New York Charity Organization Society, wrote excitedly that "enthusiasm for social service is epidemic." Social worker Felix Adler also pointed to the "high wave of service" sweeping across the nation. Even the title given to the drafting of soldiers— "selective service"—reflected this spirit of thought.

For reformers who had been struggling to improve public health and uplift morality, the war goal of making America's soldiers "fit to fight" was laden with opportunity. Ongoing battles to clean up the slums and improve personal hygiene now took on a patriotic imperative. Perhaps most noticeably, new energy infused Progressive antivice campaigns to close down "red light" districts and to insure the nation's moral and physical purity. Secretary of War Newton D. Baker wanted America's soldiers to have an "invisible armor," or "a set of social habits," that would protect them from venereal disease and moral debauchery in training camps and abroad. According to literature distributed to the soldiers, "A German bullet is cleaner than a whore," "You must keep your bodies clean and your hearts pure," and military leaves were "NOT in order that you may SOW WILD OATS, but to give you an opportunity to improve your health, and your education." An article in the December 1918 *Delineator* magazine announced that America had produced "the cleanest body of fighting men the world has ever seen."[32]

This was moral territory in which William Jennings Bryan could flourish. "If a man . . . disobeys the laws of morality he becomes a degenerate," the *Commoner* reported. No loyal citizen should forget "his first duty of allegiance to his own country," and thus end up in social exile. "Safeguarding the morals of the men in camp"—this was a goal that Bryan identified for himself on the very day that America entered the war. When he addressed troops it was frequently about morality and the "social evil" of prostitution. He suggested that prostitutes, those who "spread disease for pay," should be jailed throughout the war.[33]

Predictably, given his almost visceral reaction against trusts and Wall Street, he also urged the placement of legislative restraints on profits and industrial power. He thus favored taxing war profits or, as he also described it, drafting money. And, although he again got nowhere, he resurrected his idea for government ownership of the railroads, with the federal government controlling interstate lines and the states running local lines.

But especially important to Bryan were the causes of woman suffrage and Prohibition. Prior to the war he had ranked them, along with peace, as the "great reforms." The antiliquor and suffrage campaigns both received enormous boosts during the war years. President Wilson, for example, in 1918 described a suffrage amendment to the Constitution as "a vitally necessary war measure." Bryan had spoken for woman suffrage as early as 1890, and in 1914 had actively supported a suffrage bill in Nebraska on grounds of simple equity, saying that his wife should enjoy the same liberties as he did. He was also certain that women's influence on politics would accelerate "the triumph of every righteous cause."[34]

Like most suffragists of the era, he saw the vote as a weapon for motherhood. Just as Frances Willard of the Women's Christian Temperance Union spoke of politics as "enlarged housekeeping," he argued that the ballot would help the mother "protect her home and save her child" from "wicked men." Surely, he reasoned, a mother should be able to mold "the environment that may determine whether her child will realize her hopes or bring her gray hairs in sorrow to the grave."[35] Initially, he had preferred that women receive the vote through state action, but by the war years he was pressuring Congress to pass a federal amendment and send it out for ratification. In mid-1919, Congress finally acted; ratification occurred the following year.

Bryan believed that the suffrage amendment was slow in coming because the liquor interests opposed it. This gave him yet another reason for escalating his battle against the saloon. In 1910, of course, he had splintered Nebraska's Democrats with that issue. But even then he had not endorsed national Prohibition and had helped keep the dry question out of presidential politics. His antiliquor commitments had continued to grow, however. In 1915 he had appeared on the same platform as the famed revivalist Billy Sunday, who had sworn "to fight the saloon interests until hell freezes over and then fight them on the ice." At a huge Prohibition rally that year in Philadelphia, with a choral group singing, "William, William Jennings Bryan, we'll all drink grape juice yet," the Commoner had been the featured speaker. At the end of his speech, he had raised his glass of water aloft and asked the audience to stand and pledge "support to the cause of water."[36]

In 1916 he had once again fought vigorously to close the saloons in Nebraska. His affection for Prohibition now compared, he said, with what he would feel for a new "child born in our family." By then he was convinced that a constitutional amendment was necessary to allow "sober people" to prevail. Although still respectful of states' rights, he concluded that the dry issue was not something over which states should exert independent control. "The highest good to the greatest number" was a principle that cut across state boundaries. Although he had not dwelled upon the liquor cause when campaigning for Wilson in 1916, after the election he immediately announced his intention to make "the national Democracy dry." He was convinced that Democrats would not watch their party "be buried in a drunkard's grave." Several days later he predicted that, if a Prohibition amendment were not part of the Constitution by 1920, the dry issue would be a critical factor in that year's presidential election. Describing the liquor interests as "the most mercenary, the most tyrannical group that ever entered politics," he summoned good Democrats to align themselves with "the mother, the child, the home and humanity."[37]

Once America entered the war, demands for grain helped to make liquor an endangered species. Among the alleged sins of the liquor interests was now a lack of patriotism, and Bryan quickly picked up this theme. Rising to rhetorical heights, he asserted that purveyors of alcohol would "make drunkards of the entire army and leave us defenseless against a foreign foe." In mid-1917 the *Independent* magazine described him as "America's leading advocate of prohibition." Confident that Progressive ideals had made the saloon "an outlaw, a fugitive from justice," he believed that "the new emancipation is at hand." The war for democracy in this sense seemed to be advancing social measures as well. When the House of Representatives in December

1917 joined the Senate in approving the Prohibition amendment, a happy Bryan smiled down from the press gallery. During the subsequent fight for ratification in the states, he served as president of the National Dry Federation. And upon hearing of the Eighteenth Amendment's ratification on 16 January 1919, he rejoiced that "the greatest moral reform of the generation has been accomplished."[38]

As America moved decisively toward woman suffrage and Prohibition, the war armistice on 11 November 1918 raised Bryan's hopes even more. He saw an opportunity to ensure that this would be "the last war, the beginning of a peace that will endure."[39] Anxious to be part of the nation's diplomatic delegation at Paris, he was jolted when Wilson did not appoint him.

Subsequently, he became deeply involved in the debates over the peace settlement that Wilson brought back from Europe. The proposed League of Nations, which the president considered the heart of the treaty, engendered the largest controversy, especially in the Senate. Bryan was himself initially suspicious of the league idea. His concerns resembled those of Progressive Republicans such as senators Robert La Follette, George Norris, California's Hiram Johnson and Idaho's William E. Borah. To these reformers, the international organization would simply implicate the United States in schemes of the victorious European powers. It might, for example, place America on the side of the British against Irish revolutionaries. Certainly it would violate George Washington's and Thomas Jefferson's advice against "entangling alliances," perhaps making America a servant of Old World empires.

In 1919, however, Bryan changed his mind about the league. He concluded that it would in fact be an instrument for keeping peace by monitoring a system that resembled his conciliation treaties. Unlike the treaty's leading Progressive foes, he increasingly downplayed the league's potential use of force and emphasized its investigative and deliberative roles. As an example of international cooperation, it would help bury the traditional "balance of power" concept that he believed was as outdated "as the arbitrary power of kings." He had maintained, when he was negotiating his conciliation agreements, that a cooling-off period would allow reason to prevail and thus prevent war. He now concluded that the league, as an agency to facilitate discussion, would similarly render conflict unnecessary. Dropping his previous objections to it, he advocated the league's creation, "no matter in what form." Its police powers, in his opinion, would be purely symbolic.[40]

When disagreements over the league brought the Senate and Wilson to an impasse, Bryan broke with the president. Wilson, partially paralyzed by a stroke in September 1919, rejected anything short of unconditional ratification of the treaty. Bryan contended, as he had in 1899 when endorsing the settlement with Spain, that a treaty was essential in order to end the fighting officially. As before, he reasoned that ratification would still allow opportunities to improve upon the peace agreement. On another level, he was anxious to remove the treaty issue from the upcoming 1920 elections lest it distract from domestic reform topics and produce "a sham battle over foreign questions."[41]

In late 1918 and early 1919, he lobbied furiously with members of Congress and implored the sequestered president to accept a compromise settlement. "Bryan has come back," observed Secretary of Interior Franklin Lane. But the Commoner failed to convince either Wilson or his opposition to give ground. In March 1920 the Senate rejected the treaty a second time. That November, when Republican Warren G. Harding defeated Democrat James Cox in the presidential race, Bryan blamed Wilson for laying "the foundation for disaster."[42]

After eight years, the Democrats were again out of power. Bryan's inveterate optimism nevertheless survived. He predicted that the Democratic party, "normally a progressive party," would soon "gather about it the progressive forces of the nation." But William Allen White believed that by 1920 Bryan's place in his party had in fact become "a rather sad, lonely one," and that a new generation was emerging "to whom 1896 was but a tale that is told." Such an assessment did not augur well for Bryan as he prepared for what he called "the coming struggle."[43]

# 8

## AMERICA'S DON QUIXOTE

### (1920–1925)

"The world broke in two in 1922 or thereabouts," wrote novelist Willa Cather, a contemporary of William Jennings Bryan. Although her choice of the year 1922 was purely symbolic, she correctly sensed that American culture was undergoing a profoundly significant transformation, and she filled her fiction with sad tributes to the vanishing virtues of the Great Plains. Similarly, the hate and ugliness that followed the outbreak of war in 1914 had so disillusioned the famed Social Gospel minister Walter Rauschenbusch that he predicted sadly, "I cannot expect to be happy again in my lifetime."[1]

Bryan, in contrast, welcomed the decade of the 1920s. He believed that it was "a glorious period in which to live," and that schoolchildren would come to see it as "some Golden Age of the past and express regret that they did not live their brief span in those days." His words were unintentionally ironic because, as Cather and Rauschenbusch suspected, the United States was changing irrevocably—and in large part at the expense of Bryan's cultural landscape. Walter Lippmann's description of the Commoner as "the true Don Quixote of our politics" was particularly telling by the twenties. According to Lippmann, Bryan moved "in a world that had ceased to exist" and tilted against nothing less than "the modern world" itself. The triumphant new order, with its large economic organizations and growing complexity, "upset the old life of the prairies, made new demands upon democracy, introduced specialization and science . . . destroyed village loyalties . . . and created the impersonal relationships" so different from what Bryan had known.[2]

In the face of such changes, Bryan fought as fiercely as ever to salvage the nation's democratic traditions. Three decades of battling for reform had only strengthened his respect for America's common citizens. No major politician was more dedicated to their rights or sympathetic to their needs.

In January 1920 he outlined "A People's Constitution" at the Nebraska constitutional convention. Among his proposals were prohibitions against monopolies and gambling, the election of judges, a public legal counselor for poor people, improved highways, limits on campaign spending, primary elections, and a single moral standard "enforced impartially against both sexes." Particularly striking was his defense of labor, for which he advocated collective bargaining, a minimum wage, and profit sharing. A wave of strikes following the war, along with considerable public and governmental hysteria against alleged radicalism, had produced an environment unsympathetic to workers' organizations. But, whereas many critics of labor viewed the strikes as products of bolshevism, Bryan was inclined to see management's pursuit of "conscienceless profits" as the primary cause of industrial disputes. He credited labor unions for saving American wage earners from economic serfdom and reminded opponents of workers' organizations that "capital is organized."[3]

In the slumping economy of the early twenties, he also championed farmers and consumers. He attacked the Republican tax reform plan, which dramatically reduced rates for people in the higher income brackets. Such "unblushing piracy" in favor of the manufacturing interests demonstrated that "big business is in control."

Reminding Democrats in 1921 that they must "take the people's side of every question," he sought to ensure the party's commitment to "progressive principles." To accomplish this, he advocated a series of state and regional conventions at which reform Democrats would plan strategies and agendas. He spelled out a "National Legislative Program," a familiar list to those long accustomed to his advocacy of such reforms as banishing monopolies and establishing a referendum on war. Noting that "all the avenues of information are in private hands," he also recommended a bipartisan "National Bulletin" that the government would send free to all libraries, schools, towns, and officials. It would provide factual information about new laws and pending legislation, and would divide editorial space among competing political parties and factions. The time had also arrived, he believed, to establish cabinet departments for health and education.[4]

Now in his sixties, Bryan remained as steadfastly committed to reform as he had been earlier in his career. His perseverance in fighting against "the rule of the rich" was especially significant, given the sagging fortunes of progressivism during the administrations of Warren G. Harding and Calvin Coolidge. It helped to buoy the spirits of bewildered reformers such as William Allen White, who feared that progressivism had lost its energy, and that the nation "was tired of issues, sick at heart of ideals and weary of being noble." Bryan, for example, in one of his many lectures, stunned a respectable gathering of Kansas City realtors with a sharp rebuke: "Stop your stealing! Drive your profiteers out of business!"[5]

Bryan's rhetoric contained its old bite, but by the twenties it had taken on a somewhat ritualistic character. In some respects his responses to problems appeared almost mechanical. According to one observer, Robert Littell, writing for the reform-oriented magazine, the *New Republic*, his style had a "certain wound-up, clock-like quality." Even in private conversation, "he seemed to be addressing a large and attentive audience." Radical journalist John Reed had already noted this tendency during an interview with the Commoner in 1916. Although Reed respected him for having "always been on the side of democracy," he found Bryan's conversational style distracting: "He spoke as a public man, in the careful phrasing of an address. . . . Hardly ever did he say a natural impulsive thing; and when he did, he quickly revised it—made it formal and lifeless." William Allen White observed the same trait and speculated that Bryan "really touched life less and less as the years went by. He spoke more and more as an oracle, and put barriers against intimacies." Even among associates, he sounded too often "like a man in a trance, or masked, who proclaimed his wisdom in high-flown words."[6]

While Bryan, at least to a few people who knew him, seemed increasingly concerned with appearances and effects, some of his actions threatened to turn his progressivism into a pose. In 1919 for example, he associated himself part-time with a Washington, D.C., law firm that specialized in securing American loans for Latin America. This placed him in some unlikely financial circles. At one point he received fees from none other than the Standard Oil Corporation for helping that company and other Americans secure compensation for damages suffered during the Mexican Revolution.

Similarly, Bryan's lecture to the Kansas City realtors against profiteering had a hollow ring given his own real estate ventures. At one point he owned nine houses in five states, including a five-hundred-acre summer place in Asheville, North Carolina. It was to Florida, however, that he turned more and more attention. At least since 1910, he had invested in property there, and in 1912 he had established a winter home on Biscayne Bay so that Mary could escape Nebraska's bitter cold. In 1921, largely because of her failing health, the Bryans made a major decision to change their permanent legal residence from Nebraska to Florida. By then Mary had developed arthritis so badly that she was in constant pain and increasingly an invalid. The move not only took them from the state that for more than three decades had provided Bryan's political base; it also doomed the *Commoner*, which last appeared in April 1923. In Florida, Bryan never himself actually sold real estate, but he became a paid booster for a realtor named George Merrick. In one year alone, Merrick, the developer of Coral Gables, sold almost $100 million worth of property. As a publicist for Merrick's ventures, Bryan received up to $250 per lecture. Standing on a podium overlooking a sunlit pool, and preceding the dancing "shimmy girl," Gilda Gray, he acclaimed the brilliant future of the "Magic City" of Miami.

He was entirely sincere when touting the virtues of Florida, a state that treated him well indeed. In 1925 he sold his Bay Biscayne property for an incredible profit of between two and three hundred thousand dollars and moved to a smaller place in Coconut Grove. Much distressed about rumors that he was now a millionaire, he claimed that he was worth only half that much and was guilty of no more of a "sin" than having his home increase in value because of the economic and population growth of the area.

By the 1920s the man who had once said that no one could honestly earn a million dollars contended that it was possible to "amass five hundred million in a lifetime" and still serve society. His own difficulties in juggling service and profit were perhaps most evident in the syndication of the weekly Bible lessons of his huge, outdoor Sunday school class in Miami. In his opinion, certainly, the over twenty-thousand-dollar annual income he received for his column was not excessive or unreasonable. And syndication allowed him to conduct what he happily described as "the largest Bible class in the world." It nevertheless provided some basis for William Allen White's judgment that he had become "an emeritus statesman," turned "old and fat and seedy."[7]

White's assessment was overly harsh, but age and a fading celebrity status were unquestionably affecting Bryan. So too were problems with diabetes, an illness that was then untreatable. Although his furious schedule suggested that his energy was unflagging, fatigue was also beginning to wear him down.

Bryan's last years, appropriately enough, suggested a great deal about the fate of progressivism, which, in the words of H. L. Mencken, was "now down with the wasting disease." In the mid-1920s an "unsettled and confused" William Allen White decided that "people are deaf to reform," and *Survey* magazine raised the question "What Happened to the Pre-War Radicals?" Progressivism, like Bryan, was showing the effects of age. It was losing its longtime leaders; Theodore Roosevelt died in 1919, and Woodrow Wilson in 1924. Others, such as Frederic Howe, who by 1925 felt "unobligated to movements or to reforms," had grown discouraged with the obstacles to social justice. Some concluded that reform had gone far enough and became staunch defenders of the political status quo against allegedly radical special interest groups such as labor. Bryan, of course, was not among those who had fallen victim to cynicism or who feared "radicalism." As the oracle of "Magic Miami," Bryan had unquestionably developed new interests, but few could doubt his genuinely Progressive credentials within the Democratic party or his continuing dedication to popular rule.

It was especially Bryan's growing concern with cultural issues that aligned his last years with those of progressivism. A striking aspect of politics during the 1920s was the intrusion of matters involving beliefs and ways of life. This development played havoc with the coalition-building processes that had been so essential to Progressive reforms.

Far from being a monolithic movement, progressivism consisted of numerous floating coalitions that gathered around specific causes. The nature of the various coalitions depended on the issues involved. Advocates for tenement housing reforms, for example, included medical professionals worried about public health, moralists alarmed by the apparent spiritual corruption of slum residents, construction industries attentive to new building opportunities, and city boosters concerned that ugly urban settings would drive away customers, tourists, and investors. Similarly, the Pure Food and Drug Act of 1906 had emerged from the joint efforts of doctors and pharmacists attempting to strengthen their professions and to protect the public, of Prohibitionists who opposed the alcoholic content of cure-all medicines, of drug companies desiring national protection against potentially more radical local laws, of muckraking journalists in search of sensational stories, and of politicians hoping to strengthen governmental powers. Such alliances among diverse groups and classes had by 1920 produced a massive amount of legislation at all levels of government.

As cultural issues involving religious values, ethnicity, and personal habits pressed more and more to the surface, coalitions gave way to collisions. Prohibition was a prominent example of this, and an issue with which Bryan had direct experience. His early political successes had owed much to his ability to build a coalition among, for example, reform Democrats and Populists. Yet in 1910, his embracing of Prohibition had shattered Nebraska's Democratic party, separating him— "the Beerless Leader," as some critics called him —from such people as his old Populist ally James Dahlman.

Immigration restriction, another cultural issue, also drove reformers apart. Congressman Fiorello LaGuardia, who represented New York City's immigrant neighborhoods, admired and worked with western Progressives; yet he broke with them over the 1924 Immigration Restriction Act. The act's restrictive quotas discriminated against southern and eastern Europeans—who included LaGuardia's ancestors. He had no sympathy for people who wanted to ensure that "proper" racial types entered America. Observing sardonically that his dog came from "a distinguished family tree," he added that the animal was still "only a son of a bitch." Bryan, however, supported immigration restriction, and not simply because he wanted to protect American workers from cheap immigrant labor. One of the reasons he left Nebraska, for example, was his fear that the state's "large foreign element may not be only against prohibition but other moral issues." Florida was congenial for him in part because he was interested in "a southern state where there is but little of the foreign born element."[8]

At the 1924 Democratic National Convention, Bryan stood at the center of a cultural storm that battered his party. For years, divisions between the southern and western agrarian groups, on the one hand, and the northeastern, urban, immigrant machines on the other, had threatened to tear the party to pieces, and Bryan's many encounters with the New York City press and Tammany Hall politicians had culminated in his 1923 declaration that "no reform ever started in New York."[9] It was to that city that he came a year later as a Florida delegate, and it was there that he endured his most trying moments at the podium.

His first troubles came when he spoke against including in the Democratic platform a specific repudiation of the Ku Klux Klan—a resurgent force in American politics. He had no intention of defending the Klan, whose anti-Catholic and anti-Semitic bigotry he abhorred. But he favored a plank that reaffirmed in general terms the ideal of religious freedom and rejected "any effort to arouse religious or racial dissensions." He saw nothing to gain from singling out the Klan, and feared that such a move would needlessly divide the party. Appealing for unity, he declared that "anybody can fight the Ku Klux Klan, but only the Democratic Party can stand between the common people and their oppressors in this land." His speech elicited furious disapproval from large sections of the audience, and only the scantiest of majorities agreed with him. By a mere one vote the delegates decided not to single out the Klan for special attack. In the meantime, large numbers of foreign-born Americans in the galleries had booed the Commoner roundly.[10]

Bryan's greatest discomfort was yet to come. As the Democrats staggered through 103 ballots to name their presidential candidate, the split between the urban and rural wings of the party widened drastically. From the outset the convention resembled a religious gathering in which warring denominations squared off against each other. Emotions over subjects such as Prohibition ran so strongly that the keynote speaker's reference to the country's need for Paul Revere evoked a storm of protest; angry drys thought he had spoken of the nation's need for "real beer." The choice of the northeastern city faction was New York's governor Alfred E. Smith, an Irish-American Catholic who had grown up in New York City, a man who had worked his way into politics through Tammany Hall, and a staunch foe of Prohibition. His chief opponent was William Gibbs McAdoo, a dry who had served as Woodrow Wilson's secretary of the treasury. "McAdoodledoo," as his critics dubbed him, arrived at the convention saying that New York City (where he had once lived) was corrupt, selfish, greedy, "re-actionary, sinister, unscrupulous, mercenary, and sordid." With the convention deadlocked on the thirty-eighth ballot, Bryan rose to speak. Convinced that Smith represented nothing more than the de-testable liquor, Wall Street, and Tammany Hall factions, he asked the restless and irritable listeners in the convention hall to support McAdoo.

The next few minutes must have been among the most unpleasant in Bryan's life. Boos, jeers, barbed comments such as "Who is paying you?," chants for Smith, and shouts that he was a "hypocrite" and should "get out" continually interrupted him. At one point Montana's senator Thomas Walsh, who was chairing the convention, cleared the galleries in an effort to restore order.

As Bryan, sweat glistening on his face, struggled to combat the hecklers, the contrasts were striking between that moment and the glorious occasion almost three decades earlier when his Cross of Gold speech had electrified the audience. The technology was different for one thing. In 1896 there had not even been a public address system; in 1924 a battery of microphones amplified speeches throughout the hall and also provided a rudimentary national radio hookup. The set-ting and Bryan had also changed. As Arizona's senator Henry Ashurst watched Bryan straining against the noisy opposition, he sadly com-pared the Commoner of '96, "with raven locks and frame of oak," to the person he was now watching—"no longer handsome, eyes like occult jewels . . . a crotchety, crabbed, played-out man." After the convention, a tearful Bryan conceded to Alabama's senator Thomas Heflin that never had he felt such humiliation.[11]

Eventually, the badly fractured Democratic party settled on a com-promise candidate—Wall Street attorney and former West Virginia representative John W. Davis. To the end, Bryan had tried to prevent the selection of Davis because of his legal services for J. P. Morgan. As the convention concluded, a weary Bryan found some solace in the Progressive features of the platform, which he had again helped to write, and in the surprising choice of his brother Charles, governor of Nebraska, as Davis's running mate. During the campaign, the Commoner stumped through fifteen states for the ticket, only to see Republican Calvin Coolidge sweep to victory.

Bryan's observation after the 1924 Democratic debacle that "the sun will shine again" told far more about his personal resiliency than about the troubles still ahead.[12] They existed primarily along the cultural fault line above which Progressive coalitions, the Democratic party, and American politics generally were crumbling. An issue in the twenties that assumed for many people the same highly charged symbolic meaning as, for example, Prohibition, concerned the Darwinian theory of evolution. As religious fundamentalists and "modernists" or "liberals" faced off, Bryan became an adversary of some of his early supporters, including the famed defense attorney Clarence Darrow.

Bryan had first expressed uneasiness about Darwinism around 1905, even though he preferred at the time not to argue the matter. In his famous "Prince of Peace" Chautauqua address, he expressed reservations about the evolutionary theory of creation—at least insofar as it applied to humans. He worried mainly that it would cause people to lose a sense of God's presence and would provide the rationale "by which the strong crowd out and kill off the weak."[13] Obviously aware that John D. Rockefeller and other defenders of the new corporate order were applying Darwin's survival-of-the-fittest ideas to society, he feared the brutalizing effects of Darwinism on political democracy and social justice. Here in his opinion was a major threat to reform. It justified an economic jungle both at home, where a Rockefeller could demonstrate his "fitness" by driving out competition and controlling an industry, and abroad, where nations engaged in deadly struggle and ruthlessly tried to impose their wills on others. The doctrine of the fittest, in Bryan's estimation, encouraged industrial exploitation, war, and imperialism—evils against which he never tired of battling.

Starting around 1915, he viewed Darwinism's baneful effects with growing alarm. His earlier reservations hardened into determined opposition. He found persuasive a Baptist minister's book claiming that German militarism and the resulting world war flowed naturally from what Bryan described as "this doctrine of the strongest." By the 1920s he was saying that Darwinism was "the basis of the world's most brutal war," as well as growing class conflict in industry. It jeopardized Christian faith by substituting unbridled individualism for service and love. "By paralyzing the hope of reform, it discourages those who labor for the improvement of man's condition." In 1921, he devoted an oft-repeated lecture to nothing else but "The Menace of Darwinism."[14]

By then he was convinced that Darwinism was largely responsible not only for the reactionary politics that threatened progressivism, but also for a decline in morality across the nation. Of special concern to him were reports that young people in high schools and colleges were losing their religious faith. He had read with shock the 1916 study by James Leuba, a Bryn Mawr psychology professor, contending that most students entered college believing in a personal God but, "on leaving college, from 40 to 45 percent . . . deny or doubt the fundamental dogmas of the Christian religion." Mary Bryan recalled the impact on him also when a sobbing mother described how her son had "lost his faith." According to Mary, her husband believed staunchly in the separation of church and state, "but his soul arose in righteous indignation" as he read letters from parents claiming that public schools were smothering their children's religious values. In his opinion, this meant that the state was in fact teaching against religion, and that atheists and evolutionists were enjoying something against which democratic reformers had long battled—special privileges. "Convinced," in his wife's words, "that the teaching of evolution as a fact instead of a theory caused the students to lose faith," Bryan resolved to change the situation. "The greatest menace to the public school system today," he told Nebraska's constitutional convention in 1920, "is . . . its Godlessness. We have allowed the moral influences to be crowded out. . . . We cannot afford to have the faith of our children undermined."[15]

"Shall the people rule?" That had been the overarching question of the Commoner's 1908 campaign, and that was the fundamental query he raised again in his crusade against teaching Darwinism as a scientific fact. In a 1925 sermon, "They Have Taken My Lord," he asserted that no one could "rightly demand pay from the taxpayers for teaching their children what they do not want taught. The hand that writes the paycheck rules the school." In this respect, he echoed one of the nation's most cherished political beliefs: the right of popular rule. None other than Bryan's hero, Thomas Jefferson, had warned that "to compel a man to furnish contributions of money for the propagation of opinions which he disbelieves is sinful and tyrannical."[16]

Many academics, scientists, and others who had no quarrel with democracy, were nevertheless appalled at the suggestion that taxpayers should dictate the subject matter of the classroom. This could quickly reduce facts of any kind to majority whim. Walter Lippmann, for example, believed that Bryan's "dogma of majority rule" meant "that all men are equally good biologists before the ballot box." Democracy had itself "become an absurd tyranny" if the assumption was "that the opinion of fifty-one percent is in some high fashion the true opinion of the whole hundred percent." If fifty-one out of one hundred people voted that Darwinian theory was incorrect, it did not mean that they were better biologists; it simply meant "that there are more of them." Lippmann urged that biologists, experts in their field, should decide how to teach biology.[17]

To Bryan, and many Americans who rallied to him, expertise in itself had no magic aura. The Commoner had no grudge against scientists; in his opinion, they had done much to benefit society. As always, however, he remained on guard against elites of any kind that presumed to act or speak for the people. Too many times he had observed self-appointed leaders dismissing and degrading the wisdom of common citizens. In 1896, for instance, advocates of the gold standard had attacked his followers as "the unthinking mass of the Democratic party"—"a mob," representing a "body of ignorance" and "defects of character."[18] So too had "sophisticated" people snickered at humble folk who rattled in wagons over many miles of bumpy roads to attend Chautauqua lectures. And so too did the big-city, eastern journalist H. L. Mencken of Baltimore, one of Bryan's chief critics, lampoon the "booboisie" and the "yokels" of agrarian America.

Bryan wanted the people to be as free from the coercion of what he called "a scientific soviet" as from high society snobs, Wall Street bankers, or disdainful journalists such as Mencken. Scholars had one vote each, the same as anyone else. The Commoner was not willing to let the eleven thousand members of the American Association for the Advancement of Science "dictate to the rest of us. Can a handful of scientists rob your children of religion and turn them out atheists?" Some "109,000,000 people on the other side" would most assuredly not accept this. He agreed with the Catholic editor Benedict Elder, who said that in public schools "the common judgment of the plain people is not to be scorned." Indeed, Bryan could not resist pointing out that many of the scientists had been "educated at the expense of the toiling masses."[19]

Once again, Bryan was digging in social soil that was as emotionally and symbolically rich as free silver had been earlier. In 1896, a compelling question had involved the role of money and wealth in a democracy. By the 1920s, a related issue concerned the power of experts. The issue had haunted America's political culture for almost a century. During the early 1800s, for instance, debates had swirled around the authority of licensed physicians as opposed to practitioners of folk medicine, and religious reformer Alexander Campbell had criticized "clerical aristocrats" who failed to recognize that individuals could on their own discover God's word in the New Testament. As "the common man" became a political and cultural centerpiece in the nineteenth century, celebrations of the wisdom of rank-and-file citizens were everywhere familiar, from elections to popular fiction, melodramas, revival meetings, and P. T. Barnum's famed museums.

The incredible proliferation of specialized knowledge in the decades after Bryan's birth nevertheless posed a serious dilemma. On the one hand, a flood of human benefits flowed from this new knowledge in many areas, ranging from communications and transportation to medicine. Here, indeed, was evidence of progress and reason for optimism; science and learning were opening unprecedented opportunities for social betterment. On the other hand, however, were ominous developments. Between 1870 and 1920 more than two hundred professional societies emerged to serve the needs of educators, attorneys, scientists, medical doctors, social scientists, and other trained experts. This virtual revolution in knowledge and professional expertise raised questions about the prerogatives, domain, and authority of common citizens. By 1923, the Reverend Baxter F. McLendon voiced the fears of many nervous individuals: "This is an age of new things, so many new discoveries—so many new inventions—so many combinations that the people are all at sea."[20]

It was one thing for scientists to apply their new discoveries to technological matters; it was quite another for experts to tread onto the more subjective terrain of values and habits. Walter Lippmann in the 1920s, for example, pointed out some implications that the knowledge explosion had for education. No longer was teaching, in his opinion, a mere matter of passing on to students "a completed body of knowledge." The rapid accumulation of new information rendered knowledge "forever tentative and forever incomplete." As a result, schoolchildren could no longer simply memorize received wisdom; they needed to learn to raise questions. This meant that good teaching had to press beyond transmitting ancient truths; it had "to develop wise habits." Lippmann was excited at the prospects, but many other people worried that the schools would ignore teaching moral basics. Indeed, by the 1920s many Americans were convinced that public education was encouraging moral softness, social permissiveness, and "intellectual flapperism."[21]

At issue ultimately were the claims and wishes of grass-roots Americans in the face of the new expertise. If matters of faith and values also became the domain of experts, what authority still rested with the rank and file? Bryan typically drew the line in the people's defense. "A religion that didn't appeal to any but college graduates," he contended in the 1920s, "would be over the head of 99 percent of our people. The God I worship is the God of the ignorant as well as the God of the learned man." And for Americans who worried that a small band of arrogant intellectuals, full of foreign ideas and un-American ideals, were endangering the nation's most basic beliefs, Bryan advanced his own conspiracy theory. He warned in 1923 not only that scientists hoped "to set up an oligarchy in free America," but, even worse, it would be "the most tyrannical that has been attempted in history."[22]

As Bryan plunged into several southern states on behalf of proposals to ban the teaching of Darwinism as fact, his old ally Clarence Darrow watched sadly. The famed attorney suspected that, deep down, Bryan "was frightened out of his wits lest, after all, the illusions of his life might be only dreams." In that respect, Darrow compared the Commoner to "the traditional boy passing the graveyard at night—he was whistling to keep up his courage."[23]

Darrow sensed correctly that more was at stake for Bryan than the place of Darwinism in the schools. During the 1920's, as in the 1890s, much about America seemed to be coming unstuck. Traditional intellectual and cultural reference points wavered as familiar ways collided jarringly with such developments as the new ethic of commercialism and leisure. "We are unsettled to the very roots of our being," observed

Walter Lippmann perceptively as early as 1914. "There isn't a human
. . . that doesn't move in a strange situation." Most troubling to many
people was "the wreckage of old creeds," broken loyalties, and change
so rapid that it rendered experience a liability. "There are no prece-
dents to guide us," Lippmann wrote, "no wisdom that wasn't made for
a simpler age."[24]

Many Americans anxiously agreed with Lippmann. When Willa
Cather in 1923 viewed Nebraska's history, she commented regretfully
on "the ugly crest of materialism" so apparent—"too much prosperity,
too many moving-picture shows, too much gaudy fiction," and people
more concerned with spending money than earning it, with "buying
things instead of making anything." From her perspective, "the splendid story of the pioneers" was over, and "no new story worthy to take
its place" had commenced. No wonder she believed that the world
had broken in two. Progressive journalist George Creel, who had
spent most of his childhood in small Missouri towns, viewed modern
economic and social trends with similar distaste. "The march of in-
dustrialism," he wrote, had placed machines above the previously independent craftsmen; and the automobile had brought a "plague of
hot-dog stands, filling-stations, 'tourists' homes,' and the obliteration
of boundaries." He lamented the perceived decline of "character" in
American life. In the old days, for example, "when people married
they stayed married, not leaping to another bed at the first irritation
or disagreement, for the home was the keystone in the social arch."
And he mourned the erosion of traditional certainties. Before the on-
slaught of the twentieth century, he believed, "life presented no soul-
tearing problems necessitating a call for psychiatrists, for there were
things that decent people did and things they did *not* do. And all knew
what they were." The poignancy of such references to a lost America
suggested powerfully the deeply felt concerns of many people about
the fate of old values and creeds in the twentieth century.[25]

Change was assuredly not new in American life. Jeremiads to a passing world had been evident since the first generation of colonists. And
while a departed past had stirred anxieties among some Americans,
many others had cheered their country precisely because it seemed
ever new, a place of fresh starts, and a model of progress. The very
word *progressive* attested to the continued faith in benign change, as
did Theodore Roosevelt's "New Nationalism" and Woodrow Wilson's
"New Freedom."

But seldom before the 1920s had change seemed so overpowering, so pervasive, so threatening to familiar values. Agrarian and village America had long felt the encroachments of an urban culture but never so mercilessly as in the twenties. In this context, movements such as those of the revived Ku Klux Klan and religious fundamentalism were in large part products of an endangered culture in recoil. Rural fundamentalists struggled to maintain a sense of community in the face of disrupting forces from the outside. And in the cities themselves, fundamentalism appealed strongly to groups on the margins—primarily among transient, working-class people who, lacking social prestige and political power, tried to find a protected place in the Kingdom of God.

Appropriately enough, Bryan, longtime champion of the nation's underdogs and "losers," was once again ready to stand with them. Since the 1890s he had resisted the emerging corporate economy symbolized by Wall Street and its minions, such as the eastern press. More and more, however, his speeches and writings included another theme: the defense of old cultural certainties against decay and decline.

Along with many Americans, he was apprehensive about the apparent weakening of the traditional moral order, with its firmly established guidelines, its celebration of the work ethic, and its emphasis on self-discipline. As Bryan's own career demonstrated so well, the combined heritages of evangelical faith and the republicanism of the nation's revolutionary era had persisted with remarkable strength into the twentieth century. Basic to republicanism, and bolstered by the evangelical tradition, was a vision of the virtuous citizen—independent, hardworking, self-sacrificing, and alert to the snares of "luxury."

In the emerging urban, commercial world of the twentieth century a massive shift in values was under way. Previously, because of the scarcity of goods and rapid cycles of boom and bust, the ability to "save for a rainy day" had demonstrated good character as well as sound economic sense. But the array and variety of goods in the modern industrial society rendered previously laudable habits such as frugality downright subversive. If people did not take advantage of the new abundance through constant purchases, they could jeopardize the national economy. Moreover, in the emerging consumer economy, buying on credit signified economic approval, not poor planning or a tragic emergency. Benjamin Franklin's once sage advice "A penny saved is a penny earned" might still be a part of folk wisdom, but it was assuredly not what the new advertising industry recommended. From the industrial citadels on New York's Madison Avenue, the word went out that people should not deny themselves comfort and plea-sure. As the twentieth century unfolded, advertising focused less on the quality of products than on the quality of the purchasers' lives— their status, their psychological well-being, and their happiness. In-deed, the new consumer ethic suggested that shopping was an end in itself; it was fun. By 1916 advertisements thus promised that shoppers would find nothing less than "adventure" in Piggly-Wiggly grocery stores.

Other monuments to the new commercial culture included amuse-ment parks such as Coney Island and Atlantic City. Whereas the old-er, producer-oriented culture from which Bryan had come extolled self-control, composure, dignity, and the useful application of one's "leisure" time, the Coney Island ethic was playful, permissive, even reckless. "I AM HAVING A H . . . OF A GOOD TIME AT CONEY ISLAND," read one greeting card. People went there for a holiday from the rules, decorum, and demands of the workplace. The idea was to shed re-straints and to be more relaxed, even in terms of dress. Hence a daring turn-of-the-century postcard showed five young women smiling flir-tatiously as they raised the hems of their bathing dresses to display their stockinged legs. In 1913, one magazine referred to changing sex-ual mores by noting that it was "Sex O'Clock in America."

By the twenties, silent movies were opening an even wider public window onto alternative worlds—worlds often alarmingly risqué to defenders of traditional virtues. Those guardians of morality and so-briety, the Keystone Kops, for example, struggled haplessly against fun-filled and unrestrained adversaries. Comedians such as Charlie Chaplin, Stan Laurel, and Oliver Hardy laid waste to decorum and cultivated manners. And Cecil B. DeMille, in more than fifty films between 1914 and 1929, not only offered peeks into new life-styles but also suggested the pleasures of eroticism as a means of invigorating marriages. Movie posters bearing titles such as Gypsy Blood, Social Secretary, and Pleasure Mad intimated strongly that old expectations of responsibility and respectability were in trouble.

Bryan's concern with the moral tenor of the nation had been evi-dent for several decades. "Have the people returned to the worship of the Golden Calf?" he had wondered in 1899 when he addressed the issue of imperialism. "This republic has not spent its substance in riotous living," he had reminded his audiences. Speaking about "The Old-Time Religion" at the Winona, Indiana, Bible conference in 1911, he lamented that "the abundance of our wealth" had skewed thinking toward "material comforts" and away from the status of the soul.[26]

His legendary sloppiness in dress provided ample evidence of his disdain for what to him was "foolish fashion." He thus urged women to rely upon their "native tenderness" rather than passing styles. Mary Bryan expressed her distaste in 1913 for "the absence of dress above the waist" among some females: "I sat near a young woman at table a few evenings ago and every time she moved I had an awful fear that her right breast would fall out over its very filmy barriers." She could not understand how any real gentleman could respect such an exhibition. If Bryan himself found such attire alluring, he certainly hid his interests well. William Allen White believed that he "seemed not to know that there was another sex than his." White, who had seen him many times in differing circumstances, "never caught in his eye the wayward spark from a hidden fire in his heart."[27]

In Bryan's opinion, people should concentrate their thoughts and efforts on the "power to do good." Anything that detracted from that goal was reprehensible. His recommended New Year's Resolution in a 1917 collection of his essays was to pledge oneself to being more useful: *"To this end I will give up any practice or habit that tends to weaken my body, impair the strength of my mind or lower my moral purpose."* This meant, of course, not drinking liquor. Even "exercise for its own sake," according to one campaign biography, was not part of "Bryan's schedule of living." One of his objections to prizefighting was that "time is too precious for men who are seeking real progress to waste it" in such a brutalizing manner. Similarly, he urged young readers to leave alone "the yellow back novel" and "literary trash" such as "'blood and thunder' Indian and detective stories." For boys he recommended books that were educational, fired "worthy ambitions," emphasized morality, and taught "wholesome lessons without being namby-pamby." Indeed, he claimed that dime novels with their lurid tales had turned some youngsters into criminals.[28]

His major complaint against "the gambling vice" was that it cultivated a something-for-nothing ethic. "The man who becomes addicted to this vice soon ceases to be a producer because he cannot content himself with the slow returns of legitimate effort." This was so on the Wall Street stock exchange, as well as at the card table or race track. "The inventor of the 'gold brick' died penniless recently," Bryan once joked, "but his invention is still being used with great success on Wall Street."[29]

While the Commoner was ever on guard against things harmful to body and morals, he applauded "habits of industry." He urged boys to summon up the self-discipline and will necessary to "transform a sluggish and slothful creature into one alert, quick and active." If they took care of gardens during summer vacations, for example, they could be members of "The Producers' Club." Country youths who grew up on a farm automatically developed the correct "habits of application" in contrast with "the money worshiping portion of the nation's population" who, through greed and cheating, constituted "organized wealth."[30]

Among the greatest threats to the republic was "a corrupting commercialism" that placed getting rich above civic duties. It was "slimily" dragging the family "from dishonor to divorce and back again" amid "the clinking of our gold." This "worship of mammon," this lamentable tendency of a "money-mad" people, allowed plutocracy to run riot. It stirred "the excesses of the purse proud." It was also turning the Sabbath into "a day of merry-making and jollification" and encouraging a stock-gambling "mania" that undermined social obligations. A three-column headline of a 1904 *Commoner* editorial stated that America was being "WARPED BY COMMERCIALISM."[31]

Bryan, reminiscent of republicans such as Samuel Adams and Thomas Paine in the revolutionary era, tended to blame social and economic elites for social corruption. He believed that "speed madness" on the highways was an example of senseless thrill seeking by the "fashionable set." "There is no place in this country for the idle rich," he asserted in 1903. Such people ignored their obligations to society and the needy. They engaged in "high living" for their own "selfish enjoyment" and were "intoxicated with the glitter and pomp of imperialism."[32]

In all of this was a message of simplicity—a message that harkened to the distant past of American culture. Certainly it had been evident in the ideology of republicanism and the Christian social ethic of nineteenth-century evangelicalism; and it had strongly marked the

Populist and Progressive movements. One writer in 1904 had placed the "tyranny of things" next to trusts and urban bosses on the nation's enemy list. Other examples were legion, whether it was Henry Demarest Lloyd, whose *Wealth against Commonwealth* was a reform classic, recommending "a thorough, stalwart resimplication of life"; or the Social Gospel minister Washington Gladden warning against self-indulgence and waste; or economist Thorstein Veblen attacking "conspicuous consumption" and "ostentatious display"; or moral reformer and art professor Irene Sargent stating that personal extravagance produced "rapid degeneration and decay"; or one of the founders of American scouting, Ernest Thompson Seton, who held up "the simple life of primitive times" in contrast to the "money grubbing" and "'city rot'" that were eroding the nation's character; or Theodore Roosevelt, who constantly spurred his patrician counterparts to beware of "a love of ease and luxury." Magazines in the Progessive era were packed with articles against waste, whether on the job or even during leisure time. The Country Life Movement, which got under way in 1908, and the growing concern with conservation also signaled the continuing appeal of the old dream of combining American prosperity with self-denial and civic virtue.[33]

As much as any Progessive, Bryan rejected "too much style" in favor of "a simpler life." On several occasions he recommended *The Simple Life*, a popular book in 1901 by Charles Wagner, a French Protestant minister. Wagner's successful American lecture tour in 1904, at the behest of President Roosevelt, had expanded his already large audience. Bryan believed that the popularity of this "apostle of simplicity" was one sign that the United States was undergoing a "moral awakening."[34]

But as with many Progressives, Bryan's optimism invariably competed with his fears of corruption, irresponsibility, vice, and the loss of old values. In 1906 a writer in the *Outlook* resigned himself to the inexorable march of the new urban, commercial culture; he doubted that the "revolt against wealth as the supreme aim of life" would triumph because "the tendencies in the other direction are far too powerful, the opportunities too tempting." Two years earlier, Bryan had already complained that "one by one the poetic things of life are smashed."[35]

Long before the 1920s, then, Bryan had bemoaned many social and cultural trends in America. On the subject of marriage in an era of growing divorce, he had noted his willingness to seem like an "old fogy." Regarding some of the new advice on child rearing, he had indicated his preference for "the old fashioned methods of the mothers." During an era in which Coney Island symbolized new forms of amusement, he had opposed any kind of enjoyment that might "become a dissipation and consume time that might be better employed" toward "physical perfection, intellectual strength or moral worth." At a time when the new motion pictures carried titles such as *Who's in the Bedroom?* he regretted the death of a legitimate stage actor who "never stooped to the suggestive, but ever strived for cleanliness and morality." And in 1914, when he and his Sunday school class viewed a movie about the biblical Joseph, he recommended the deletion of several sexually explicit scenes.[36]

In his 1916 interview with John Reed, Bryan's discomfort with the developing intellectual world was equally apparent. Despite new forms of art and music, the Commoner adhered resolutely to the familiar sights and sounds of his youth. His favorite music included either traditional hymns or sentimental tunes; his preferred paintings were ones that hung in Young Men's Christian Association buildings; his reading choices came from the Bible, Thomas Jefferson, or George Bancroft. When Reed, mentioning such relatively modern poets as Keats, asked his opinion about literature "that is sheer sensual beauty, without any moral purpose," Bryan wanted to drop the subject.[37]

In a time of great intellectual upheaval, Bryan's compass remained true to the reference points of republican ideology and evangelical Protestantism. Like so many of his generation, he accepted the traditional wisdom that the universe is moral; that desirable consequences flow naturally from good intentions and good deeds; that individuals are rational; that human reason, will, and example are decisive; that religion, economics, and politics are inseparable; that fate is purposeful, not a matter of blind chance; and that events are understandable in personal terms. It was a worldview by which several generations had tried to make sense of themselves and their environment.

Tremors had begun to shake that worldview long before the nineteenth century ended. Some thinkers, having difficulty spotting any direct connection between human motives and what actually happened, began to forge an ironic view. It seemed from this perspective that sometimes, for no particular reason, bad motives in fact produce

good results, while the best of intentions sometimes generate horrendous consequences. Also under growing scrutiny was the assumption,
so essential to Bryan and the cultural tradition from which he came,
that individual character counted. Increasingly, modern thinkers, reflecting the influence of Karl Marx and Sigmund Freud, talked about
historical "forces" or the role of the irrational. And to an emerging
group of modern writers and artists, the old ideal that a narrative or a
painting could capture reality appeared little more than an illusion.
The fragmentation of knowledge, society, and "truth" itself seemed to
require new artistic imperatives and standards. To the despair of Progressives, the new schools of painters and sculptors talked more and
more of art for art's sake, and of the artists' responsibility to their
creative selves, not to morality or society. Here, certainly, was a world
beyond Bryan's comprehension.

Although Bryan was hardly a careful explorer of this developing
cultural continent, he was not oblivious to it. The considerable pub-
licity surrounding the famed Armory Show in 1913, with its modernist
sculpture and paintings, including Marcel Duchamp's much-discussed
*Nude Descending a Staircase,* could hardly have escaped him. And by
the 1920s, a flurry of writings reflective of shifting intellectual dis-
course had started filtering down at least to periodicals such as
*Harper's* and the *Atlantic Monthly.* A young thinker such as Walter
Lippmann concluded by the end of the decade that "the acids of mod-
ernity" were dissolving nothing less than the "feeling of certainty itself." Another, Joseph Wood Krutch, provided a bleak assessment of
"the modern temper." With despair and resignation, Krutch wrote
that civilizations die from trying to act decently "quite as surely as
they die of debauchery," that certitude was nothing more than a
"phantom," and that the human cause was "lost."[38]

Virtually all of William Jennings Bryan's public life had been a fight
against huge, impersonal forces. In his campaigns against the trusts
and imperialism, he had typically resorted to explanations that good
revolutionary republicans such as Sam Adams would have appreciated.
He pointed to conspiracies on the part of designing, selfish individuals, or to the intrusions of "alien" modes of thought, whether from
England's financial district and its commitment to the gold standard,
or from Old World militarism and imperialism. But by around 1916,
he was struggling against more than corrupt individuals and interests
who endangered republican virtue and God's design. He was also

squaring off against a shifting intellectual universe that seemed bent on removing both God and a rational, virtuous citizenry from the center of human affairs.

"The enemy's country," as he called it, was in the end less geographical than cultural and intellectual. Ultimately, it seemed to foster a sensibility that jeopardized not only his own perceptions but, indeed, the very cultural matrix from which he had come. Emotionally, he could not abide a universe of chance and ambiguity. "There is only one side to a moral issue," he liked to say, "and that is the moral side." According to Mary Bryan, "his freedom from doubt" was his great source of strength. "Others might waver, drift, and struggle," she wrote, but he "went serenely on, undisturbed." According to the Omaha *World-Herald*, with which he had once been associated, he seemed immune to life's shadows and uncertainties. "There was in life for him truth and error. They were easily distinguishable. There was no twilight zone in between. Where he stood was truth's side and with all his power he battled for the Lord."[39]

Not surprisingly, he took aim at what he increasingly perceived as the strongest threat to such truth, and the main source of "alien" ideas: Darwinism. "All the ills from which America suffers can be traced back to the teaching of evolution," he emphatically told a group of Seventh Day Adventists in 1924. Given such an interpretation, the zeal of his commitment to what he called "a duel to the death" against Darwinism was entirely predictable. Once again, the Commoner sallied forth to protect the people from an insidious foe that would render them and their ideals irrelevant.[40]

Perhaps because the stakes seemed so high, or perhaps because he was wearing down, his usual good nature, equanimity, and tolerance sometimes gave way to nastiness and even demagoguery. In the early 1920s, when a group of students at Brown University booed him, he uncharacteristically stomped off the platform. When the president of the University of Wisconsin, Edward A. Birge, a zoology professor who was also a deacon of the First Congregational Church and taught a Bible class, took issue with his interpretations of Darwin, Bryan announced snidely that the university should print handbills admitting that "our class rooms furnish an arena in which a brutish doctrine tears to pieces the religious faith of young men and young women; parents of the children are invited to witness the spectacle." Noting that a

Yale professor reputedly turned his students into atheists, Bryan advocated investigating "the effect of some of the things that are taught in these days by those who call themselves scientists." Warming to his subject, he pressed on, insinuating that "a multitude of highly paid teachers" were purveyors of a "sham intelligence that leads men away from God." He inquired into processes of hiring university professors that failed to consider "the strength of their spiritual lives." And, in an unfair jab at Wisconsin's Birge, he said that a young, impressionable college student should "not need to have men like the President of the University of Wisconsin ridicule the beliefs of his father, mother and grandparents." Convinced that organizations such as the National Education Association and the American Library Association were "poisoning young minds" by deliberately extending "anti-Christian propaganda" into the schools, he declared in 1921 that "the supreme need of the day is to get back to God." "To your tents, O, Israel!" he cried.[41]

Over the next several years Bryan resembled a one-man army against Darwinism. He thrilled defenders of the "old-time religion" in various states by speaking and lobbying intensely for laws to ban the teaching of evolution as a scientific truth. He was unquestionably a key motivating force in the drive that produced thirty-seven anti-evolution bills in twenty states during the 1920s. In a two-hour attack on Darwinism before a packed Raleigh, North Carolina, auditorium in 1923, for example, he reportedly "stung Tar Heel Democracy into a frenzy of loyalty." He warned against sending innocent schoolchildren to Darwin's fate: an atheist's grave. Unwilling to defer to so-called scientific experts, he challenged any "son of an ape to match cards" with him. Spurred on by bursts of loud applause, he even claimed that a Kentucky professor who had questioned his intelligence was now unemployed.[42]

In notable ways, his starring role among religious fundamentalists was incongruous. Certainly, like them he believed that religious truths rested on an infallible Bible. Unlike the leadership of such groups as the World's Christian Fundamentals Association, however, he was a political liberal whose religious allies had typically been Social Gospelers devoted to the practical, reform applications of Christianity. As late as 1919 he had called the liberal Federal Council of Churches the "greatest religious organization in our nation"—an interpretation squarely at odds with that of religious conservatives.[43] Yet his growing apprehensions about Darwinism made possible a working alliance, at least on the issue of evolution, with fundamentalists who did not share his Progressive reform commitments.

During the 1920s he aligned himself ever more conspicuously with theological conservatives in the Presbyterian church in opposition to the "modernists." In 1923, he even actively sought the moderatorship of the church's General Assembly, losing by a narrow margin on the third ballot. Less than graceful in defeat, he told reporters that the assembly was in the grasp of the church's "liberal machine"—a religious counterpart to the urban boss system. The machine received support from "the college men," "practically all the evolutionists," and "nearly all of the colored delegates." Refusing to give ground, he threw the gathering into turmoil by introducing a resolution that would prohibit any of the Presbyterian church's educational funds from going to schools or colleges that taught Darwinism as fact "or any other evolutionary hypothesis that links man in blood relationship with any other form of life." When the thousand delegates defeated the resolution by a two-to-one margin, he sank dejectedly to his seat. But when the convention subsequently directed the New York presbytery not to allow regular preaching on the part of Dr. Harry Emerson Fosdick, a leading theological modernist and professor at Union Theological Seminary, Bryan declared "a great victory." Fosdick, whom he had privately described as a religious Jesse James, was now "within reach of our stick."[44]

Such was the backdrop for Bryan's celebrated trip to Dayton, Tennessee, in the summer of 1925 for a courtroom showdown with the forces of materialism, atheism, and elitism. Leaders of the World Christian Fundamentals Association, hoping to take advantage of Bryan's prominence, recruited him as one of the prosecutors in a trial involving Tennessee's new antievolution law. Bryan himself had addressed the state legislature earlier on behalf of the statute, even though he believed the one- to five-hundred-dollar penalty for teaching Darwinian evolution was unnecessary. Certainly he bore no personal malice against John T. Scopes, the young high school instructor who had agreed to teach Darwinism so that opponents of the law could test its constitutionality in the courts. Indeed, Bryan was willing to pay Scopes's fine.

By enlisting Bryan's services, the Christian Fundamentals Association was in some ways simply hoping to use the Commoner's famous name. But he was no one's pawn. Insofar as popular opinion judged him the nation's leading fundamentalist voice, he exerted his own influence, keeping fundamentalism at least somewhat open to reform politics and the Social Gospel.

Just as his presence influenced the fundamentalist movement, it also transformed the famed "monkey trial" into a national media event. From the moment he arrived in tiny Dayton, some forty miles north of Chattanooga, the Scopes trial was front-page news. The anticipated confrontation between the Commoner and the battery of well-known defense attorneys, including Dudley Field Malone, Arthur Garfield Hays, and—most prominently—Clarence Darrow, piqued public interest even beyond the United States. This was exactly what the shrewd local promoters in Dayton had hoped would happen. They knew that the town's slumping economy could benefit from outside attention.

From the outset, the trial was thus a staged affair—for Dayton's entrepreneurs, the contending sides in the case, and the press. Scopes himself was the high school's athletic coach; as only a substitute biology teacher, he was not even sure he had been teaching evolution on the day of his arrest. The press, well aware of the popular appeal of the "monkey trial," converged on the area. Around two hundred reporters and sixty-five telegraph operators were on hand, along with a radio hookup for the first national broadcast of an American trial. Also present were numerous tourists, various cranks, and novelty peddlers, hawking such items as stuffed cotton monkeys. A group of Holy Rollers shouted, "Thank God I got no education. Glory be to God."

Bryan, a pith helmet sheltering him from the sun, wandered Dayton's dusty streets before the trial, enjoying enormous affection and local support. One young reporter who interviewed him over breakfast observed that the years were taking their toll. He noted the Commoner's bulging midriff and the bald head that "glistened in the early morning light." As the journalist looked at Bryan's thin, tightly pressed lips, he recalled stories about the man's mouth being so wide that he "could whisper in his own ear."[45]

But Bryan was not in Dayton to whisper. He was there to thunder against the "Godlessness" that he had identified as public education's worst threat, and on behalf of what he defined as the central issue of the trial: the right of people in a democracy to determine what their children learn in school. "Our purpose and our only purpose," he said on the eve of the trial, "is to vindicate the right of parents to guard the religion of their children." The question, quite simply, was "who shall control our public schools?" He hoped the trial would help to educate the people, in whose hands he believed the decision ultimately rested, about the issues involved.[46]

Unfortunately for Bryan, the trial ended without that issue receiving much attention and on a considerably lower plane of debate than he had advocated. This was partly his own fault, as his speech on the fifth day demonstrated. In the stifling heat of the crowded third-floor courtroom, he rose, trembling and agitated. For over an hour he delivered a lengthy statement asking the court to prohibit expert testimony from scientists regarding evolution and the law. Because Tennessee's citizens had spoken through their legislature, Bryan argued that "it isn't proper to bring experts in here to try to defeat the purpose of the people of this state." He soon resorted to the mannerisms of the Chautauqua tent, addressing the audience as "my friends," and eliciting applause and shouts of "amen." Prior to the trial, he had suggested that the issue of evolution might not even be involved in the case. Now, however, he brought it front and center. He ridiculed "the absurdities of Darwinism" and defended the authority of the Bible on such subjects as the virgin birth and Christ's resurrection.[47]

Although Bryan returned to his seat with the audience clearly on his side, the reply of defense attorney Dudley Field Malone brought him up short. The Commoner's flicking palm-leaf fan was perhaps as much a sign of his discomfort with Malone's impassioned remarks as it was a defense against the heat and flies. For twenty minutes Malone, who had worked in the State Department under Bryan, respectfully but forcefully took his "old chief and friend" to task. He chided Bryan, who in his opinion had been one of the nation's greatest moral forces, for unbecoming attacks on America's underpaid teachers. He spotted a double standard in the objections of Bryan, himself not a citizen of Tennessee, to outsiders entering the state to discuss the issues. He suggested that Bryan misrepresented many scientists who in fact were God-fearing church members, trying with conviction and honesty to reconcile science and religion. And he intimated that Bryan, deep down, feared that the people would make the wrong choice. Malone assured him that "the truth always wins and we are not afraid of it." Placing himself on the side of "fundamental freedom in America," Malone asked several times, "Where is the fear?" The audience that Bryan had rendered spellbound now responded enthusiastically to Malone. The Commoner himself was obviously moved. When the court adjourned for the day, he approached his former assistant. "Dudley," he said, "that was the greatest speech I have ever heard." Malone's response was both touching and poignant. "Thank you, Mr. Bryan, I am sorry that it was I who had to make it."[48]

Four days later, on Monday, 20 July, the trial deteriorated into a judicial circus. With the court now meeting on the courthouse lawn, Bryan, in a bizarre turn of events, took the witness stand to testify about the truth of the Bible. Under the merciless grilling of Darrow, the Commoner began to lose his composure. As Darrow baited him with queries about the literal truth of such scriptural accounts as Jonah and the whale, the rattled Bryan lurched to his feet, objecting to his antagonist's "slurring of the Bible." Darrow, shaking his fist in Bryan's face, shouted back, "I am examining you on your fool ideas that no intelligent Christian on earth believes."

In retrospect, Darrow wrote that Bryan had resembled "a wild animal at bay," lunging in a desperate attempt "to get even with an alien world." Recalling his earlier enthusiasm for the Commoner, Darrow regretted that Bryan had become "the idol of all Morondom." But he shrugged off any second thoughts about his harsh courtroom treatment of his former political ally by remembering how Bryan "had busied himself tormenting intelligent professors with impudent questions about their faith, seeking to arouse the ignoramuses and bigots to drive them out of positions." Mary Bryan was furious at Darrow's "abusive" treatment of her husband, but she privately conceded that William's performance on the witness stand had "made him appear more ignorant than he is."[49]

Bryan had hoped to have the last word during the final summations and, in fact, viewed his prepared comments as his life's "mountain peak." But Darrow, by waiving the defense's right to offer a closing argument, shrewdly denied him the opportunity to make his statement. From the beginning, of course, the defense had not intended to prove Scopes's innocence, but instead to overturn the antievolution law in an appeal to a higher court. Eventually, the Tennessee Supreme Court overruled Scopes's hundred-dollar fine on a technicality but left the antievolution statute alone.

The Commoner was not around for the outcome. On 26 July, five busy days after the Dayton trial ended, he died in his sleep while taking an afternoon nap. Shortly before, he and Mary had discussed what she described as "the narrow margin" separating a legitimate defense of religion, as well as the people's right to govern, from "an encroachment on individual religious belief." Bryan, confident that he could respect that thin line, indicated that he intended to keep up the good fight.[50]

To the end he had no doubts that he spoke for the great majority of Americans. "My dear brother Bryan," a resident of Smackover, Arkansas, had written him during the Scopes trial, "fight them evolutions until hell freezes over and then give them a round on the ice. God bless you."[51]

Not everyone, of course, had been so supportive. The Commoner had also been the target of savage criticism, especially from H. L. Mencken. The rural-baiting journalist from Baltimore had ridiculed him as a fraud, a "buffoon," a preacher of "theological bilge," "a zany," "a peasant come home to the barnyard," and "a tinpot pope in the coca-cola belt." But Bryan could take comfort in knowing that Mencken had also labeled Tennessee's hill people as "morons," "hillbillies," "gaping primates of the upland valleys," and "one-horse, village" hicks who enjoyed "the tune of cocks crowing on the dunghills." In fact, a week before he died, Bryan had reassured the plain folk at a Sunday evening gathering in Pikeville, Tennessee, that they would outlast the reporters who viewed them condescendingly as yokels and bigots. Characteristically, the Commoner found in that audience what many others missed: "a humanity" with its own worth and dignity.[52]

As William Allen White observed, he always had a "curious instinct" for sensing "when things were wrong." That instinct had again and again guided him into the camps of people anxious about the future—people worried that events were rendering them superfluous.[53]

On another level, of course, despite his own fame and remarkable success, he knew something himself about losing. Born midway through one century, he died as another was taking shape. A son of devout parents from Illinois farm country, and the product of a nineteenth-century, village setting, he had taken seriously the lingering

202

values of America's republican ideology and evangelical faith. He had struggled to put into practice oft-spoken national ideals that affirmed the virtues of democracy, the common people, and those who demonstrated the "habits of industry." To his death he had battled plutocracy and privilege. The emerging economy of large-scale corporations, commercialism, and a consumer ethic had baffled and worried him. Bryan wanted it to be different.

And so too would have most of the thousands of people who in late July 1925 watched a special funeral train carrying the Commoner's body to its final resting place in Arlington National Cemetery. As the sun rose over the Tennessee hills, the train started its trek to the nation's capital. All day and through the night, at stations and along the tracks, plainly dressed country people paused sadly in tribute to the man who had in so many ways been their advocate. They had lost a friend. And, although they may not have realized it, they were mourning the end of an era as well.

# CHRONOLOGY

| | |
|---|---|
| 19 March 1860 | William Jennings Bryan born in Salem, Illinois. |
| 1875–1881 | Schooling at Whipple Academy and Illinois College, Jacksonville, Illinois. |
| 1881–1883 | Law school, Union College of Law, Chicago. |
| 1883–1887 | Practices law in Jacksonville. |
| 1 October 1884 | Marries Mary Baird. |
| 1 October 1887 | Moves to Lincoln, Nebraska. |
| 1890 | Elected to U.S. House of Representatives. |
| 1892 | Reelected to House of Representatives. |

| | |
|---|---|
| 1894 | Chooses not to seek third term in House; unsuccessful Democratic nominee for Senate. |
| 1896 | Cross of Gold speech; receives Democratic and Populist nominations for president; loses election to William McKinley. |
| 13 July 1898 | Becomes colonel in Nebraska's Third Regiment during Spanish-American War. |
| 10 December 1898 | Resigns from military service on day the United States and Spain sign treaty. |
| 1900 | Receives Democratic presidential nomination; loses election to McKinley. |
| 1901 | Founds the *Commoner*. |
| 1904 | Plays major role at Democratic convention. |
| September 1905–August 1906 | World tour. |
| 1908 | Receives Democratic presidential nomination; loses election to William Howard Taft. |
| 1910 | Actively joins Prohibition movement. |
| 1912 | Plays major role at Democratic convention. |
| 1913–1915 | Secretary of state. |
| 8 June 1915 | Resigns as secretary of state out of concern that the United States is headed toward war. |
| 8 June 1915–6 April 1917 | Works strenuously as private citizen to keep United States out of war. |
| 1917–1919 | Works in support of U.S. war effort and Progressive reforms such as Prohibition and woman suffrage. |
| 1919–1920 | Advocates ratification of Versailles treaty and U.S. entry into League of Nations. |

# NOTES AND REFERENCES

### INTRODUCTION: THE GHOST AT THE CONCERT

1. Quotation in Ferenc Szasz, "William Jennings Bryan, Evolution, and the Fundamentalist-Modernist Controversy," *Nebraska History*, 56 (Summer 1975): 275.

2. White quoted in Dixon Merritt, "Bryan at Sixty-Five," *Outlook*, 140 (3 June 1925): 182.

### 1. FORMATIVE YEARS (1860–1887)

1. William Jennings Bryan, *The Memoirs of William Jennings Bryan* (New York: Haskell House, 1925), 10.

2. Bryan, *Memoirs*, 11, 13; Roosevelt quoted in Lawrence W. Levine, *Defender of the Faith, William Jennings Bryan: The Last Decade, 1915–1925* (New York: Oxford University Press, 1965), 246; Mary Bryan in *Memoirs*, 454.

3. William Lee Miller, "The Seminarian Strain," *New Republic*, 9 July 1984, 18.

4. Bryan, *Memoirs*, 40, 90, 246–48.

5. Bryan, *Memoirs*, 10; William Jennings Bryan, *The First Battle: A Story of the Campaign of 1896* (Chicago: W. B. Conkey, 1896), 57; Bryan, *Speeches of William Jennings Bryan*, 2 vols. (New York: Funk & Wagnalls, 1909), 1:67.

6. Herndon quoted in Paxton Hibben, *The Peerless Leader: William Jennings Bryan* (New York: Farrar & Rinehart, 1929), 59.

7. John Thomas, *Alternative America: Henry George, Edward Bellamy, Henry Demarest Lloyd and the Adversary Tradition* (Cambridge: Harvard University, 1983), 5, 13; Cushing Strout, *The New Heavens and New Earth: Political Tradition in America* (New York: Harper & Row, 1974), 53–55, 226; Mary Baird Bryan, "Life of William Jennings Bryan by His Wife," in *First Battle*, by Bryan, 34–35.

8. Bryan, *Memoirs*, 22–26, 34–35, 41.

9. Bryan, *Memoirs*, 17, 40, 43; Louis W. Koenig, *Bryan: A Political Biography of William Jennings Bryan* (New York: Putnam's, 1971), 23.

10. Bryan, *Memoirs*, 17–18, 241–42.

11. Bryan, *Memoirs*, 52–56.

12. Don Harrison Doyle, *The Social Order of a Frontier Community: Jacksonville, Illinois, 1825–70* (Urbana: University of Illinois Press, 1978), 138.

13. Bryan, *Memoirs*, 13. Doyle, *The Social Order of a Frontier Community*, 255–59, on "inverted boosterism."

14. Mary Baird Bryan, "Life of William Jennings Bryan," 40.

15. Mark Twain in Carl S. Smith, *Chicago and the American Literary Imagination 1880–1920* (Chicago: University of Chicago Press, 1984), 1.

16. Kipling in Smith, *Chicago and the American Literary Imagination*, 158; Bryan to Mary, 29 January 1882, quoted in *Memoirs*, 228.

17. Quotation in Koenig, *Bryan*, 43.

18. Quotations in Hibben, *Peerless Leader*, 101, and Bryan, *Memoirs*, 63.

## 2. POLITICAL BEGINNINGS (1887–1892)

1. Quotation in R. Hal Williams, *Years of Decision: American Politics in the 1890s* (New York: Wiley, 1978), 45.

2. Bryan to Mary, 3 April 1891, in *Memoirs*, 225–26

3. Quotation in Stanley B. Parsons, *The Populist Context: Rural vs. Urban Power on a Great Plains Frontier* (Westport, Conn.: Greenwood Press, 1973), 17.

4. Quotations in H. Roger Grant, *Self-Help in the 1890s Depression* (Ames: Iowa State University Press, 1983), 4, and Raymond Arsenault, *The Wild Ass of the Ozarks: Jeff Davis and the Social Bases of Southern Politics* (Philadelphia: Temple University Press, 1984), 32.

5. Quotation in Bruce Palmer, *"Man Over Money": The Southern Populist Critique of American Capitalism* (Chapel Hill: University of North Carolina Press, 1980), 21.

6. Quotations in O. Gene Clanton, *Kansas Populism: Ideas and Men* (Lawrence: University Press of Kansas, 1969), 68; Palmer, *"Man Over Money,"* 16, 37.

7. Quotation in Parsons, *The Populist Context,* 69.

8. Palmer, *"Man Over Money,"* 3–49, 71–80; quotations 31–32, 76.

9. Bryan, *Memoirs,* 456, on the mission; Levine, *Defender of the Faith,* 218.

10. Quotations in Robert C. McMath, Jr., *Populist Vanguard: A History of the Southern Farmers' Alliance* (Chapel Hill: University of North Carolina Press, 1975), 10–11.

11. Bryan quoted in Eric F. Goldman, *Rendezvous with Destiny: A History of Modern American Reform* (New York: Knopf, 1952; rev. reprint ed., 1977), 50–51; Palmer, *"Man Over Money,"* 36, on a "Bryan Populist."

12. Harold I. Ickes, *The Autobiography of a Curmudgeon* (New York: Reynal & Hitchcock, 1943; reprint ed., Chicago: Quadrangle, 1969), 78.

13. Quotations in Williams, *Years of Decision,* 7, 46.

14. Quotations in Clanton, *Kansas Populism,* 77, 190–91.

15. Leon W. Fuller, "Colorado's Revolt Against Capitalism," *Mississippi Valley Historical Review* 21 (December 1934): 345–46.

16. Bryan, *Speeches,* 1:6, 73.

17. Ibid., 22–23, 36, 40, 43, 61.

18. Ibid., 53, 60, 68–69, 71, 74.

19. Quotation in Koenig, *Bryan,* 95.


### 3. "FIRST BATTLE" (1893–1896)

1. Quotations in Smith, *Chicago and the American Literary Imagination,* 110–11.

2. Quotation in Williams, *Years of Decision,* 54.

3. Walter Lippmann, *Drift and Mastery* (New York: Mitchell Kennerly, 1914; reprint ed., Englewood Cliffs, N.J.: Prentice-Hall, 1961), 135.

4. Morgan quoted in J. Rogers Hollingsworth, *The Whirligig of Politics: The Democracy of Cleveland and Bryan* (Chicago: University of Chicago Press, 1963), 26.

5. Quotation in Goldman, *Rendezvous with Destiny*, 33. Bryan was referring to an ancient but rare custom by which some Hindu women drowned one of their children at the mouth of the Ganges to fulfill religious vows. See R. C. Majumdar, et al., *An Advanced History of India* (London: Macmillan, 1958), 822.

6. Editor in Paolo E. Coletta, *William Jennings Bryan: Political Evangelist, 1860–1908* (Lincoln: University of Nebraska Press, 1964), 75; Morton in Koenig, *Bryan*, 110.

7. Bryan, *First Battle*, 76–121.

8. Quotation in Williams, *Years of Decision*, 95.

9. Quotation in Robert W. Cherny, *A Righteous Cause: The Life of William Jennings Bryan* (Boston: Little, Brown & Co., 1985), 47.

10. Twain quoted in Gordon S. Wood, "Politics without Party," *New York Review of Books*, 10 October 1984, 20.

11. Quotations in Hollingsworth, *Whirligig of Politics*, 26–27.

12. Bryan, *Memoirs*, 106–7, 110.

13. Wilson in Williams, *Years of Decision*, 109; Cleveland in Hollingsworth, *Whirligig of Politics*, 42; minister in Stanley L. Jones, *The Election of 1896* (Madison: University of Wisconsin Press, 1964), 213; Whitney in Robert F. Durden, *The Climax of Populism: The Election of 1896* (Lexington: University Press of Kentucky, 1965), 18–19.

14. Coletta, *Political Evangelist*, 132–33.

15. Bryan, *Memoirs*, 113–15; Coletta, *Political Evangelist*, 139.

16. Ickes, *Autobiography*, 78.

17. Josephus Daniels, *Editor in Politics* (Chapel Hill: University of North Carolina Press, 1941), 165.

18. Ray Stannard Baker, *American Chronicle* (New York: Scribner's, 1945), 61–63.

19. William Allen White, *The Autobiography of William Allen White* (New York: Macmillan, 1946), 278.

20. Thomas quoted in Gilbert C. Fite, "Election of 1896," in *History of American Presidential Elections*, ed. Arthur Schlesinger, Jr., and Fred L. Israel, 4 vols. (New York: Chelsea House, 1971), 2: 1808; McKinley in Williams, *Years of Decision*, 112–113.

21. Quotation in Clanton, *Kansas Populism*, 186.

22. Watson in Williams, *Years of Decision*, 114.

23. Watson in Hollingsworth, *Whirligig of Politics*, 66; Lease in Clanton, *Kansas Populism*, 282n.

24. Quotations in Durden, *The Climax of Populism*, 24–25.

25. Quotation in Jones, *The Election of 1896*, 250.

26. Donnelly in Martin Ridge, *Ignatius Donnelly: The Portrait of a Politician* (Chicago: University of Chicago Press, 1962), 357.

27. Newspaper quotation in Durden, *The Climax of Populism*, 70; Lloyd quoted in Koenig, *Bryan*, 217.

28. Weaver in Bryan, *First Battle*, 276–79; convention vote in *New York Times*, 26 July 1896. Durden, *The Climax of Populism*, 42–43, and Jones, *The Election of 1896*, 258–59, refute the "conspiracy" interpretation, but see Peter H. Argersinger, *Populism and Politics: William Alfred Peffer and the People's Party* (Lexington: University Press of Kentucky, 1974), 263–66.

29. Clanton, *Kansas Populism*, 171–83.

30. Argersinger, *Populism and Politics*, esp. 302–11; Donnelly, 265.

31. Weaver in Bryan, *First Battle*, 279; on Waite, James Edward Wright, *The Politics of Populism: Dissent in Colorado* (New Haven: Yale University, 1974), 183–210; Darrow in Jones, *The Election of 1896*, 253; on Debs, Nick Salvatore, *Eugene V. Debs, Citizen and Socialist* (Urbana: University of Illinois, 1982), 158.

32. Durden, *The Climax of Populism*, 79–80.

33. White, *Autobiography*, 278–79.

34. "The Political Menace of the Discontented," *Atlantic Monthly*, 77 (October 1896): 447.

35. Quotations in Dixon Wecter, *The Hero in America: A Chronicle of Hero-Worship* (New York: Scribner's, 1941), 368–71.

36. White, *Autobiography*, 279; Wecter, *The Hero in America*, 368.

37. McMath, *Populist Vanguard*, 62–64, 75–76, 81; Peter H. Argersinger, "Pentecostal Politics in Kansas: Religion, the Farmers' Alliance, and the Gospel of Populism," *Kansas Quarterly* 1 (Fall 1969): 24–35; Palmer, "Man Over Money," 22–27, 126–37.

38. Quotations in Argersinger, "Pentecostal Politics in Kansas," 27, 29–31, 35.

39. Richard Reeves, "The Ideological Election," *New York Times Magazine*, 19 February 1984, 26, on the big vs. little guys theme; Lease in Clanton, *Kansas Populism*, 77; Nebraska Populist in Jones, *The Election of 1896*, 4–5.

40. Bryan, *First Battle*, 304, 319, 354, 365, 446, 467, 560, 589, 594–96.

41. Bryan, *First Battle*, 560; James Turner, "Understanding the Populists," *Journal of American History* 67 (September 1980): 354–73.

42. Newspaper quoted in Clanton, *Kansas Populism*, 189; Bryan, *First Battle*, 344, 467.

43. Conservative opposition in Coletta, *Political Evangelist*, 162, 172, and in Bryan, *First Battle*, 471–76; Norton in Durden, *The Climax of Populism*, 114.

44. Cather in Don M. Wolfe, *The Image of Man in America*, 2d ed.

(New York: Crowell, 1970), 221; description quoted in Goldman, *Rendezvous with Destiny*, 50; Altgeld in Durden, *The Climax of Populism*, 135n.

45. Bryan, *First Battle*, 594; Donnelly in Durden, *The Climax of Populism*, 163. Lawrence Goodwyn, *Democratic Promise: The Populist Moment in America* (New York: Oxford University, 1976), on populism as a "movement culture." Goodwyn, however, sharply dismisses Bryan's place within that culture.

46. Bryan, *First Battle*, 205, 378.

47. Quotations in Bryan, *First Battle*, 452, 578.

48. McKinley in Williams, *Years of Decision*, 116, and Coletta, *Political Evangelist*, 167.

49. Bryan, *First Battle*, 617–18, 625.

50. Hill in Matthew Josephson, *The Politicos, 1865–1896* (New York: Harcourt, Brace, 1938), 687; Bryan, *First Battle*, 617–18.

51. Bryan, *First Battle*, 617–18.

52. W. Lance Bennett and William Haltom, "Issues, Voter Choice, and Critical Elections," *Social Science History* 4 (November 1980): esp. 392–14; McKinley quotations, 408–10; Bryan in Fite, "Election of 1896," 1822.

53. Gilbert C. Fite, "William Jennings Bryan and the Campaign of 1896: Some Views and Problems," *Nebraska History* 47 (September 1966): 247–64; quotation, 262.

54. Roosevelt quoted in James MacGregor Burns, *The Power to Lead: The Crisis of the American Presidency* (New York: Simon & Schuster, 1984), 136.

55. John Wanant and Karen Burke, "Estimating the Degree of Mobilization and Conversion in the 1890s: An Inquiry into the Nature of Electoral Change," *American Political Science Review* 76 (June 1982): 360–70.

## 4. STUMBLING TOWARD THE TWENTIETH CENTURY (1897–1900)

1. Quotations in Koenig, *Bryan*, 266, 271.

2. Quotation in Robert W. Cherny, "Anti-Imperialism on the Middle Border, 1898–1900," *Midwest Review* 1 (1979): 23.

3. Quotation in Robert Dallek, *The American Style of Foreign Policy* (New York: Knopf, 1983), 12.

4. Quotation in William Jennings Bryan, *Republic or Empire?: The Philippine Question* (Chicago: Independent Co., 1899), 9.

5. Quotation in Bryan, *Republic or Empire*, 48.

6. Quotations in Bryan, *Republic or Empire*, 12; Koenig, *Bryan*, 283.

7. Koenig, *Bryan*, 285.

8. Quotations in Bryan, *Republic or Empire*, 13, and J. R. Johnson, "Imperialism in Nebraska, 1898–1904," *Nebraska History* 44 (1963): 145.

9. Hoar quoted in E. Berkeley Tompkins, *Anti-Imperialism in the United States: The Great Debate, 1890–1920* (Philadelphia: University of Pennsylvania Press, 1970), 176; Bryan in *Republic or Empire*, 15, 55.

10. Hoar in Goran Rystad, *Ambiguous Imperialism: American Foreign Policy and Domestic Politics at the Turn of the Century* (Stockholm: Scandinavian University Books, 1975), 241–42.

11. Quotation in Tompkins, *Anti-Imperialism in the United States*, 203.

12. Morton quoted in Johnson, "Imperialism in Nebraska," 147; Dawes quoted in Coletta, *Political Evangelist*, 244.

13. On Indiana, see Rystad, *Ambiguous Imperialism*, 86–139.

14. William Jennings Bryan, "The Issue for 1900," *North American Review* 170 (June 1900): 753–71.

15. Ally quoted in Rystad, *Ambiguous Imperialism*, 184; Bryan in Koenig, *Bryan*, 296.

16. Quotations in William Jennings Bryan, *The Second Battle* (Chicago: W. B. Conkey, 1900), 160–61, 168, 170, and Rystad, *Ambiguous Imperialism*, 179, 184.

17. Quotations in Rystad, *Ambiguous Imperialism*, 137, 170, 202.

18. Tompkins, *Anti-Imperialism in the United States*, 140–60.

19. Quotations in Johnson, "Imperialism in Nebraska," 148; Rystad, *Ambiguous Imperialism*, 270, 279.

20. Breidenthal's quotation in Cherny, "Anti-Imperialism on the Middle Border," 28; Bryan's in Walter LaFeber, "Election of 1900," in *History of American Presidential Elections*, 3: 1890.

21. Altgeld in Koenig, *Bryan*, 328; Bryan in LaFeber, "Election of 1900," 1883.

22. Creelman quoted in Rystad, *Ambiguous Imperialism*, 179; on Mary Bryan, Coletta, *Political Evangelist*, 260.

23. Coletta, *Political Evangelist*, 259.

24. Roosevelt quoted in Rystad, *Ambiguous Imperialism*, 201.

25. "Acceptance Speech by William Jennings Bryan, Indianapolis, August 8, 1900," in *History of American Presidential Elections*, 3: 1943–56.

26. Bryan, *Second Battle*, 202.

27. Bryan, *Speeches*, 1: 9–16.

28. William Jennings Bryan, *First Battle*, 93, 95, 372–73, 432–33, 476–77, 561.

29. Bryan, *Speeches*, 2: 15–16.

30. Bryan quoted in Arthur B. Ogle, "Above the World: William Jennings Bryan's View of the American Nation in International Affairs," *Nebraska History* 61 (Summer 1980): 164, and in "Acceptance Speech, August

8, 1900," 1947; David Healy, *US Expansionism: The Imperialist Urge in the 1890s* (Madison: University of Wisconsin Press, 1970), 119, on Lodge and Theodore Roosevelt.

31. Roosevelt's quotation in Rystad, *Ambiguous Imperialism*, 225–26.

32. William Jennings Bryan, *Letters to a Chinese Official* (New York: McClure, Phillips & Co. 1906), 45–46; poem in Richard E. Welch, Jr., *Response to Imperialism: The United States and the Philippine-American War, 1899–1902* (Chapel Hill: University of North Carolina Press, 1979), 102.

33. Bryan in *History of American Presidential Elections*, 3: 1948; Clark in Rystad, *Ambiguous Imperialism*, 49.

34. Bryan, *Speeches*, 2: 8; "Acceptance Speech, August 8, 1900," 3: 1946, 1951, 1953.

35. Bryan, *Republic or Empire*, 63, 85.

36. Bryan, *Republic or Empire*, 17, 23–24.

37. Bryan, "Acceptance Speech, August 8, 1900," 3: 1953.

38. White quoted in LaFeber, "Election of 1900," 3: 1884.

39. "Acceptance Speech by President William McKinley, Canton, Ohio, July 12, 1900," in *History of American Presidential Elections*, 3: 1938–42.

40. Stuart Creighton Miller, *"Benevolent Assimilation": The American Conquest of the Philippines, 1899–1903* (New Haven: Yale University Press, 1982), 141–43; John Morgan Gates, *Schoolbooks and Krags: The United States Army in the Philippines, 1898–1902* (Westport, Conn.: Greenwood, 1973), 163, 173; Daniels quoted in Koenig, *Bryan*, 331.

41. "Acceptance Speech by President William McKinley," 3: 1940; Hay quoted in Coletta, *Political Evangelist*, 283.

42. Roosevelt quotations in Rystad, *Ambiguous Imperialism*, 274; Edmund Morris, *The Rise of Theodore Roosevelt* (New York: Coward, McCann & Geoghegan, 1979), 552; Lewis L. Gould, *The Presidency of William McKinley* (Lawrence: Regents Press of Kansas, 1980), 229; Hanna in Koenig, *Bryan*, 341.

43. Quotations in LaFeber, "Election of 1900," 3: 1903; Koenig, *Bryan*, 332.

44. George Creel, *Rebel at Large: Recollections of Fifty Crowded Years* (New York: Putnam's, 1947), 56; Hay quoted in Coletta, *Political Evangelist*, 276.

45. Roosevelt quoted in William Allen White, *Masks in a Pageant* (New York: Macmillan, 1928), 256, and Hollingsworth, *The Whirligig of Politics*, 180.

46. Quotations in Koenig, *Bryan*, 341, 344.

47. E. A. Ross, *Seventy Years of It: An Autobiography* (New York: Appleton-Century, 1936), 62.

48. Herbert Croly, *The Promise of American Life* (1909; reprint ed., Cambridge, Mass.: Harvard University Press, 1965), 169.

49. Quotations in Daniel B. Schirmer, *Republic or Empire: American Resistance to the Philippine War* (Cambridge, Mass.: Schenkman, 1972), 219; Ray Ginger, *Altgeld's America, 1890–1905* (1958; reprint ed., Chicago: Quadrangle Books, 1965), 340.

## 5. PROGRESSIVE LEADER (1901–1908)

1. Bryan, *Letters to a Chinese Official,* 47–48.

2. Quotations in William Allen White, *Autobiography,* 431–32; Justin Kaplan, *Lincoln Steffens, A Biography* (New York: Simon & Schuster, 1974), 23; Frederic C. Howe, *The Confessions of a Reformer* (1925; reprint ed., Chicago: Quadrangle, 1967), 17, 55; Bryan, *Memoirs,* 232.

3. Sinclair quoted in Kaplan, *Lincoln Steffens,* 117–18.

4. Bryan, *Memoirs,* 227; Bryan, *Letters to a Chinese Official,* 73, 76–77, 79, 88–89; Willard H. Smith, "William Jennings Bryan and the Social Gospel," *Journal of American History* 53 (June 1966): 54.

5. Ferenc M. Szasz, "The Stress on 'Character and Service' in Progressive America," *Mid-America* 63 (October 1981): 145–56. Bryan quotations in Franklin Modisett, ed., *The Credo of the Commoner* (Los Angeles: Occidental College, 1968), 10, 14–15, and Bryan, *Speeches,* 2: 241, 285.

6. Richard L. Metcalfe, ed., *The Real Bryan* (Des Moines, Iowa: Personal Help Publishing Co., 1908), 87–89; on Ruth Bryan, Koenig, *Bryan,* 361.

7. Quotation in *Commoner,* 23 January 1901, 7.

8. William Allen White, *Masks in a Pageant,* 265.

9. Quotations in John Whiteclay Chambers II, *The Tyranny of Change: America in the Progressive Era, 1900–1917* (New York: St. Martin's, 1980), 61, 123.

10. *Commoner,* 23 January 1901, 1; *The Credo of the Commoner,* ed. Modisett, 43–44, 50, 53–54; Cherny, *A Righteous Cause,* 186.

11. Bryan, *Speeches,* 2: 165, 169, 178; Levine, *Defender of the Faith,* 198–99.

12. Bryan, *Memoirs,* 249–50, on the Utah experience.

13. Silas in Cherny, *A Righteous Cause,* 15; Bryan in Willard H. Smith, *The Social and Religious Thought of William Jennings Bryan* (Lawrence, Kans.: Coronado Press, 1975), 54, 58; on Washington, Miller, "Benevolent Assimilation," 123.

14. Quotation on reform in Levine, *Defender of the Faith,* 226.

15. Bryan, *Memoirs*, 145; *The Credo of the Commoner*, ed. Modisett, 93–94; Coletta, *Political Evangelist*, 309.

16. *Commoner*, 23 January 1901, 1, 5.

17. Charles Edward Russell, *Bare Hands and Stone Walls: Some Recollections of a Side-Line Reformer* (New York: Scribner's, 1933), 299–317.

18. Ibid., 319–20.

19. Harry P. Harrison, *Culture under Canvas: The Story of Tent Chautauqua* (New York: Hastings House, 1958), 156, 158; Bryan quoted in "On the Chautauqua Circuit," reprinted, from the July 1916 *Lyceum Magazine*, in *Commoner*, November 1916, 28.

20. Harrison, *Culture under Canvas*, 157–58, 162–64.

21. Ibid., 157–61; Bryan, *Memoirs*, 287–88.

22. White, *Masks in a Pageant*, 261, 264, 268.

23. Quotations in Page Smith, *America Enters the World: A People's History of the Progressive Era and World War I* (New York: McGraw-Hill, 1985), 76–77, 80, 92.

24. See, e.g., his more famous Chautauqua addresses, "The Value of an Ideal" and "The Prince of Peace," in Bryan, *Speeches*, 2: 235–90.

25. Quotation in William Harbaugh, "Election of 1904," in *History of American Presidential Elections*, 3: 1974.

26. Congressman quoted in Koenig, *Bryan*, 371.

27. Bryan quotations in Hollingsworth, *The Whirligig of Politics*, 208–9; Coletta, *Political Evangelist*, 311–12; Koenig, *Bryan*, 359, 366, 373; John B. Wiseman, "Dilemmas of a Party Out of Power: The Democracy, 1904–1912" (Ph.D. diss., University of Maryland, 1967), 22; on Telluride, Stephen W. Sears, et al., *Hometown U.S.A.* (New York: American Heritage Publishing Co., 1975), 216–17; Flagg in Horace Samuel Merrill and Marion Galbraith Merrill, *The Republican Command, 1897–1913* (Lexington: University Press of Kentucky, 1971), 172–73.

28. Quotations in Harbaugh, "Election of 1904," 3: 1978–79; Creel, *Rebel at Large*, 56.

29. Bryan, *Memoirs*, 146–52; other quotations in Wiseman, "Dilemmas of a Party Out of Power," 37–38, and in Koenig, *Bryan*, 383.

30. Harbaugh, "Election of 1904," 3: 1976–77; Bryan, *Speeches*, 2: 50–62.

31. Cleveland in Harbaugh, "Election of 1904," 3: 1984; Bryan, *Memoirs*, 154–55.

32. Bryan, *Memoirs*, 156; White in Paul Glad, *The Trumpet Soundeth: William Jennings Bryan and His Democracy, 1896–1912* (Lincoln: University of Nebraska Press, 1960), 158.

33. Quotation in Harbaugh, "The Election of 1904," 3: 1994.

34. Bryan in Glad, *The Trumpet Soundeth*, 161; White, *Autobiography*, 390, 428; German in Smith, *America Enters the World*, 97–98.

35. White, *Autobiography*, 281–82, 388–89.

36. Roosevelt in Glad, *The Trumpet Soundeth*, 90, and Harbaugh, "Election of 1904," 3: 1966.

37. Newspaper quoted in Wiseman, "Dilemmas of a Party Out of Power," 50; Bryan in William Jennings Bryan, "The Future of the Democratic Party," *Outlook* 78 (19 December 1904): 927; in Glad, *The Trumpet Soundeth*, 162, and in Lewis L. Gould, *Reform and Regulation: American Politics, 1900–1916* (New York: Wiley, 1978), 127.

38. Bryan, *Speeches*, 2: 63–91.

39. Russell, *Bare Hands and Stone Walls*, 237.

40. Quotations in Richard L. McCormick, "The Discovery That Business Corrupts Politics: A Reappraisal of the Origins of Progressivism," *American Historical Review* 86 (April 1981): 263–64.

41. Arsenault, *The Wild Ass*, 47, 63–72; Bryan, *Speeches*, 2: 89; David Sarasohn, "The Democratic Surge, 1905–1912: Forging a Progressive Majority" (Ph.D. diss., University of California, Los Angeles, 1976), 43.

42. Croly, *The Promise of American Life*, 158; quotations on race in Wiseman, "Dilemmas of a Party Out of Power," 77; Roosevelt in Merrill and Merrill, *The Republican Command*, 231.

43. Bryan, *Speeches*, 2: 92–99, 138–40.

44. Quotations in Wiseman, "Dilemmas of a Party Out of Power," 96.

45. Sarasohn, "The Democratic Surge," 74–76.

46. Quotation in Wiseman, "Dilemmas of a Party Out of Power," 115.

47. Bryan, *Speeches*, 2: 100–19.

48. Coletta, *Political Evangelist*, 423.

49. Brisbane quoted in Josephus Daniels, *Editor in Politics* (Chapel Hill: University of North Carolina Press, 1941), 550; Croly, *The Promise of American Life*, 157; White, *Autobiography*, 509.

50. Bryan quotation in Howe, *Confessions of a Reformer*, 132.

51. Bryan, *Speeches*, 2: 120–42; Coletta, *Political Evangelist*, 428, on Rockefeller.

52. Bryan, *Speeches*, 2: 143–63.

53. Daniels, *Editor in Politics*, 548.

54. Quotations in Sarasohn, "The Democratic Surge," 95; Paolo E. Coletta, "Election of 1908," in *History of American Presidential Elections*, 3: 2084; Gould, *Regulation and Reform*, 82–83.

55. Koenig, *Bryan*, 454.

56. Ickes, *Autobiography*, 46.

57. Ibid., 50.

58. Quotations in Sarasohn, "The Democratic Surge," 106–7; Bryan in Cherny, *A Righteous Cause*, 171.

## 6. POLITICAL MISSIONARY (1909–1914)

1. Howe, *Confessions*, 131.
2. Riis quoted in Paul Boyer, *Urban Masses and Moral Order in America, 1820–1920* (Cambridge, Mass.: Harvard University Press, 1978), 176.
3. Bryan quotation in Bryan, *Memoirs*, 306; Mary, 334.
4. Ibid., 205–6; *Commoner*, 5 September 1902, 2–3; Harrison, *Culture under Canvas*, 162.
5. Bryan quoted in Koenig, *Bryan*, 76.
6. Quoted in Bryan, *Memoirs*, 290.
7. Quotation on the Tract in Boyer, *Urban Masses and Moral Order*, 25; Lincoln and other quotations in Norman H. Clark, *Deliver Us from Evil: An Interpretation of American Prohibition* (New York: Norton, 1976), 3, 22.
8. Miner's quotation in Thomas J. Noel, *The City and the Saloon: Denver, 1858–1916* (Lincoln: University of Nebraska Press, 1982), 85.
9. Raymond Robins, "Prohibition, Why, How, Whither," undated ms. in Herbert Hoover Presidential Library, West Branch, Iowa, Name File, Box 927.
10. *Commoner*, November 1914, 1, and 19 November 1909, 1; Robins, "Prohibition, Why, How, Whither."
11. *Commoner*, 18 February 1910, 1.
12. Bryan quotations in Paolo E. Coletta, *William Jennings Bryan: Progressive Politician and Moral Statesman, 1909–1915* (Lincoln: University of Nebraska Press, 1969), 10, 13–14; Levine, *Defender of the Faith*, 109–10.
13. Quotation in *Commoner*, 13 February 1901, 5.
14. Quotations in Coletta, *Progressive Politician*, 15, and Koenig, *Bryan*, 472.
15. Mary Bryan in Bryan, *Memoirs*, 327; White, *Autobiography*, 328–29.
16. Quotation in Koenig, *Bryan*, 466.
17. Newspaper and Gore in Wiseman, "Dilemmas of a Party Out of Power," 152, 168.
18. Bryan's letter to Clark in Bryan, *Memoirs*, 163; Clark's response in Coletta, *Progressive Politician*, 33; other quotations in Wiseman, "Dilemmas of a Party Out of Power," 201, 203.
19. Quotation in Sarasohn, "The Democratic Surge," 204.
20. Bryan, *Memoirs*, 159.

21. Wilson quotations in Coletta, *Progressive Politician*, 27–29, 39, and Glad, *The Trumpet Soundeth*, 168; McAdoo in Sarasohn, "The Democratic Surge," 242.

22. Bryan, *Memoirs*, 160; William Jennings Bryan, *A Tale of Two Conventions* (New York: Funk & Wagnalls, 1912), 81, 84.

23. Bryan, *Tale of Two Conventions*, 201–2, 206; White, *Autobiography*, 477–78, 480.

24. Bryan, *Tale of Two Conventions*, 112, 114, 118–19, 148, 150–51, 158–59.

25. Bryan quotations in Coletta, *Progressive Politician*, 57, and Bryan, *Memoirs*, 170; Bryan, *Tale of Two Conventions*, 152, on the telegrams.

26. Sladen quoted in Sarasohn, "The Democratic Surge," 266–67; Bryan in *Tale of Two Conventions*, 167, 206.

27. Bryan, *Memoirs*, 176; Bryan, *Tale of Two Conventions*, 172–75; listener quoted in Glad, *The Trumpet Soundeth*, 171; Bryan quoted in Page Smith, *America Enters the World*, 326.

28. James M. Cox, *Journey through My Years* (New York: Simon & Schuster, 1946), 133; Bryan, *Memoirs*, 177; Koenig, *Bryan*, 490.

29. Bryan quoted in Smith, *America Enters the World*, 328.

30. Wilson quoted in John Milton Cooper, Jr., *The Warrior and the Priest: Woodrow Wilson and Theodore Roosevelt* (Cambridge, Mass.: Harvard University Press, 1983), 181; reporter in Sarasohn, "The Democratic Surge," 271–72.

31. Quotation in Arthur S. Link, *Wilson: The New Freedom* (Princeton, N.J.: Princeton University Press, 1956), 7.

32. House in ibid., 9; David F. Houston, *Eight Years with Wilson's Cabinet, 1913 to 1920*, 2 vols. (New York: Doubleday, 1926), 1: 60.

33. Bryan in Coletta, *Progressive Politician*, 136; Wall Street quotation in Link, *Wilson: The New Freedom*, 216.

34. Wilson quoted in Coletta, *Progressive Politician*, 135.

35. Quotations in Link, *The New Freedom*, 104, 114.

36. Criticisms quoted in Rachel West, *The Department of State on the Eve of the First World War* (Athens: University of Georgia Press, 1978), 28–30.

37. Quotations in Coletta, *Progressive Politician*, 99; Bryan, *Memoirs*, 302.

38. Bryan, *Memoirs*, 188.

39. *Nation* quoted in West, *The Department of State*, 36; Mark Sullivan, *Our Times*, 6 vols. (New York: Scribner's, 1926–35), 5: 149; Page in Smith, *America Enters the World*, 406.

40. Quotations in West, *The Department of State*, 32, 71, 74.

41. Quotations in ibid., 35, 74.

42. Quotations in William Jennings Bryan, *Republic or Empire*, 10; Richard Challener, "William Jennings Bryan," in *An Uncertain Tradition: American Secretaries of State in the Twentieth Century*, ed. Norman A. Graebner (New York: McGraw-Hill, 1961), 92; Koenig, *Bryan*, 515.

43. On the Czar, Bryan, *Memoirs*, 317; on teaching the natives, *The Real Bryan*, ed. Metcalfe, 248–50.

44. Bryan quoted in Charles D. Tarlton, "The Styles of American International Thought: Mahan, Bryan, and Lippmann," *World Politics* 17 (1965): 598; Bryan, *Republic or Empire*, 18, 49; Houston, *Eight Years with Wilson's Cabinet*, 1: 66.

45. Bryan, *Memoirs*, 359.

46. Wilson in Arthur S. Link, *Woodrow Wilson: Revolution, War, and Peace* (Arlington Heights, Ill.: AHM, 1979), 10; Bryan to Wilson, 28 October 1913, in Bryan, *Memoirs*, 359–60.

47. Bryan to Woodrow Wilson, 28 October 1913, in *William Jennings Bryan: Selections*, ed. Ray Ginger (Boston: Bobbs-Merrill, 1967), 159–60; and quotation in Lloyd C. Gardner, *Safe for Democracy: The Anglo-American Response to Revolution, 1913–1923* (New York: Oxford University Press, 1985), 42.

48. Mary in Bryan, *Memoirs*, 356.

49. Quotations in Kendrick A. Clements, *William Jennings Bryan: Missionary Isolationist* (Knoxville: University of Tennessee Press, 1982), 85, 89.

50. Quotations in Coletta, *Progressive Politician*, 207; Clements, *Missionary Isolationist*, 95; D. H. Lawrence, *Studies in Classic American Literature* (1923; reprint ed., New York: Viking, 1951), 59.

51. Quotation in Koenig, *Bryan*, 503.

52. Quotation in Link, *The New Freedom*, 282.


## 7. PEACE, WAR, AND REFORM (1914–1920)

1. Bryan quoted in Ogle, "Above the World," 165.

2. On Bryan and San Francisco, *Commoner*, 7 December 1906, 2.

3. Roosevelt quoted in Cooper, *The Warrior and the Priest*, 277; *New York Times*, 27 June 1914.

4. Quoted in Bryan, *Memoirs*, 390.

5. Quotations in *Commoner*, June 1915, 3; July 1915, 2.

6. Bryan quoted in Bryan, *Republic or Empire*, 63; Watson in John Milton Cooper, Jr., *The Vanity of Power: American Isolationism and the First World War, 1914–1917* (Westport, Conn.: Greenwood, 1969), 186.

7. Kenyon quoted in Cooper, *Vanity of Power*, 108.

8. Bryan quoted in Coletta, *Progressive Politician*, 264, and Merle

Curti, *Bryan and World Peace,* Smith College Studies in History 16 (Northampton, Mass: Smith College, 1931), 192.

9. Bryan quotation in Bryan, *Memoirs,* 421; Page in Ernest R. May, "Bryan and the World War, 1914–1915" (Ph.D. diss., University of California, Los Angeles, 1951), 408.

10. Quotations in Coletta, *Progressive Politician,* 341; William G. McAdoo, *Crowded Years, the Reminiscences of William G. McAdoo* (Boston: Houghton-Mifflin, 1931), 336.

11. Houston, *Eight Years with Wilson's Cabinet,* 1: 146.

12. Roosevelt quoted in Cooper, *The Warrior and the Priest,* 271–72; Lane in May, "Bryan and the World War," 434; McAdoo in *Crowded Years,* 336; cartoon in Mark Sullivan, *Our Times,* 5: 157.

13. Quotations in Cooper, *The Warrior and the Priest,* 290, and Levine, *Defender of the Faith,* 24–25.

14. *Commoner,* July 1915, 2, 11.

15. Ibid., 11.

16. Ibid., 11–12.

17. *Commoner,* October 1915, 1.

18. Norris quoted in Cooper, *Vanity of Power,* 197; war profits statistics in David P. Thelen, *Robert La Follette and the Insurgent Spirit* (Boston: Little, Brown & Co., 1976), 129.

19. Quotations in Bryan, *Memoirs,* 432; Koenig, *Bryan,* 554.

20. White, *Autobiography,* 508–10.

21. Bryan in Levine, *Defender of the Faith,* 22, 55, and John Reed, "Bryan on Tour," *Collier's,* 20 May 1916, 12.

22. Quotation in Curti, *Bryan and World Peace,* 234.

23. Bryan quotation in Bryan, *Speeches,* 1: 75–76.

24. Wilson quoted in Levine, *Defender of the Faith,* 57; Bryan in Curti, *Bryan and World Peace,* 236.

25. *Times* in Curti, *Bryan and World Peace,* 237.

26. *New York Times,* 23 April 1916.

27. Quotations in Koenig, *Bryan,* 565; Levine, *Defender of the Faith,* 79.

28. Wilson quoted in Link, *Wilson: Revolution, War, and Peace,* 67.

29. Bryan quoted in Levine, *Defender of the Faith,* 89; Norris and La Follette in Walter A. Sutton, "Bryan, La Follette, Norris: Three Mid-Western Politicians," *Journal of the West* 8 (1969): 625–27.

30. Bryan quoted in Cooper, *Vanity of Power,* 168, and Paolo E. Coletta, *William Jennings Bryan, Political Puritan, 1915–1925* (Lincoln: University of Nebraska Press, 1969), 55.

31. Lindbergh quotation in Bruce L. Larson, *Lindbergh of Minnesota:*

A *Political Biography* (New York: Harcourt, Brace, Jovanovich, 1973), 204–5; Bryan in Levine, *Defender of the Faith*, 94–95.

32. Quotations in Allan M. Brandt, *No Magic Bullet: A Social History of Venereal Disease in the United States since 1880* (New York: Oxford University Press, 1985), 58, 101, 109, 118.

33. *Commoner*, November 1917, 1; Bryan quoted in Coletta, *Political Puritan*, 57, 59.

34. William Jennings Bryan, "A Single Moral Standard," *Collier's*, 13 March 1920, 7; Wilson quotation in Koenig, *Bryan*, 572.

35. Bryan, *Memoirs*, 506.

36. Quotations in Koenig, *Bryan*, 558.

37. Quotations in William Jennings Bryan, "Why I Am for Prohibition," *Independent*, 17 July 1916, 89, and Levine, *Defender of the Faith*, 115–17.

38. Quotations in William Jennings Bryan, "Prohibition," *Independent*, 19 May 1917, 332, and Levine, *Defender of the Faith*, 119, 124–25.

39. Quotation in Coletta, *Political Puritan*, 85.

40. Quotations in ibid., 88.

41. Quotation in ibid., 94.

42. Lane quoted in ibid., 96; Bryan in Koenig, *Bryan*, 591.

43. White, *Masks in a Pageant*, 271–72; Bryan quoted in Koenig, *Bryan*, 592, and Levine, *Defender of the Faith*, 175.


## 8. AMERICA'S DON QUIXOTE (1920–1925)

1. Cather quoted in Warren Susman, *Culture as History: The Transformation of American Society in the Twentieth Century* (New York: Pantheon, 1984), 105; Rauschenbusch in Strout, *The New Heavens and New Earth*, 243.

2. William Jennings Bryan, "A Single Moral Standard," 36; Lippmann, *Drift and Mastery*, 80–81.

3. Levine, *Defender of the Faith*, 197, 199, on labor quotations.

4. Koenig, *Bryan*, 598, on Democrats; William Jennings Bryan, "A National Bulletin," *Forum* 65 (April 1921): 455, on the press.

5. White, *Autobiography*, 597; quotation on realtors, Levine, *Defender of the Faith*, 195.

6. Robert Littell, "The Commoner," *New Republic*, 17 February 1926, 361; John Reed, "Bryan on Tour," 43; White, *Masks in a Pageant*, 276.

7. Bryan quotations in Hibben, *The Peerless Leader*, 374, and Koenig, *Bryan*, 593; White, *Masks in a Pageant*, 274, 276.

8. LaGuardia in Arthur Mann, *LaGuardia: A Fighter against His Times*,

*1882–1933* (Philadelphia: Lippincott, 1959), 187–89; Bryan in Coletta, *Political Puritan,* 116.

9. Quotation in Levine, *Defender of the Faith,* 293.

10. Plank and Bryan quotations, ibid., 310, 312.

11. Ashurst quoted in Koenig, *Bryan,* 624.

12. Bryan quoted in Levine, *Defender of the Faith,* 321.

13. Bryan, *Speeches,* 2: 269.

14. Quotations in Levine, *Defender of the Faith,* 262; Ferenc M. Szasz, *The Divided Mind of Protestant America, 1880–1930* (University, Ala.: University of Alabama Press, 1982), 109, 129.

15. Leuba quoted in Smith, *Social and Religious Thought,* 187; Mary Bryan in Bryan, *Memoirs,* 459, 479; Bryan in Koenig, *Bryan,* 606.

16. Bryan quoted in C. Allyn Russell, *Voices of American Fundamentalism: Seven Biographical Studies* (Philadelphia: Westminster Press, 1976), 182; Jefferson in Robert A. Garson, "Political Fundamentalism and Popular Democracy in the 1920's," *South Atlantic Quarterly* 76 (Spring 1977): 232.

17. Walter Lippmann, *Men of Destiny* (New York: Macmillan, 1927), 55, 58–59.

18. Quotation in "The Political Menace of the Discontented," 449–51.

19. On the "scientific soviet," Levine, *Defender of the Faith,* 289; on scientists dictating, Allen Birchler, "The Anti-Evolution Beliefs of William Jennings Bryan," *Nebraska History* 54 (1973): 550; Elder in Paul Carter, "The Fundamentalist Defense of the Faith," in *Change and Continuity in Twentieth-Century America: The 1920's,* ed. John Braeman et al. (Columbus: Ohio State University Press, 1968), 201; *Commoner,* January 1923, 2, on the "toiling masses."

20. McLendon quoted in Willard B. Gatewood, Jr., ed., *Controversy in the Twenties: Fundamentalism, Modernism, and Evolution* (Nashville: Vanderbilt University Press, 1969), 5.

21. Lippmann in ibid., 251–52; "intellectual flapperism," 219.

22. Quotations in Szasz, *The Divided Mind of Protestant America,* 133–34.

23. Clarence Darrow, *The Story of My Life* (New York: Scribner's, 1932), 250.

24. Lippmann, *Drift and Mastery,* 92–93.

25. Willa Cather, "Nebraska: The End of the First Cycle," *Nation,* 5 September 1923, 238; Creel, *Rebel at Large,* 24.

26. For Bryan on the "golden calf," Bryan, *The Second Battle,* 99, 101; at Winona, George M. Marsden, *Fundamentalism and American Culture: The Shaping of Twentieth-Century Evangelicalism, 1870–1925* (New York: Oxford University Press, 1980), 133–34.

27. "A Serious Indictment," *Commoner*, 14 November 1902, 43; Mary quoted in Coletta, *Progressive Politician*, 99n; White, *Autobiography*, 510.

28. William Jennings Bryan, *Heart to Heart Appeals* (New York: Revell, 1917), 49; on exercise, quotation in Paul F. Boller, Jr., *Presidential Campaigns* (New York: Oxford University Press, 1984), 190; on prizefighting, *Commoner*, 1 July 1910, 1; on literature, ibid., 3 January 1902, 5; 7 November 1902, 2; 18 March 1904, 4.

29. *Commoner*, 31 May 1901, 3; 24 March 1905, 3; 17 May 1901, 6.

30. *Commoner*, 19 June 1903, 2; 14 August 1903, 30; Bryan, *Heart to Heart Appeals*, 181.

31. *Commoner*, 18 January 1907, 4; 22 February 1901, 6; 15 January 1907, 2; 8 April 1904, 3.

32. *Commoner*, 5 September 1902, 6; 23 October 1903, 1–2; 5 June 1903, 2.

33. Quotations in David E. Shi, *The Simple Life: Plain Living and High Thinking in American Culture* (New York: Oxford University Press, 1985), 177–78, 185, 207.

34. *Commoner*, 5 June 1902, 2; 25 January 1907, 2.

35. Quotations in Shi, *The Simple Life*, 213; *Commoner*, 27 May 1904, 19.

36. Quotations in *Commoner*, 10 March 1905, 2; 23 January 1903, 5; May 1914, 5; 8 May 1903, 16.

37. Reed, "Bryan on Tour," 45.

38. Walter Lippmann, *A Preface to Morals* (New York: Macmillan, 1929), 19–20; Joseph Wood Krutch, *The Modern Temper* (1929; reprint ed., New York: Harcourt, Brace & World, 1956), 31, 126, 169.

39. Bryan quoted in Levine, *Defender of the Faith*, 120; Mary in Bryan, *Memoirs*, 457; *World-Herald* in Smith, *Social and Religious Thought*, 214.

40. Quotations in Richard Hofstadter, *Anti-Intellectualism in American Life* (1963; reprint ed., New York: Vintage Books, 1966), 125, and Coletta, *Political Puritan*, 239.

41. *Commoner*, June 1921, 3; August 1921, 2.

42. Quotations in Willard B. Gatewood, Jr., *Preachers, Pedagogues, and Politicians: The Evolution Controversy in North Carolina, 1920–1927* (Chapel Hill: University of North Carolina Press, 1966), 99–100.

43. Quotation in Szasz, *Divided Mind of Protestant America*, 113.

44. Quotations in Robert Moats Miller, *Harry Emerson Fosdick: Preacher, Pastor, Prophet* (New York: Oxford University Press, 1985), 121–22.

45. W. B. Ragsdale, "Three Weeks in Dayton," *American Heritage* 26 (1975): 39.

46. Quotations in Hofstadter, *Anti-Intellectualism in American Life*, 125; Levine, *Defender of the Faith*, 331, 341.

47. *The World's Most Famous Court Trial: Tennessee Evolution Case* (Cincinnati: National Book Co., 1925), 172, 175.

48. *The World's Most Famous Court Trial*, 183–88; Malone and Bryan in Koenig, *Bryan*, 646.

49. Darrow, *The Story of My Life*, 249, 267, 276–77; Mary Bryan in Coletta, *Political Puritan*, 269.

50. Mary in Bryan, *Memoirs*, 485–86.

51. Dixon Wecter, *The Hero in America*, 374.

52. Mencken in Coletta, *Political Puritan*, 256–57, Russell, *Voices of American Fundamentalism*, 186, and Marsden, *Fundamentalism and American Culture*, 187.

53. White, *Masks in a Pageant*, 277.

# BIBLIOGRAPHIC ESSAY

Primary and secondary materials on William Jennings Bryan are voluminous. His autobiography *The Memoirs of William Jennings Bryan* (New York: Haskell House, 1925) has notable strengths and weaknesses. He died before finishing it, so two-thirds of the contents are in fact Mary Baird Bryan's reflections on her husband's life and brief selections from his speeches and letters. Although it conveys something of Bryan's personality and includes important basic information, especially about his early life, it is necessarily incomplete, and often raises more questions than it answers.

Many of his speeches and writings are in published form. William Jennings Bryan, *Speeches of William Jennings Bryan*, 2 vols. (New York: Funk & Wagnalls, 1909), contains a useful biographical sketch written by Mary Baird Bryan as well as some forty selections. These include his major statements in Congress as well as significant early political and Chautauqua speeches, such as "The Value of an Ideal" and "The Prince of Peace." *Heart to Heart Appeals* (New York: Revell, 1917) is one of several anthologies that he compiled that contain additional segments from his political and Chautauqua writings and addresses. Ray Ginger, ed., *William Jennings Bryan: Selections* (Indianapolis:

Bobbs-Merrill, 1967), has snippets of varying lengths from a variety of Bryan's essays and speeches. For the years between 1896 and 1908, Richard Metcalfe, ed., *The Real Bryan* (Des Moines, Iowa: Personal Help Publishing Co., 1908), similarly provides a wide-ranging assortment of excerpts.

From 1901 until 1923, an indispensable source is the *Commoner*, Bryan's newspaper; it is full of information about his activities and includes his major addresses. Published weekly until 1913, and then monthly until 1923, it is also an essential document of Progressive reform. Although Bryan did not write all the editorials or essays, they clearly reflect his thinking. Franklin Modisett, ed., *The Credo of the Commoner* (Los Angeles: Occidental College, 1968), uses brief segments from the paper, and also from the *Memoirs* and a few other writings, to illustrate Bryan's philosophy and opinions on subjects ranging from religion to labor, the income tax, and the Philippines.

William Jennings Bryan, *The First Battle: A Story of the Campaign of 1896* (Chicago: W. B. Conkey, 1896), is an invaluable collection of documents that includes substantial extracts from many of Bryan's campaign speeches, as well as Mary Bryan's brief biographical sketch of her husband. *The Second Battle* (Chicago: W. B. Conkey, 1900) is much less satisfying. It is an uneven collection that recycles large chunks of *The First Battle* and includes little on the 1900 campaign itself. Around eighty pages of *Republic or Empire?: The Philippine Question* (Chicago: Independence Company, 1899) is an anthology of his speeches and writings during 1898–99 on American expansion, but the bulk of the book consists of the works of other leading antiimperialists. A *Tale of Two Conventions* (New York: Funk & Wagnalls, 1912) is Bryan's rendition of the 1912 Democratic and Republican conventions and includes useful excerpts from speeches, magazines, and newspapers. His *Letters to a Chinese Official, Being a Western View of Eastern Civilization* (New York: McClure, Phillips & Co., 1906), provides excellent insights into Bryan's Americanism; it is also an interesting example of Progressive reform thought.

Essays by contemporaries that are particularly insightful about Bryan are in William Allen White, *Masks in a Pageant* (New York: Macmillan, 1928); Walter Lippmann, *Drift and Mastery* (New York: Mitchell Kennerley, 1914; reprint ed., Englewood Cliffs, N.J.: Prentice-Hall, 1961), and *Men of Destiny* (New York: Macmillan, 1927); Herbert Croly, *The Promise of American Life* (New York: Macmillan, 1909; reprint ed., Cambridge, Mass.: Harvard University Press, 1965); John Reed, "Bryan on Tour," *Collier's*, 20 May 1916, 11–12, 40–47; Charles E. Merriam, *Four American Party Leaders* (New York: Macmillan, 1926); and Edward G. Lowry, *Washington Close-Ups: Intimate Views of Some Public Figures* (Boston: Houghton-Mifflin, 1921). William Allen White, *The Autobiography of William Allen White* (New York: Macmillan, 1946), includes much good information on Bryan. Other memoirs with useful material on Bryan and the times include Clarence Darrow, *The Story of*

*My Life* (New York: Scribner's, 1932); Frederic C. Howe, *The Confessions of a Reformer* (New York: Scribner's, 1925; reprint ed., Chicago: Quadrangle, 1967); Ray Stannard Baker, *American Chronicle: The Autobiography of Ray Stannard Baker* (New York: Scribner's, 1945); Josephus Daniels, *Editor in Politics* (Chapel Hill: University of North Carolina Press, 1941); George Creel, *Rebel at Large: Recollections of Fifty Crowded Years* (New York: Putnam's, 1947); and Harold I. Ickes, *The Autobiography of a Curmudgeon* (New York: Reynal & Hitchcock, 1943; reprint ed., Chicago: Quadrangle, 1969).

Among the early biographies of Bryan, the most famous is Paxton Hibben, *The Peerless Leader: William Jennings Bryan* (New York: Farrar & Rinehart, 1929), which was completed after Hibben's death by C. Hartley Grattan. Although it still has its uses, especially regarding Bryan's early life, it is for the most part relentlessly critical. In contrast, Wayne C. Williams, *William Jennings Bryan* (New York: G. P. Putnam's Sons, 1936), is completely uncritical.

Richard Hofstadter, *The American Political Tradition and the Men Who Made It* (New York: Knopf, 1948), is a justifiably influential book that includes an unjustifiably scathing assessment of Bryan. Hofstadter conceded his interpretive debt to Hibben's biography. Dixon Wecter, *The Hero in America: A Chronicle of Hero-Worship* (New York: Scribner's, 1941), has an interesting chapter on Bryan's grass-roots popularity but concludes unfairly that after 1896 "Bryan's life was an anticlimax." A more recent sketch is John Garraty, "Bryan," *American Heritage* 13 (December 1961): 4–11, 108–15, which stresses the Commoner's political courage and principles, but faults him for his inability to grow. Ray Ginger, in his introduction to *William Jennings Bryan: Selections*, argues unfairly that there was not much to Bryan that could grow in the first place and that, indeed, his mind "resembled cooked oatmeal." Paul Glad, ed., *William Jennings Bryan, A Profile* (New York: Hill & Wang, 1968), is a useful collection of secondary essays with a perceptive introduction. Merle Curti, *Bryan and World Peace*, Smith College Studies in History 16 (Northampton, Mass.: Smith College, 1931) is an admirable early effort that treats Bryan as a "conscientious and intelligent critic of the war system."

Since 1960, Bryan has been the subject of some outstanding scholarly work, notable for its balance and understanding. Paolo E. Coletta has led the way with numerous articles and a three-volume biography, *William Jennings Bryan* (Lincoln: University of Nebraska Press, 1964–69), that is prodigiously researched and packed with information. In terms of sheer detail, it is the standard work on the Commoner. Louis W. Koenig, *Bryan: A Political Biography of William Jennings Bryan* (New York: Putnam's, 1971), is a highly readable one-volume biography of "the founder of the modern Democratic party" and "the apostle of the deprived." Koenig makes a good case, but perhaps narrows too much the cultural distance that separated Bryan from the sidewalks of New York. A brief treatment is Robert W. Cherny, *A Righteous Cause: The Life of William Jennings Bryan* (Boston: Little, Brown & Co. 1985), which is particularly good on the social world in which Bryan grew up and in evaluating his role as a crusader.

Three books are exceptionally notable studies of important aspects of Bryan's life. Paul W. Glad, *The Trumpet Soundeth: William Jennings Bryan and His Democracy, 1896–1912* (Lincoln: University of Nebraska Press, 1960), insightfully explores the "middle border" culture from which he came and convincingly argues that he was the leader of the political opposition from 1896 until 1912. Glad's book helped introduce Bryan as a subject who deserved more appreciative attention than Hofstadter and others had given him. Lawrence W. Levine, *Defender of the Faith, William Jennings Bryan: The Last Decade 1915–1925* (New York: Oxford University Press, 1965), treats Bryan's controversial last years with sensitivity and compassion, and successfully rebuts earlier interpretations by showing the continuities in the Commoner's career. Kendrick A. Clements, *William Jennings Bryan, Missionary Isolationist* (Knoxville: University of Tennessee Press, 1982), is the best source on Bryan's foreign policy, and it shrewdly traces the "missionary" theme through his life.

Willard H. Smith, *The Social and Religious Thought of William Jennings Bryan* (Lawrence, Kans.: Coronado Press, 1975), is thoughtful and informative, especially on the subjects of race, the Social Gospel, and fundamentalism. Arthur B. Ogle, "Above the World: William Jennings Bryan's View of the American Nation in International Affairs," *Nebraska History* 61 (Summer 1980): 153–71, perceptively places Bryan within the context of the patriotic nationalism of his times. Also useful for understanding Bryan and world affairs are Edward H. Worthen, "The Mexican Journeys of William Jennings Bryan, A Good Neighbor," *Nebraska History* 59 (1978): 485–500; Roger Daniels, "William Jennings Bryan and the Japanese," *Southern California Quarterly,* 48 (1966): 227–40; and Selig Adler, "Bryan and Wilsonian Caribbean Penetration," *Hispanic American Historical Review* 20 (1940): 198–226.

On Bryan's early years, Paolo E. Coletta, "The Youth of William Jennings Bryan," *Nebraska History* 31 (March 1950): 1–24, and George R. Poage, "College Career of William Jennings Bryan," *Mississippi Valley Historical Review* 15 (September 1928): 165–82, have useful additional information. Donna M. Oglio, "The American Reformer: Psychological and Sociological Origins; A Comparative Study of Jane Addams, Louis Dembitz Brandeis and William Jennings Bryan" (Ph.D. dissertation, City University of New York, 1979), applies psychohistorical analysis to Bryan. The results are mixed. She infers from his writings that he was basically insecure and unhappy as a child, and in this respect her arguments are suggestive and provocative. But her assessment of his relationship with his domineering father ultimately seems forced and strained.

For an understanding of the social setting in which Bryan spent his high school and college years, Don Harrison Doyle, *The Social Order of a Frontier Community: Jacksonville, Illinois, 1825–70* (Urbana: University of Illinois Press, 1978), is excellent. On the ideological tradition of republicanism, the literature is huge and growing. See Robert E. Shalhope, "Republicanism and Early American Historiography," *William and Mary Quarterly* 39 (April 1982): 334–56, for a valuable overview that also urges the necessity of seeing republicanism "as a cultural system." Nick Salvatore, *Eugene V. Debs, Citizen and Socialist* (Urbana: University of Illinois Press, 1982), and John Thomas, *Alternative America: Henry George, Edward Bellamy, Henry Demarest Lloyd and the Adversary Tradition* (Cambridge: Harvard University Press, 1983), show the continuing influence of republican thought in the late nineteenth century. On the Protestant evangelical strain, also a much-discussed subject, one of the best guides is Paul Boyer, *Urban Masses and Moral Order in America, 1820–1920* (Cambridge: Harvard University Press, 1978). Good on the fusion of religion and politics is Cushing Strout, *The New Heavens and New Earth: Political Religion in America* (New York: Harper & Row, 1974).

James C. Olson, *History of Nebraska* (Lincoln: University of Nebraska Press, 1966), is informative on developments underway in Nebraska during Bryan's early years there. Important quantitative studies of the political turmoil in Nebraska from the 1880s into the twentieth century are Stanley B. Parsons, *The Populist Context: Rural vs. Urban Power on a Great Plains Frontier* (Westport, Conn.: Greenwood, 1973), and Robert W. Cherny, *Populism, Progressivism, and the Transformation of Nebraska Politics, 1885–1915* (Lincoln: University of Nebraska Press, 1981). An outstanding guide to the literature that focuses on the ethnocultural bases of the political parties is Richard L. McCormick, "Ethno-Cultural Interpretations of Nineteenth-Century American Voting Behavior," *Political Science Quarterly* 89 (June 1974): 351–77.

On the changing interpretations of politics in the late nineteenth century, see Richard L. McCormick, "The Party Period and Public Policy: An Exploratory Hypothesis," *Journal of American History* 66 (September 1979): 279–98, and the essays by Paul Kleppner and Walter Dean Burnham, in *The Evolution of American Electoral Systems*, ed. Kleppner et al. (Westport, Conn.: Greenwood, 1981). A readable, brief survey is R. Hal Williams, *Years of Decision: American Politics in the 1890s* (New York: Wiley, 1978). Walter T. K. Nugent, *Money and American Society 1865–1880* (New York: Free Press, 1968), makes sense of the complicated history of the money question and says that silver became "the great weapon of a holy war."

In recent years populism has produced a rich and fertile field of literature. Martin Ridge, "Populism Redux: John D. Hicks and *The Populist Revolt*,"

*Reviews in American History* 13 (March 1985), 142–54, provides a brief historiographical overview of some of the recent writing. Lawrence Goodwyn, *Democratic Promise: The Populist Moment in America* (New York: Oxford University Press, 1976), is extremely suggestive regarding populism as a "movement culture," but he dismisses Nebraska's version as a "shadow movement" and is highly critical of fusion and of Bryan (a "pragmatic traditionalist" and phony Populist). Robert Cherny, "Lawrence Goodwyn and Nebraska Populism: A Review Essay," *Great Plains Quarterly* 1 (1981): 181–94, is an important corrective that argues a strong case for Nebraska's Populist claims.

Particularly enlightening on the ideological dimensions of the farmers' movement are Bruce Palmer, *"Man Over Money": The Southern Populist Critique of American Capitalism* (Chapel Hill: University of North Carolina Press, 1980); Steven Hahn, *The Roots of Southern Populism: Yeoman Farmers and the Transformation of the Georgia Upcountry, 1850–1890* (New York: Oxford University Press, 1983); and O. Gene Clanton, *Kansas Populism: Ideas and Men* (Lawrence: University of Kansas Press, 1969).

On the 1896 election, Stanley L. Jones, *The Presidential Election of 1896* (Madison: University of Wisconsin Press, 1964), is thorough and judicious. Paul W. Glad, *McKinley, Bryan, and the People* (New York: Hill & Wang, 1964), places the election in the context of the era's dominant myths about agrarianism and self-made individualism. For a persuasive argument that the election story was not a simplified one of Populist sacrifice and Democratic gain, see Robert F. Durden, *The Climax of Populism: The Election of 1896* (Lexington: University Press of Kentucky, 1965). A shrewd assessment of the strengths of Bryan's campaign and the difficulties he confronted is Gilbert Fite, "William Jennings Bryan and the Campaign of 1896: Some Views and Problems," *Nebraska History* 47 (September 1966): 247–64. Fite's "Election of 1896," in *History of American Presidential Elections*, ed. Arthur M. Schlesinger, Jr., and Fred L. Israel, 4 vols. (New York: Chelsea House, 1971), 2: 1787–1825, is a readable narrative that shows "Bryan was the strongest candidate the Democrats could have put in the race."

On the importance of 1896 within the shifting party "systems" in American politics, the writings of Walter Dean Burnham are basic. *The Current Crisis in American Politics* (New York: Oxford University Press, 1982) is a convenient collection of his essays.

On imperialism and antiimperialism at the turn of the century, good places to start are Stuart Creighton Miller, *"Benevolent Assimilation": The American Conquest of the Philippines, 1899–1903* (New Haven: Yale University Press, 1982), and Richard E. Welch, Jr., *Response to Imperialism: The United States and the Philippine-American War, 1899–1902* (Chapel Hill: University of North Carolina Press, 1979). Most studies focus on the northeastern expressions of antiimperialism, so Robert W. Cherny, "Anti-Imperialism on the

Middle Border, 1898–1900," *Midwest Review* 1 (1979): 19–34, is a notable corrective. Gerald Linderman, *The Mirror of War: American Society and the Spanish-American War* (Ann Arbor: University of Michigan Press, 1974), nicely describes the cultural importance of the role of state national guard and volunteer units.

Goran Rystad's excellent *Ambiguous Imperialism: American Foreign Policy and Domestic Politics at the Turn of the Century* (Stockholm: Scandinavian University Books, 1975), is a careful, detailed treatment of the 1900 election and the extent to which a foreign policy issue affected it. Walter LaFeber, "Election of 1900," in *History of American Presidential Elections*, ed. Schlesinger and Israel, 3: 1877–1917, is a fine overview that shows how McKinley shrewdly manipulated foreign policy to his political advantage.

Studies of Democratic party politics, and Bryan's role, include J. Rogers Hollingsworth, *The Whirligig of Politics: The Democracy of Cleveland and Bryan* (Chicago: University of Chicago Press, 1963); John J. Broesamle, "The Democrats from Bryan to Wilson," in *The Progressive Era*, ed. Lewis Gould (Syracuse: Syracuse University Press, 1974), 83–113; and Arthur S. Link, *Wilson: The New Freedom* (Princeton, N.J.: Princeton University Press, 1956). Link is indispensable on Wilson and his era. Also useful are essays on the elections of 1904 through 1924 in *History of American Presidential Elections*, ed. Schlesinger and Israel, vol. 3.

Helpful guides to the historical literature on progressivism are David M. Kennedy, "Overview: The Progressive Era," *Historian* 37 (May 1975): 453–68, and Daniel T. Rodgers, "In Search of Progressivism," *Reviews in American History* 10 (December 1982): 113–32. Excellent reminders of the strong religious bent of progressivism are Clyde Griffen, "The Progressive Ethos," in *The Development of an American Culture*, ed. Stanley Coben and Lorman Ratner, 2d ed. (New York: St. Martin's, 1983), and Robert M. Crunden, *Ministers of Reform: The Progressives' Achievement in American Civilization, 1889–1920* (New York: Basic Books, 1982). On progressivism in terms of coalition politics, start with John Buenker's essays in *Progressivism*, ed. Buenker, John C. Burnham, and Robert Crunden (Cambridge, Mass.: Schenkman, 1977). David P. Thelen, *Robert La Follette and the Insurgent Spirit* (Boston: Little, Brown & Co. 1976), probes the struggle between the insurgent and modernizing wings of the movement. Robert H. Wiebe, *The Search for Order, 1877–1920* (New York: Hill & Wang, 1967), examines the organizational tendencies of progressivism that were interwoven with the knowledge explosion at the turn of the century. Insightful on the timing and texture of progressivism is Richard L. McCormick, "The Discovery that Business Corrupts Politics: A Reappraisal of the Origins of Progressivism," *American Historical Review* 86 (April 1981): 247–74, which also stresses the unexpected and ironical results of the reform movement. On Prohibition, see

James H. Timberlake, *Prohibition and the Progressive Movement, 1900–1920* (Cambridge, Mass.: Harvard University Press, 1963), and Norman H. Clark, *Deliver Us from Evil: An Interpretation of American Prohibition* (New York: Norton, 1976).

Helpful in understanding the organizational changes underway in the State Department in the early twentieth century is Waldo H. Heinrichs, Jr., "Bureaucratization and Professionalism in the Development of American Career Diplomacy," in *Twentieth-Century American Foreign Policy,* ed. John Braeman et al. (Columbus: Ohio State University Press, 1971), 119–206. Rachel West, *The Department of State on the Eve of the First World War* (Athens: University of Georgia Press, 1978), is sharply critical of Bryan as a "well meaning amateur." Besides Kendrick's and Curti's books, useful treatments of Bryan as secretary of state are Richard Challener, "William Jennings Bryan," in *An Uncertain Tradition: American Secretaries of State in the Twentieth Century,* ed. Norman A. Graebner (New York: McGraw-Hill, 1961), 79–100, and Anonymous (J. V. Fuller), "William Jennings Bryan," in *American Secretaries of State and Their Diplomacy,* ed. Samuel F. Bemis (New York: Cooper Square Publishers, 1929). Ernest R. May, "Bryan and the World War, 1914–1915" (Ph.D. dissertation, University of California, Los Angeles, 1951), rests on careful primary research and argues forcefully that "Bryan was the real architect of American foreign policy during the early months of the world war."

To understand the dilemmas that Bryan faced when viewing a world of war and revolution, see these thoughtful treatments of the Wilson administration and foreign policy: N. Gordon Levin, Jr., *Woodrow Wilson and World Politics: America's Response to War and Revolution* (New York: Oxford University Press, 1968); Arno J. Mayer, *Political Origins of the New Diplomacy* (New Haven: Yale University Press, 1959); Arthur S. Link, *Woodrow Wilson: Revolution, War, and Peace* (Arlington Heights, Ill.: AHM, 1979); and Lloyd C. Gardner, *Safe For Democracy: The Anglo-American Response to Revolution, 1913–1923* (New York: Oxford University Press, 1985).

John Milton Cooper, Jr., *The Vanity of Power: American Isolationism and the First World War, 1914–1917* (Westport, Conn.: Greenwood, 1969), carefully shows that isolationism was far from monolithic and is insightful on reformers like Bryan. On World War I and progressivism at home, see especially Allen F. Davis, "Welfare, Reform and World War I," *American Quarterly* 29 (Fall 1967): 516–33.

On the effects of the cultural clashes of the 1920s on politics, see David Burner, *The Politics of Provincialism: The Democratic Party in Transition, 1918–1932* (New York: Knopf, 1967). Perceptive and evenhanded treatments of fundamentalism include Paul Carter, "The Fundamentalist Defense of the Faith," in *Change and Continuity in Twentieth-Century America: The 1920's*, ed. Robert Bremner et al. (Columbus: Ohio State University Press, 1968), 179–214; George M. Marsden, *Fundamentalism and American Culture: The Shaping of Twentieth-Century Evangelicalism, 1870–1925* (New York: Oxford University Press, 1980); and Ferenc M. Szasz, *The Divided Mind of Protestant America, 1880–1930* (University: University of Alabama Press, 1982), which has two excellent chapters on Bryan. Willard B. Gatewood, Jr., ed., *Controversy in the Twenties: Fundamentalism, Modernism, and Evolution* (Nashville: Vanderbilt University Press, 1969), is an outstanding collection of primary documents with commendable introductions. C. Allyn Russell, *Voices of American Fundamentalism: Seven Biographical Studies* (Philadelphia: Westminster, 1976), 162–89, and Allen Birchler, "The Anti-Evolutionary Beliefs of William Jennings Bryan," *Nebraska History* 54 (1973): 545–59, are fine discussions of Bryan's religious views. Irvin G. Wyllie, "Bryan, Birge, and the Wisconsin Evolution Controversy, 1921–1922," *Wisconsin Magazine of History* 35 (Summer 1952): 294–301, shows Bryan at his most irresponsible and demagogic.

On the Scopes trial, *The World's Most Famous Court Trial: Tennessee Evolution Case* (Cincinnati: National Book Co., 1925) is a published edition of the proceedings. Ray Ginger, *Six Days or Forever?: Tennessee v. John Thomas Scopes* (Boston: Beacon Press, 1958), is a readable account.

Especially useful for understanding the growth of the modern commercial culture are Lewis A. Erenberg, *Steppin' Out: New York Nightlife and the Transformation of American Culture, 1890–1930* (Westport, Conn.: Greenwood Press, 1981); John F. Kasson, *Amusing the Million: Coney Island at the Turn of the Century* (New York: Hill & Wang, 1978); T. J. Jackson Lears, "From Salvation to Self-Realization: Advertising and the Therapeutic Roots of Consumer Culture, 1880–1930," in *The Culture of Consumption: Critical Essays in American History, 1880–1980*, ed. Lears and Richard W. Fox (New York: Pantheon, 1983), 3–38; and Lary May, *Screening Out the Past: The Birth of Mass Culture and the Motion Picture Industry* (New York: Oxford University Press, 1980).

Very helpful introductions to the shifting intellectual worlds are Gordon S. Wood, "Conspiracy and the Paranoid Style: Causality and Deceit in the Eighteenth Century," *William and Mary Quarterly* 39 (1982): 401–41, a superb essay that helps to distinguish between the Enlightenment and modern views; Dorothy Ross, "The Liberal Tradition Revised and the Republican Tradition Addressed," in *New Directions in American Intellectual History*, ed. Paul Conkin and John Higham (Baltimore: Johns Hopkins University Press,

1979), 116–31, that insightfully treats the "shift in historical consciousness" between the 1880s and 1920s; and Fred H. Matthews, "Historians and the Eclipse of Civil Religion: Progressivism in Recent American Historiography," *Historical Reflections* 10 (Summer 1983): 245–67, a perceptive analysis of the Progressive era transition from republican assumptions to modernist thought.

# INDEX

xvi, 103–4, 184–86; military career of,
74–76; "money power," opposition to,
34, 45, 52–53, 62–63, 81, 82, 90,
113, 138–39, 142–43; moralism of, xv,
4, 20, 21, 63, 81, 85, 97, 98, 99, 110,
116, 126, 131–33, 139–40, 144, 148–
52, 156, 170–73, 189–96; move to
Florida by, 178; move to Nebraska by,
17–18; nationalism of, 6, 52–53, 81,
85–89, 148–51, 153–54, 156, 161,
169–70; and "New Freedom," 142–44;
and New York City, dislike of, 161,
164, 181; and neutrality policy, 154,
156–59; optimism of, 5, 11–12, 21,
71, 97, 99, 100, 109–10, 127, 152,
153, 156, 174, 175, 183, 194, 196;
oratorical abilities of, xiv, 25–26, 35–
36, 38–39, 50–54, 107–9, 139–40,
141; and Paris peace delegation, 173;
personal traits of, xv, 9, 10–13, 15,
25–26, 104, 108, 127–28, 145–46,
154–55, 196; political skills of, xiv,
25–26, 30, 35, 46–47, 84, 120, 139,
180; and populism, xv, 30–32, 43, 44,
46, 52, 56–65, 79; presidential
candidacies of, xiv, 54–70 (1896), xiv,
83–95 (1900), xiv, xv, 120–25 (1908);
and progressivism, xv, 97–103, 109–
10, 124–25, 135, 138–44, 157, 176–
83; and Prohibition, 21, 126–33, 140,
146, 171–73, 180, 181, 191; and race,
88–89, 103–4, 120, 148, 154, 181,
198; and railroads, 24, 114, 116, 118–
20, 171; religious beliefs of, xv, xvii,
2–5, 7, 14, 72, 85, 99, 148, 184, 187,
194, 197, 200, 202; republican
ideology of, 6, 72, 84–85, 189, 191,
192–93, 194, 195, 203; resignation of
from Cabinet, xiv, 159–60; and role of
government, xv, xvi, 31, 65, 73, 111,
116, 118–23, 127, 142–43; and
science, 5, 10, 185; as Secretary of
State, xiv, 126, 141–42, 144–60;
senatorial ambitions of, 46, 135; and
Social Gospel, xvii, 99–100; and
socialism, 119, 124; and special
privilege, xv, 31–32, 38–39, 184; and
tariff reform, 25, 36, 92, 122, 135–36,
138; and taxing war profits, 171;
tolerance of, 104, 127–28, 181; travels

of, 105, 116, 135, 149; and treaty with
Spain (1899), 77–78, 174; and treaty
concluding World War I, 174; and
village America, 1–2, 5, 10–13, 31–
32, 70, 75, 109, 122, 176, 202; wealth
of, xiv, 104–5, 135, 178–79; and
woman suffrage, 171; and World War
I, xiv, 156–69

Bryan, William Jennings, Jr., 26, 134
"Bryan Populists," 32
Butler, Marion, 56, 94
Butt, Archie, 123


California alien land law, 154–55
campaign disclosure laws, 121, 138
campaign regulations, xv
Campbell, Alexander, 186
Campfire Girls, 100
Carnegie, Andrew, 6
Cather, Willa, 64, 175, 188
Catholics, 104, 132, 181
Chamber of Commerce, 24
Chaplin, Charlie, 190
Chautauqua, xiv, 106–9, 128, 135, 137,
146, 183, 185, 200
Chicago: as Bryan's residence, 16–17;
Bryan's views of, 16–17; characterized,
16–17, 41
Chicago Municipal Lodging House, 130
*Chicago Tribune,* 50
China, 147
Chinda, Sutemi, 155
Chinese exclusion, 104
Christian benevolence, 4
Christian Endeavor, 100
civil service, 144
Clark, Champ, 88–89, 136–37, 140–41
Clayton Anti-Trust Act, 142
Cleveland, Grover, 25, 42–49 passim, 65,
66, 69, 73, 90, 110, 111, 113, 124,
137
Coinage Act of 1873, 33–34
*Collier's,* 124
Colorado, 37–38, 59
*Commoner, The,* 105–6, 116, 120, 134,
136, 155, 163, 170, 178, 192
Coney Island, 190, 194
Congregational church, 132
"conservative populism," xvii

239

# ABOUT THE AUTHOR

LeRoy Ashby is professor of history at Washington State University. His publications include *The Spearless Leader: Senator Borah and the Progressive Movement in the 1920's* (1972), *Saving the Waifs: Reformers and Dependent Children, 1890–1917* (1984), and a coedited anthology, *The Discontented Society: Interpretations of Twentieth-Century American Protest* (1972). In 1983 he received the first Washington State University award for teaching excellence.